TRENDS AND ISSUES IN DEVELOPMENTAL PSYCHOLOGY

TRENDS AND ISSUES IN DEVELOPMENTAL PSYCHOLOGY

Edited by

PAUL MUSSEN
JONAS LANGER
MARTIN COVINGTON

Department of Psychology
University of California, Berkeley

HOLT   New York   Chicago   San Francisco
RINEHART   Atlanta   Dallas   Montreal
and WINSTON   Toronto   London   Sydney

PREFACE

Most of the articles in this volume were prepared for lectures, seminars, or colloquia at the University of California, Berkeley, and are being published for the first time.

While the articles were prepared independently of each other, all reflect the current, burgeoning interest in cognitive development. Most of the authors address themselves directly to theoretical and research issues related to factors affecting cognitive development. A few of the articles, dealing mainly with socialization, are not focused primarily on cognitive concepts or theories, but even these show the influence of cognitive theory, offering cognitive explanations of moral development (for example, Rosenhan and Turiel) or exploring the effects of molar factors—such as school assignment or physical stature—on intellectual, academic, and occupational performance.

The contents of this book can be divided into several sections, each dealing with a fundamental or core problem. Thus, the first four articles deal with *mechanisms* or *processes* of critical importance in cognitive development. In the first, "Learning Cognitive Structures," Piaget's co-workers Inhelder and Sinclair present findings from their experimental attempts to accelerate the transition from one cognitive stage to the next by means of special training. The results were notably unsuccessful; even after conscientious, systematic training, subjects at a preoperational level did not acquire the logical structures necessary for real understanding of the notion of conservation. Only a few subjects, already at an intermediate level, achieved the "threshold of concrete operations." The authors' conclusion—"learning is subordinate to the laws of development and development does not consist in a mere successive accumulation of bits of learning"—has important theoretical and practical implications

v

relevant to questions about the mechanisms underlying transitions between stages and about educational programs.

"Disequilibrium as a Source of Development," by Langer, critically analyzes and clarifies the concepts of *equilibrium* and *disequilibrium* which, in a number of theoretical systems, are used as explanations of progressive change. The author views the child as "an active operator whose actions are the prime generator of his own psychological development. . . . He will change only if he feels, consciously or unconsciously, that something is wrong." Furthermore, theoretical considerations and the results of several experimental studies strongly suggest that both *affective* and *organizational* (intellectual) disequilibrium are necessary conditions for the child's engagement in the adaptive, constructive mental activities that constitute the sources of cognitive change and development.

Wapner's article, "Organismic-Developmental Theory," describes some of his recent work in a research program initiated at Clark University in collaboration with the late Heinz Werner. The wide applicability of Werner's orthogenetic principle (that development consists of "increasing differentiation and hierarchic integration") was demonstrated in experiments on the development of learning and of the perception of self:object (or self:environment) relations. Studies involving normal and retarded children and normal and psychopathological adults demonstrate that *how* and *what* subjects learn, and the extent to which they differentiate between body and object space, depend on the level of their cognitive organization—on the cognitive operations available to them.

In the fourth article, "Developing the Skills of Productive Thinking," Olton and Crutchfield focus their attention on the effects of special training on thinking and problem solving of children approximately twelve years old. Their training program, described in some detail in this article, emphasizes the skills required for original and independent thinking—*how*, rather than *what*, to think. The remarkable success of the program indicates that, once the basic capacities for complex thinking have emerged, training may considerably enhance the child's ability and readiness to use complex cognitive processes efficiently and effectively.

The next two articles deal with moral development—from a cognitive point of view in Turiel's "Developmental Processes in the Child's Moral Thinking," and from a more behavioristic perspective in Rosenhan's "Some Origins of Concern for Others." Turiel examines and elucidates a number of concepts basic to the analysis of conscience and moral thinking. Moral development is assumed to be "a self-constructive process involving changing conceptions and emotions." Several empirical studies lead the author to conclude that Kohlberg's six stages form an invariant sequence in the development of moral judgment and that progress from one stage to the next involves cognitive restructuring and displacement of earlier stages. Even if children are systematically exposed to moral concepts that are at different stages above the cognitive level they have already achieved, they will assimilate only those that are a little above their own level: they cannot incorporate the reasoning involved in stages further above and they reject thinking that is at stages below their own.

Rosenhan's paper is concerned with antecedents of altruism and socially oriented, prosocial behavior. The research reported stresses the importance of observation of models and of rehearsal in facilitating the acquisition of these kinds of behavior, but cognitive variables also play a role. For example, a model's altruistic behavior is "cognitively processed" by the observer, who will imitate and incorporate this behavior only if he possesses "certain relatively well-formed cognitive and affective structures."

The final two articles deal with the social contexts in which development occurs. Thus, in "A Model for the Understanding of School as a Socializing Agent," Himmelweit and Swift provide a comprehensive model for ordering variables that affect the child's socialization and report the results of a twelve-year longitudinal study highlighting the enduring effects of secondary school placement. Their data show that the subjects' later intellectual functioning, self-concepts, attitudes, orientations, academic and occupational histories were more highly influenced by the type of school attended (grammar or secondary modern) and the "stream" to which they were assigned, than by their social class backgrounds, abilities, or motivations.

The final article, "Relation of Body Size, Intelligence Test Scores, and Social Circumstances" by Tanner, reviews the extensive literature on the relationships among intelligence test scores (often regarded as global measures of cognitive ability), height, upward social mobility, and small family size. Possible explanations of these correlations are explored, but it is impossible to determine ". . . whether the tall, bright, upward-moving children are this way primarily because of excellence of antenatal and postnatal care and intelligent, responsible feeding and upbringing, or because they inherited a gene complex that was predisposed toward developing in this direction."

Obviously these brief comments give only the barest suggestion of the contents of the articles in this volume and do not do justice to the articles' variety, richness, novelty, or flavor. Nor can such summaries convey the full impact of the most important aspect of this collection: each of the articles makes some contribution to our understanding of cognitive development and the processes underlying this development, and each of them will stimulate further thinking and research about basic issues of cognitive change and growth.

Paul Mussen
Jonas Langer
Martin Covington
University of California, Berkeley
May 1969

CONTENTS

TRENDS AND ISSUES IN
DEVELOPMENTAL PSYCHOLOGY

1

LEARNING COGNITIVE STRUCTURES

In recent years, a number of research projects on learning problems have been based on the Genevan studies of the development of intelligence, particularly those concerning the formation of concepts of conservation and of elementary logical operations. There seem to be a number of reasons for this trend. Whereas the original research was undertaken with a view to illuminating problems of developmental epistemology, the research projects that issued from it incorporated specific learning procedures which seem on the one hand to pursue pragmatic aims and on the other more theoretical aims.

Educational reforms in the field of science teaching are very topical nowadays. Educators are preoccupied with initiating children in modern scientific thinking at as early an age as possible, partly spurred by the need to provide society with enough scientists and technicians in the near future.

Those who work out the educational programs have sought leads mainly from behavioristic learning theories. However, some—and it may not be by chance that these are mainly mathematicians and physicists—have looked for the origins of scientific notions in epistemology and believe that Piaget's findings about the development of basic logical and physical concepts can point the way to understanding the child's specific difficulties in acquiring certain notions, as well as to overcoming these difficulties (as far as possible) by teaching methods adapted to the child's thinking (Bruner,1960).

Apart from the more practical interest that Piaget's work presents for educators, a great deal of attention is now paid to his work by theoretical psychologists (this renewed interest is reflected by the recent publication of a volume entitled *Piaget Rediscovered*). In the past, psychologists in various countries often found difficulty in accepting the authenticity of the facts discovered by Piaget (for instance, in

BÄRBEL INHELDER

HERMINA SINCLAIR

University of Geneva, Geneva, Switzerland

nonconservation, animism, and egocentrism) and checked his findings by proposing Piaget-type tasks to children of different environments and different ages. At present, however, the facts seem to be accepted, and though straightforward replication studies are still being carried out with children in various cultural environments, the main focus of interest and controversy has become the interpretation of the facts and the search for psychological mechanisms that have explanatory value (Bruner, 1964, 1966).

The main purpose of the Genevan learning experiments is to study in detail the psychological mechanisms that underlie and explain the transition from one structure to the next; secondary points of interest are the epistemological bearing of the facts discovered in learning studies and the possible didactic implications of these facts (Inhelder, Bovet, Sinclair, 1967).

The developmental research has already shown the main lines of succession of the different structures, as well as the specific difficulties in coordination encountered during the acquisition of operations. Conservations, the main symptoms of a budding system of operational structures, have been extensively studied both cross-sectionally and longitudinally. Moreover, logical models have provided insight into the structural organization of these systems of operations and into the way they develop. The learning experiments are more directly geared to the search for psychological processes that have explanatory value and that can illuminate the actual transitions between stages and substages as well as the links between different fields of knowledge.

This search for explanatory mechanisms entails the use of experimental methods that introduce a variation of some of the factors involved as well as different learning procedures. At least three problem areas can be distinguished.

1. *The temporal aspect of organization.* Developmental research has already shown, *grosso modo*, the order of succession and the hierarchy of the different structures. However, mental growth is essentially a time-bound, causal process and, as long as one stays within the logical framework, only atemporal phenomena can be grasped. The question has to be asked whether it is possible, in the organization of cognitive processes, to discover mechanisms that rule the rhythm of development in the manner of the regulatory mechanisms known to embryology. We used operational exercises, providing a similar experimental feedback, with children of different developmental levels, in order to decide whether the assimilatory speed is the same at different levels or whether speed is itself subject to developmental change.

2. *The developmental links between partial structures of operations.* No structure of classification or seriation, no operatory system underlying conservation notions, is formed in isolation. There is always interference and mutual interaction between the systems that are being formed. A logical analysis can provide a model of these multiple relations, but only an experimental approach can demonstrate the true psychological links and transitions. In the mind of a child who already possesses the notions of quantity, what actually happens when he starts to acquire elementary spatial concepts such as conservation of length? This question gave rise to one of our learning experiments in which we studied the interaction of logico-mathematical, physical, and spatial operations.

3. *The role of the various factors that contribute to the development of logical structures.* It evidently is impossible to explore all these factors at once, and accordingly we first focused our attention on the role of language since, for many influential psychologists in recent years, language (or systems of symbolization in general) has taken on the guise of an explanatory factor in intellectual development. Within the framework of Genevan developmental psychology, we have tried to clarify the relations between linguistic structure and semantic interpretation on the one hand, and intellectual operations on the other.

Several examples of our learning procedures will be given in this article. Despite their variety, some important principles are common to all of them, and we would like to stress the following points.

1. We always start with a diagnosis of the developmental level of our subjects by means of a pretest which, while it needs to be detailed, should not in itself constitute a learning session. Therefore, we insist on:

    a. using at least two operational structure tests;

    b. paying great attention to the way the children justify their answers (a non-conservational answer, for example, may give useful indication of the level the child has reached);

    c. exploring in detail the intermediary stages, which are of the utmost importance both for determining the initial level of development of the subjects and for obtaining an insight into the mechanisms of transition.

2. Our learning procedures vary, obviously, according to the particular concept or operation that is being studied. However, in all of them we avoid imposing definite

strategies on the child. Although the pattern of the different items stays the same, the child is encouraged to make his own choice of coordinations and our supplementary questions and suggestions can vary accordingly. Moreover, the choice of exercise items has been dictated by what we know of the spontaneous (that is, outside the laboratory) acquisition of the operations or concepts in question, either from previous developmental research or from specific preliminary exploration on a small group of subjects, interviewed with a supple technique. The child is asked to anticipate the likely outcome of certain transformations and then to observe the actual outcome of the transformation (mainly in the case of conservation problems). In other cases, we aim at a step-by-step circumscription of the problem destined to make the child aware of contradictions in his arguments, and we also use a graduation of items that embody existing operational schemes to overcome the obstacles to a higher order coordination. These ingredients are, so to speak, used in different doses in the different experiments, according to the character of the operation being studied and to its place in the hierarchy of structures; however, the dosage is always systematic.

3. The final evaluation of the acquired behavior is carried out by means of posttests which, in our opinion, should satisfy several conditions.

  a. The posttests should comprise all the items of the pretest.
  b. At least one item should pertain to a structure in a different field but of the same level as the structure that was the object of the learning sessions.
  c. They should comprise at least one item pertaining to the same structure but touching a different problem (for example, conservation of weight—transitivity of weight).
  d. Special attention should be paid to the child's justification of his answers and the experimenter should make countersuggestions (usually in the following form: "But another child told me that. . .").
  e. Results should be checked for durability by a control test several weeks later.

We shall briefly describe some of our learning experiments to illustrate the points we have made. The apparent variety of these experiments is partly due to the fact that most of them are not yet completed, but it also stems directly from our determination to stay as close as possible to the child's ways of progressing, as far as we know them from previous research (Piaget and Inhelder, 1941; Piaget and Szeminska, 1952) and to the extent that we learn about them in the course of the experiments themselves.

THE TEMPORAL ASPECT OF ORGANIZATION PROCESSES

Several of our learning experiments concern conservation problems. In one experiment of this type, the following apparatus, designed by C. Fot, is used (Inhelder et al., 1966): six glasses with outlet taps at the bottom are fixed onto a vertical board, in three rows placed in vertical alignment (a and a', b and b', c and c'). The top row consists of two glasses of equal size and shape. Directly below are two more glasses, one the same as the one above it, and the other either thinner or wider than its counterpart. The bottom row is identical to the top row (Figure 1.1).

Colored liquid is poured in equal quantities into the top two glasses. The child is encouraged to manipulate the apparatus and thus can observe the closed system of transformations, either with equal or unequal quantities of liquid. One of the principal difficulties encountered by the child at the nonconservational or intermediary level springs from the fact that he centers his judgments of equality or inequality only on the states (levels) of the liquids, without being able to see these different states as moments in a reversible transformation. The experimenter may, for instance, ask the child to open the taps and fill the middle glasses (b and b')

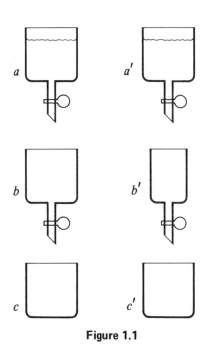

Figure 1.1

with an equal amount of liquid; if the child fills these glasses so that the level of the liquid is the same in both, and if he expects that when the liquid is let into glasses c and c' the quantity and level will again be the same, he will not only see that this is not the case, but can also observe that what is lacking in c' remained behind in a'.

What are the effects of such operational exercises on the process of structuration of operations? Without going into the details of the qualitative transformations in the thought process, we would like to emphasize the fact that the effects vary significantly with the initial developmental level of the children. Not one child who started from a truly preoperational level (we have already indicated the precautions that should be taken to establish this diagnosis of the schemes the child has at his disposal) succeeded in learning the logical operations that underlie the elementary notions of conservation of physical quantities. The majority (87.5 percent) did not make any real progress, while a minority (12.5 percent) attained an intermediary level characterized by frequent oscillations between judgments of conservation and judgments of nonconservation. The latter group attained only partial and momentary coordinations between the different centrations on isolated states or on their variation. To observe that in a continuous transformation of physical quantities nothing is lost and nothing is added is not the same thing as inferring a principle of conservation.

The situation was rather different for those children who started from an intermediary stage. Of this group, only 25 percent made no progress at all, whereas the other 75 percent benefited from the learning procedures in varying degrees. For 38.5 percent of the latter group, the acquisition of the conservation concept was no more than the extension of a structuration that had already begun at the time of the pretest. For the other 36.5 percent, however, a true progressive elaboration took place in which it is easy to follow the successive moments of integration during the learning sessions: their reasoning acquired stability and no regressions were observed between the posttest and the control test. However, when we compare the argumentation of the subjects who have acquired this concept in the learning sessions and those who have arrived at the same concept by the slower spontaneous process, we notice certain differences: the subjects who followed the learning sessions present many arguments of identity and compensation (which they had invoked even during the learning sessions) but few of the arguments of annulation by reversibility that are frequent among spontaneous learners.

On the other hand, progress due to learning sessions is far clearer with children who start from a true operational level, characterized by the acquisition of the conservation concept of quantities (in the case of the pouring of liquids), but who do not yet possess the more complex notion of conservation of weight. In spontaneous development this concept appears two or three years later than that of quantities. In this group, only 14 percent of our subjects made no progress and 86 percent acquired the notion of weight conservation. In our learning procedures the subjects not only were confronted with the discrepancy between their "anticipations" and the outcome of actual weighing, but also had to establish equalities of weight with objects of different shapes and sizes that were disposed in different ways on the scales, and to evaluate equal or unequal compositions of various objects. The majority (64 percent) of those who acquired conservation of weight were capable of performing operations of transitivity and showed that they felt a kind of logical necessity for their answers which, moreover, were based on complete reversibility. Such acquisitions are very different from the empirical solutions preferred by those children who, starting from a preoperational level as in Smedslund's (1959) experiments, take part in a learning procedure where the emphasis is on the observation of facts.

DEVELOPMENTAL LINKS BETWEEN
THE DIFFERENT PARTIAL STRUCTURES

Elementary Numerical and Spatial Operations

The following experiment, designed by M. Bovet (Pascual Leone and Bovet, 1967; Inhelder, Bovet, and Sinclair, 1967), differs in two ways from the preceding experiments concerning problems of physical quantities: (a) numbers refer to discrete units and length measurements to a continuum, whereas quantity and weight *both* refer to continua; (b) numerical and geometrical operations belong to two different fields of knowledge, whereas the concepts in question in the previous experiments both belong to the same field.

The learning procedure, however, follows the same plan in both experiments: starting from an already acquired operational structure, the subject is led during the learning sessions to develop a structure which, in spontaneous development, is acquired later: cross-sectional experiments have shown that problems of number conservation are solved two or three years before problems of length conservation.

One of the child's main difficulties in acquiring spatial structures, especially quantifiable spatial structures, resides in the fact that the elementary topological relationships (contiguity, order, enclosure) have to be transformed to fit a graded system of geometrical coordinates (Piaget and Inhelder, 1956); such transformation, by combining subdivision of length and displacement, leads to the concept of conservation of linear dimension—a prerequisite of the constitution of units of measurement (Piaget, Inhelder, Szeminska, 1960).

The experiment mainly concerned the following problems.

1. Can the acquisition of elementary spatial measurement be facilitated by exercises in which the child applies numerical operations to the evaluation of length? If yes, what stages does the child go through?

2. Can the child's behavior during learning sessions provide insight into the interval elapsing between the acquisition of number and length conservation, and into the specific difficulties attached to reasoning about discrete units on the one hand and about continuous quantities and dimensions on the other?

In essence, the procedure is as follows: both the experimenter and the subject have a number of matchsticks at their disposal, but the subject's matches are considerably shorter than those of the experimenter and of a different color (seven of the subject's red matches add up to the same length as five of the experimenter's green matches). The experimenter constructs either a straight or a broken line (a "road") and asks the subject to construct a line of the same length ("just as long a road"; "just as far to walk, so that two people, one on each road, would be just as tired"). Three situations are presented.

1. The first situation is the most complex: the experimenter constructs a sort of zigzag line and the subject has to construct a straight line of the same length directly underneath (Figure 1.2). The figural pregnancy of the situation suggests a topological situation where beginning and end of both lines are congruent.

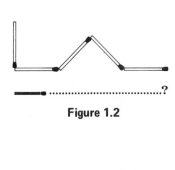

Figure 1.2

2. In the second situation the subject has again to construct a straight line of the same length as the experimenter's zigzag line, but no longer directly underneath (Figure 1.3); this facilitates the problem slightly, since there is no longer a perceptual pregnancy that suggests a topological solution.

3. The third situation is the easiest, since the experimenter's line is straight and the subject is

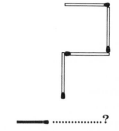

Figure 1.3

asked to construct a straight line directly underneath it (Figure 1.4). Moreover, the experimenter uses the same number of matches (five) as in situation (1) so that this situation (seven of the subject's matches are needed to make a straight line of the same length) suggests a correct solution to situations (1) and (2).

Figure 1.4

The three situations remain in front of the subject; after he has given his first three solutions, he is led to give explanations and eventually to reconsider his constructions, while the experimenter draws his attention to one situation after another.

In this experiment we interviewed a group of children—mean age, six years—chosen according to the following criteria.

1. The children had to succeed in a test of numerical conservation, consisting of the following items (Piaget and Szeminska, 1952): (a) Two identical glasses, A and B, are filled with large beads (the experimenter and the child simultaneously drop beads, one or two at a time, into the glasses). Glass B then is emptied into a narrower glass, N, or into a larger glass, L. The conservation question is asked. The beads in glass N (or L) are then poured back into B. (b) The beads in glass A are poured into L, and those in B are poured into N at the same time. The conservation question is asked again. Not only do the subjects have to give consistent conservative answers, but they also have to be able to justify their answers.

2. The subjects had to fail on a test of conservation of length, consisting of the following items: (a) Of two lengths of wire, the bigger one, A, is twisted so that its extremities are congruent with the extremities of B (Figure 1.5a). The conservation question is asked. (b) A is straightened out and again compared to B. Then A is twisted once more, this time so that B sticks out further than A (Figure 1.5b). The conservation question is asked again (Piaget, Inhelder, Szeminska, 1960). These two items are also used as a posttest immediately after the learning session.

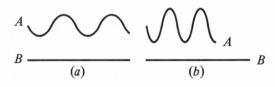

Figure 1.5

If we compare the subjects' behavior in the pretest and the posttest, we find that 35 percent of the subjects made no progress at all; of the 65 percent who profited from the learning procedure, 28 percent gave correct answers and justifications for both items of the posttest. The following reactions are typical of the behavior of the subjects during the learning sessions.

In situation (1), the most elementary solution is to construct a straight line with its extremities congruent with those of the experimenter's zigzag line (Figure 1.6). The child is convinced that the two lines are the same length, although his line is made up of four short matches, and the experimenter's line of five long matches.

In situation (2), the child has no ordinal or topological point of reference, since he has to construct his line at some distance from the experimenter's line, and so he uses the numerical reference: he constructs his line with the same number of matches the experimenter has used, regardless of the fact that his matches are shorter. When the experimenter now goes back to situation (1), the child will notice—with some embarrassment—that there he has constructed a line he judged to be of equal length which does not have the same number of elements as the model line. At this point we often see amusing compromise solutions: for instance, in situation (1) the child may break one of his matches in two, thus creating a line with the same number of elements without destroying the ordinal correspondence (Figure 1.7). Another solution, again clearly indicating the conflict between topological ordinal and numerical references, consists of adding one match but placing it vertically instead of horizontally (Figure 1.8). When the child then is asked to construct his line in situation (3), he starts by using the same number of matches (five) as the experimenter has used for his line. Since this time both lines are straight and the child's line is directly under the model line, he sees immediately that this does not give the right solution—because his matches are shorter, his line is not as long as the model line (Figure 1.9).

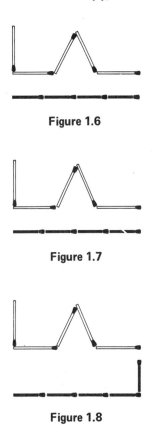

Figure 1.6

Figure 1.7

Figure 1.8

Many children are perplexed at this point and announce: "I can't do it. The red matches are smaller; it is impossible to get a road as long as the other." However, the child usually will realize after a while that the difference in length can be compensated for by using a greater number of matches and will add two, thus giving the correct solution. He is now on the way to grasping the relationship between length and number of elements. Going back to situation (2) he will say immediately: "I will have to use more red matches to get the same road because they are smaller." Those children who really acquire the concept will go even

Figure 1.9

further: they will use the knowledge gained from situation (3) (that the length of seven red matches equals that of five green matches) in situation (1), and they will use seven matches in a straight line without falling into the error of paying attention only to the ordinal aspect.

In terms of percentages of total and partial progress, the results of this experiment are midway between those of the two previously mentioned experiments. Very little progress was made by the frankly preoperational children in the learning procedure geared to the acquisition of the conservation of liquids, but more than three-quarters of the subjects who already possessed conservation of quantity acquired conservation of weight.

The main interest of this experiment resides in the fact that, as in all our learning experiments, the reactions of the children during the learning sessions show us, as through a magnifying glass, both the step-by-step developmental processes and the specific difficulties encountered by the children. Cross-sectional experiments rarely attain the fleeting, transitional stages, and although the general theory allows us to infer these gradual steps and the specific obstacles, the learning experiments show the development in a clearer and more detailed fashion.

As regards the specific problem of the links between numerical conservation and elementary measurement of continuous length, and the connected problem of the relationship between numerical and geometrical fields of knowledge, we seem justified in concluding that it is indeed possible to make use of already acquired numerical operations to lead the child to spatial operations of measurement. However, even in the case of total acquisiton, progress is slow and many obstacles are encountered in fitting the number-concept to conservation-of-length problems. In some situations, the ordinal and topological references are misleading, and before the two operational structures can strengthen each other, there is a period of conflict that can be overcome only through a constructive effort on the part of the child who discovers compensatory and coordinating actions. It is the feedback from these actions themselves that finally results in the acquisition of a structure of a higher order, and not the passive reading-off of a result.

Class Inclusion

Piaget's quantification of inclusion problems (Inhelder and Piaget, 1964) has given rise to a number of replication studies and to several learning experiments. The author of one of the latter, Kohnstamm (1963, 1967), regards the results he obtained with his learning procedure as a contradiction of Piaget's theory of development in general and, in particular, of his interpretation of the known facts regarding the class-inclusion problems in spontaneous development.

J. Pascual Leone and M. Bovet (1966) have formulated theoretical objections to Kohnstamm's method, especially to his evaluation of the quality of the progress he obtained with his subjects. This is not the place to reopen this controversy. We shall, however, describe a class-inclusion experiment of our own, which illustrates the fact that, with a very different method, we obtain as high a percentage of progress as Kohnstamm himself if we apply his criteria for success on the posttest. However, since our exigencies for the determination of the quality of an acquired behavior are much more rigorous than his, as is indicated above, we discriminate between a true acquisition of a structure, a limited operational progress, and the learning of a specific strategy—almost a trick—which permits correct answers to problems of one and the same structure.

Our class-inclusion learning experiment was undertaken with a twofold aim: (a) to study in more detail the substages in the acquisition of this concept, and (b) to study the eventual mutual influence between conservation and class inclusion. We therefore took two groups of subjects, both of which underwent identical pretests in conservation of number, liquids, substance, and in class inclusion and inter-section. We selected subjects who possessed conservation of number but none of the other conservations or class inclusion. One group received training on class-inclusion problems, the other group on conservation problems. As a posttest, both groups passed the same tests as in the pretests (except for conservation of number) plus certain additional items. Two sessions a week were held and each subject took part in five or six sessions. A control test was given three to four weeks after the posttest.[1]

The learning procedure for conservation comprised a series of items of gradually increasing difficulty, progressing from discrete units to continuous quantities, com-position of equalities and inequalities, and exercises with the Fot apparatus (the six glasses, as shown in Figure 1.1). The learning procedure for class inclusion was based on a preliminary experiment aimed at discovering substages by having the children execute verbal orders such as: "Give the boy more apples than the girl, but he must have as many pieces of fruit[2] as the girl" (in a situation where a girl-doll has two apples and three pears, or two apples, one orange, one pear, and one peach). To succeed in these acting-out items, the subject has to compare subclass and total class, as in the test question: "Are there more daisies or more flowers" in a bunch of twelve daisies and two tulips. The acting-out items are easier, however, because they do not demand comparison of a subclass to the total class in one collection only; the total class (the basket of fruit belonging to one of the dolls) remains visible as an object of comparison while the child constructs his subclasses (apples and other fruit) for the other doll. A series of items leads to questions on such comparisons in one collection: the doll has a basket containing four apples and two pears and the child is asked, "What should he say to eat the

---

[1]The experiment continues. So far we have results for only 20 subjects.
[2]The plural of *fruit* in French, the language in which the experiment was conducted, is simply *fruits*. If conducted in English, flowers or candies, for example, would have had to be used to avoid the "artificial" plural with *pieces*.

most: *I want to eat my apples* or *I want to eat my fruit*?" Finally, the same question is asked as in the class-inclusion test: "Are there more apples or more pieces of fruit in the basket?" The posttests for both groups include some items not presented in the pretest and not exercised during the learning sessions: for conservation, problems of transitivity; for class inclusion a three-stage inclusion (terriers, dogs, animals) and a question such as "Are there more dogs or more animals?" in a situation where *only* dogs are present. In that case, the usual answer "There are more animals than dogs" is no longer correct.

Though the main interest of this experiment lies in the careful analysis of each subject's reasoning and the gradual coordinations and integrations that are observed, the global results present a clear enough picture to make some general points.

1. In both groups, almost all of the subjects made progress in the concept exercised during the learning sessions: eight of the ten subjects in the inclusion group made very clear progress in the inclusion tests, although only two subjects made sufficient progress to satisfy all our criteria. Eight of the ten subjects in the conservation group made clear progress in conservation, although only two subjects achieved total acquisition. These results compare very favorably with the outcome of our other learning procedures—no doubt because of the intensive and extended training (six sessions) and because of the rather advanced initial level of the conservation training group. Most of them were already at the intermediary stage as regards conservation of quantity.

2. Progress in the exercised concept affected the subjects' reasoning about the nonexercised concept differently in the two groups. In fact, of the eight conservation group subjects who progressed clearly in conservation, only two showed progress in the inclusion tests and their progress was only partial. The other subjects showed no progress whatsoever in the class-inclusion problem, despite their success in the conservation tasks. By contrast, of the eight subjects (inclusion group) who made clear progress in the inclusion problem, four made remarkable progress in the conservation tasks, acquiring both conservation of quantity and conservation of weight. In one case, acquisition was complete, including transitivity of weight and composition of liquids and in one other case, nearly complete, including transitivity of weight; two subjects acquired conservation of quantity but not of weight. Furthermore, one other subject who made very little progress in the inclusion problem made clear progress in the conservation tasks, succeeding both in the conservation of substance and that of weight, transitivity included, although without a clear justification. Despite all our restrictions and precautions, it is nevertheless true that some of our subjects acquired a truly operational structure.

3. Once again, progress was clearly related to the initial stage of development. Even subjects who in the pretest gave only answers of nonconservation often justified their answers in a way that indicated a difference in their level of reasoning. Compare, for instance, a child who, for all the transformations of a ball of plasticine, affirms that there is no longer the same amount, but who says for the item where the one ball is divided into little pieces: "There is much more to eat with the little

bits; they are much smaller, there is a lot more of them," with a child who says "There is less to eat; those are only little bits." The first child mentions both that there are a lot of little bits and that these bits are small, and even though he is incapable of using these data for a judgment of compensation, he is no longer, as is the second child, uniquely centered on one aspect of the situation. Other subjects whom we considered more evolved although still completely nonconservational in their answers, said in the same situation: "The boy has more to eat, with all the little bits; the girl should break her ball up, too." These subjects have already shifted from centering on the final state to taking into consideration the transformation itself, and even though this does not lead them to reversibility, it does indicate an approach to the problem that is different from the simple consideration of two final states considered static.

Initial results in this experiment would point to the following conclusions. First, progress in inclusion problems, obtained in learning sessions, has far more effect on conservation tasks than vice versa; in other words, appropriate training in a mainly logical field influences the child's reasoning in more physical problems, even though these have not been touched upon in the learning sessions. However, progress in conservation tasks—even clearly operational progress—only rarely (and then only partially) influences the child's approach to logical problems.

Second, we conclude that the lower the child's initial level (even if there are only differences within one stage) the more progress tends to be limited to one specific field or even to one specific type of problem. With some children we obtained excellent results during the training sessions, but the slightly different situations in the posttest (within the same field) were already less successfully solved, and the problems in the different fields were approached in exactly the same way as during the pretest. Only the subjects who mastered the operations of class inclusion thoroughly, and who had already shown signs of decentration in the conservation pretests, could use their newly acquired logical competence to succeed in conservation tasks. Only the very exceptional child could use newly acquired conservation concepts (even if they included transitivity of weight) as a basis for solving inclusion problems.

Finally, in connection with Kohnstamm's experiments, it may be worth mentioning that we also took a group of eleven subjects for a learning experiment in class inclusion, without investigating conservation. If we apply Kohnstamm's criteria for the acquisition of the concept, nine of our eleven subjects succeed; if we demand that for success at least 1 three-stage item should be solved (terriers, dogs, animals), only six of these nine succeed; if, in addition, we take into account the arguments these six subjects give for their correct answers, only three of them satisfy our criteria; and if, finally, we demand that they should be able to solve problems where the answer has a different form (for example, the subject is shown a group of terriers and other dogs and he is asked: "Are there more dogs or more animals?") only two of our subjects succeed. In fact, we obtain a perfect Guttmann-type scale if we place our items in the following order: correct answer to simple class-inclusion problems, correct answer to three-stage class-inclusion problems, valid explanation and correct answer to a problem demanding an answer of a different form. If we apply the least exacting criterion, we (like Kohnstamm) find that 85 percent of our subjects acquire the concept. However, as soon as we investigate more closely the operational and structural value of the acquisition, we find that the subjects are incapable of applying what seemed to be a correct answer based on an operational structure to a slightly more complex situation. We also find that the subjects cannot justify their answers correctly (to say "These are all animals" or "There are only animals" is not a sufficient justification for the answer "There are more animals than dogs"). Finally we find that these insufficient justifications lead to wrong answers when the situation changes (for example, when the question "Are there more animals or more dogs?" is applied to the situation where there are only dogs). These answers are examples of either a specific strategy learned in one type of problem or of a limited operational structure, but not of the acquisition of a true operational structure.

We thus do not contest Kohnstamm's results, but we do contest his interpretation of these results as the acquisition of an operational structure by empirico-didactic methods.

THE ROLE OF LANGUAGE
IN THE ACQUISITION OF OPERATIONAL STRUCTURES

For many reasons, language has often been thought the most efficient instrument in the formation of concepts. A superficial but seductive reason is linked to educational practice: when a child does not know a fact, you tell him; when he does not understand a concept, you explain. A more profound reason lies in the fact that many authors regard social interaction as the most important factor in cognitive development, and a great deal of social transmission takes place through language. A theoretically more elaborate and slightly different version of this view is Bruner's (1966) "instrumental functionalism," with its emphasis on cognitive development as a function of the evolution of different modes of representation—the symbolic, mainly linguistic, mode being the most evolved. These views appear to have in common the idea that the child, in the course of his development, fits his experience somehow to his language (which, of course, is socially transmitted) and that the verbal representation of objects and events is what allows him to acquire concepts and operations.

Our experiments on the role of language in the acquisition of operational structures were built on the following model (Sinclair, 1967). First we tried to establish whether the acquisition of a concept or an operation is accompanied by a modification in the child's language; that is to say, in the specific expressions he uses to describe simple situations that call for the same terms as are used to express the concept. Second, since we did find such modifications (which is not at all tantamount to saying that verbal development brings about operational progress), we explored what effect the teaching of expressions used by operational children had on the operative behavior of children who in a pretest were diagnosed as frankly preoperational.

The first results of the experiments exploring the modifications that accompany operative development led to a distinction between vocabulary and structure; in other words, between the semantic and the syntactic component of language. Although this distinction may be theoretically clear, practically it is difficult to handle. Within the bounds of this paper it is sufficient to admit that vocabulary concerns the *content* of what we say (expressed, for example, in descriptive lexical items, nouns, or adjectives) and that syntactical structures concern the *form* of what we say (expressed, for example, in word order, grammatical markers, auxiliary verbs, or articles).

All our experiments on the modifications of language at the beginning of the operational period show a much closer link between syntactical structure and operativity than between vocabulary and operativity. To take our experiments concerning the conservation concept as an example, one of the arguments of the children who have acquired conservation of quantity is that of compensation: when one of two balls of plasticine is transformed into a sausage, the child says that there is still the same amount of plasticine because although the sausage may be longer, it is also thinner. One might suppose that the availability of two pairs of words for two different dimensions (long:short, thin:fat) is linked to the level of operativity, or even that the correct use of these words could lead to conservation. We actually found a certain correlation between the acquisition of these lexical items and the level of operativity, but the correlation was much higher between certain structural traits of the description given by the children and their level of operativity.

Quite frequently, frankly preoperational children, when asked to describe the difference between two pencils, one long and thin, the other short and thick, show that they possess the two pairs of words that describe the two dimensions. However, in that case, their pattern of description is the following: "This pencil is long, this one is short; this one (the first) is thin, this one (the second) is fat." The children who already had conservation, on the other hand, said in the same situation: "This one is longer and thinner (than the other one)." Instead of singling out the difference in one dimension, expressing this difference in two complete sentences, using positives, and then going on to describe the difference in the other dimension in the same way, these children expressed the differences in two dimensions in one all-embracing statement, using comparatives and a coordinated structure. In many other situations we encountered the same phenomenon: what distinguished the operational from the preoperational children was not so much the use of certain lexical items as the use of structural devices: *more* and *less* (instead of *a lot* and *a little*), comparative markers and sentence structure (Inhelder et al., 1966).

These findings were used in a second series of experiments, where we tried to teach preoperational children the patterns of expression used by the operational children. If indeed language or, in general, an adequate and efficient way of coding information, has a direct formative effect on operations, an acquisition of the superior verbal forms should result in progress in operativity.

The results of verbal training in connection with the conservation of liquids were as follows.

1. It was easy (in the sense of needing few repetitions) to teach our preoperational subjects the correct use of pairs of opposites describing different dimensions. By contrast, we found that intensive drill was necessary to make the children use comparatives and coordinated sentence structure and, despite the training, a certain number of children never acquired this use.
2. Even among the children who did acquire the superior verbal forms, progress in operativity was rare: only 5 percent of our subjects acquired conservation.

The verbal training had one clear effect: those children who passed to an intermediate operational stage (30 percent) and also many who remained clearly preoperational, had learned to center on two pertinent factors in the problem (level of the liquid and diameter of the glass). Instead of simply judging the quantity of liquid by the level, as they did in the pretest, they mentioned the covariance of the two dimensions. Yet, conservation was not achieved. They would say: "There the water goes higher because the glass is thin; the other glass is shorter and wider and there is less to drink there." Noting the covariance of dimensions is not in itself sufficient to arrive at multiplication of factors, nor to understand that they are the product of a reversible transformation.

Another experiment (Sinclair, 1967) concerned the operation of seriation of lengths. Here we tried to teach children who failed on the seriation test the following expressions used by children who succeeded: (a) the description of a series of sticks as "This one is short, this one is longer, this one is still longer, . . . , this one is the longest," and inversely, "This one is long, this one is shorter, . . . , this is the shortest"; (b) the description of a stick, B, in a series of three sticks, A, B, C, as "bigger than A and smaller than C." The results were as follows.

1. It was fairly easy to obtain the first description, "short, longer, longer, . . . ," although even here some subjects had difficulties. It was considerably more difficult to make them use the reciprocal expression for the description of the same series in the other direction, "long, shorter, shorter, ..." Finally, 85 percent eventually succeeded on the first point, 50 percent on the second.
2. Only 30 percent of our subjects succeeded in describing one stick as bigger than another and, at the same time, smaller than a third. The best the others could do was to say that stick A was smaller than stick B, and that stick C was bigger than stick B—in a sense, evading our question which was to describe B in relation to A and C, not A and C in relation to B.
3. The same subjects who succeeded on the second item also acquired the operation of seriation; 25 percent made no progress at all and the rest attained an intermediate stage.

As far as progress in operativity is concerned, these results are considerably better than in the conservation experiment. Several points have to be considered here. In the first place, the group of subjects in the seriation experiment were more advanced than those in the conservation group; 25 percent of the former were initially at an intermediate stage. Almost all subjects moved only from one substage to the next.

Our second item in the learning procedure is not simply a matter of verbal training, but much closer to an operational exercise. In fact, in the seriation operation the essential point is that the subject understands that in a series of lengths—A, B, C, D, E—element D is at the same time longer than C and shorter than E; the expression "at the same time" has to be taken in a fully psychological sense. The child is quite capable of using *longer* and *shorter* (or *bigger* and *smaller*) if these terms are applied to situations that are spatially or temporally distant. For instance, he can say that element B is longer than element A, and that element B' (of the same length as element B) is shorter than C. He can also say that B is longer than A, when he is only shown A and B, and that B is shorter than C when, after a short interval, he is shown B and C. But he often remains incapable of saying that B is longer than A and shorter than C; for this, he needs the same type of coordination and integration that is necessary for the operation itself.

Finally, the seriation experiment is different from the conservation experiment, in that conservation is never visible by itself whereas relations in a regular series are perceptible and allow a description that, in a sense, is an exact replica of the result of the operation.

It is difficult, and certainly would be premature, to draw definitive conclusions from the results of these experiments. However, the data seem to justify the following.

1. The acquisition of appropriate verbal patterns does not per se bring about the acquisition of concepts and operations. Progress from frankly preoperational level to the acquisition of an operational structure is rare, although not totally absent. On the other hand, progress from one substage to another is much less rare and becomes fairly frequent if verbal training is combined with operational exercises (as in the case of the seriation experiment). Bruner (1966), in an experiment on the conservation of quantity (done with modeling clay), reports a similar effect. We cannot agree with his interpretation (Inhelder et al., 1966), which is essentially the following: the iconic representation, linked to perception, has to be overcome; this is most efficiently done by symbolic representation (verbal expression); when the misleading perceptual cues are very strong, symbolic representation (labeling) has to be reinforced by enactive representation (manipulation) if the child is to overcome his iconic representation.

We cannot here state our reasons for disagreeing, since this would necessitate a discussion of Bruner's entire theory. However, we can suggest an interpretation of our own: operational exercises imply meaningful action on the part of the child ("action" does not necessarily mean manipulation of objects); it is the feedback from these actions that brings about operational progress. Verbal training, designed to make the child acquire patterns used by children who are already in possession of the operation in question, results (if it succeeds) in conscious use of appropriate language—and let us not forget that speaking also is a form of action. Such action can reinforce the feedback from the other coordinating actions performed by the child, especially in the case of an operation of which the result can be described in a way that is very similar to the operation itself.

2. It has often been said that, between the ages of three and six, the child acquires most of the structures of adult language. However, during that time we note a number of what P. Menyuk (1963) calls "restricted structures" in the child's language, which are only gradually eliminated. The parallelism we noticed between the verbal patterns and the level of operativity of our subjects points to the fact that an operational component is at work in the acquisition of linguistic structures. Moreover, the difficulties encountered by the subjects in the learning of certain expressions seem to be of the same nature as the difficulties encountered in the acquisition of operations: an incapacity to decenter and coordinate. Therefore, linguistic structures do not seem to be acquired uniquely according to their own laws, much less to be innate: an operational component is necessary before linguistic structures, acquired in isolated sentences, are ready to be generalized and correctly applied in all situations.

CONCLUSIONS

From these first samples of research on the learning of logical structures, we conclude that the evolution of operativity is malleable only within certain limits imposed by the laws of development. No matter whether they are exposed to a confrontation with physical experience or to verbal training, children at the preoperational level do not acquire truly logical structures and, at best, reach an intermediate level. A certain number of those who start from this latter level reach the threshold of concrete operations, and such an acquisition is an extreme case of the regulations that characterize the partial coordinations of intermediate levels. Finally, those who start from a first operational stage rapidly extend their logical structuration to more and more complex situations. This extension, however, is bound by a certain field of knowledge.

Although learning may accelerate development (within certain limits), such acceleration apparently obeys limitative conditions of assimilation which, in turn, are subject to temporal regulations reminiscent of the "chronological succession of competences" in embryology, as Waddington (Piaget, 1967) calls them. In fact, if the subject already has acquired partial logical structures, he assimilates better and more rapidly the same physical and verbal data. The more the subject is capable of establishing new relationships, the more the experiment is productive of new hypotheses.

The problem of interaction between different fields of knowledge (numerical, logical, spatial, physical) seems extremely complex, and we can do no more than draw a few, rather tentative conclusions.

First, it seems clear that the possession of an elementary invariant (conservation of number) is a prerequisite of success—even of partial success—in learning experiments in any field. Until now, we have not been able to provoke more than fugitive moments of operational structuring in children who are totally preoperational in the pretests.

Second, the possession or acquisition of a structure in one field can interact in different ways with the acquisition of structures in another field. In the case of conservation concepts, the possession of an invariant in one field certainly does not lead by easy, gradual steps to conservation in another field. On the contrary, as was shown in the experiment on number and length (and we have several other experiments of the same kind, comparing, for instance, number and quantity or weight and volume), the first effect of such learning procedures often is visible only in the appearance of explicit conflict that the child is unable to solve. However, as the learning sessions continue, the child struggles for ways to resolve the conflict. It is here that our procedures must remain supple, for the ways in which partial resolving of the conflict begins can be very different from one child to another. The awareness of contradictions seems to act as an incentive to decentration: the child begins to search for both similarities and differences between the two problems and this may finally lead him to a true new acquisition in a different field. Such new acquisitions are certainly not the result of a linear progression, where bits of new knowledge are simply added on to an existing structure.

Finally, the acquisition of a structure in one field can either aid operational progress in a different field or be without any effect whatsoever. If, as was the case in the inclusion-conservation experiment, we exercise only one field in our learning sessions and test the child's behavior in the other field at the conclusion of the experiment, both alternatives occur. Transfer of acquisition to a different field seems to depend on several factors.

Logico-mathematical progress is more apt to cause progress in the physical field than vice versa. We may suppose that this is due to the fact that, in learning procedures concerning logico-mathematical operations, the operational grouping itself is more directly acted upon, whereas in the case of conservation concepts the better coordination of reversible relationships and the integration of empirical data does not directly reflect upon the underlying operations. However, even for a transfer from the logical field to the physical field to take place, certain conditions must be fulfilled, and these conditions bring us back to the temporal aspect of the acquisition of operational structures.

In the first place, we observed, as we have already mentioned, that much depends on the initial level of the subject: the lower his level, the more a new acquisition tends to stay limited either to the particular problem or to the particular field. Before a new logical acquisition can serve as a basis for the building up of structures in physical or causal fields, a certain time of assimilation is necessary. New accommodations do not seem to take place in the case of very recently acquired assimilatory schemes. In the second place, a time element seems to intervene in the learning process itself. We were astonished to notice that several of our subjects who learned quickly and surely, without regressions or hesitations from one session to the next, showed no sign of transfer of what they had acquired to a different field, whereas other subjects, who during two or three sessions seemed to have great difficulties in progressing from one item to another and who frequently regressed from one session to another, finally showed a true mastery of the learned concept as well as transfer to another field.

Learning of the fundamental operations of thought means to *understand*.

Understanding does not consist in simply incorporating ready-made and readily available data, but rather in rediscovering them or reinventing them by one's own activity. Rediscovery is certainly facilitated by using a system of symbolization, as Bruner has emphasized, but language as such a system is but an instrument and a child must learn to use it. This learning capacity is not provided by the instrument, but by the subject.

To summarize, learning is subordinate to the laws of development, and development does not consist in a mere successive accumulation of bits of learning, since development follows structuration laws that are both logical and biological.

REFERENCES

Bruner, J. S. *The process of education*. Cambridge: Harvard University Press, 1960.

Bruner, J. S. The course of cognitive growth. *American Psychologist*, 1964, **19**, 1–15.

Bruner, J. S. et al. *Studies in cognitive growth*. New York: Wiley, 1966.

Inhelder, B., & Piaget, J. *The early growth of logic in the child (classification and seriation)*. New York: Harper, 1964. (Original ed., 1959)

Inhelder, B. et al. On cognitive development. *American Psychologist*, 1966, 21, No. 2.

Inhelder, B., Bovet, M., & Sinclair, H. Développement et apprentissage. *Revue suisse de psychologie*. 1967, **26**, No. 1, 1–23.

Kohnstamm, G. A. An evaluation of part of Piaget's theory. *Acta Psychologica*, 1963, 21.

Kohnstamm, G. A. *Teaching children to solve a Piagetian problem of class inclusion.* Mouton & Co. (Gravenhage) 1967.

Menyuk, P. Syntactic structures in the language of children. *Journal of Child Development*, 1963, 34, 407–422.

Pascual Leone, J., & Bovet, M. L'apprentissage de la quantification de l'inclusion et la théorie opératoire. Partie I. *Acta Psychologica*, 1966, 25.

Pascual Leone, J., & Bovet, M. Quelques résultats expérimentaux nouveaux. *Acta Psychologica*, 1967, **26**, 64–74.

Piaget, J., & Inhelder, B. *Le développement des quantités physiques*. Neuchâtel et Paris: Delachaux et Niestlé, 1941 (2nd ed., 1962).

Piaget, J., & Inhelder, B. *The child's conception of space*. London: Routledge and Kegan Paul, 1956. (Original French ed., 1948, Paris P.U.F.)

Piaget, J., Inhelder, B., & Szeminska, A. *The child's conception of geometry*. New York: Basic Books & Harper, 1960. (Original ed., 1948)

Piaget, J. *Biologie et connaissance*. Paris: Gallimard, 1967.

Ripple, E., & Rockastle, V. (Eds.) *Piaget rediscovered*. Report of the conference on cognitive studies and curriculum development, Cornell University, 1964.

Sinclair, H. *Acquisition du langage et développement de la pensée*. Paris: Dunod, 1967.

Smedslund, J. Apprentissage des notions de la conservation et de la transitivité du poids. *L'apprentissage des structures logiques, Etudes d'épistémologie génétique*, Paris, P.U.F. 1959, IX, 85–124.

2

DISEQUILIBRIUM AS
A SOURCE OF DEVELOPMENT[1]

A comprehensive look at developmental psychology reveals three major approaches to change: the mechanistic or behavioristic, the organismic, and the psychoanalytic views. (For a fuller discussion of these three theoretical perspectives, see Langer, 1969.)

Only one of these perspectives, the mechanistic stimulus-response view, does not include some concept of an equilibration process to account for progressive change, whether short-term (local) change or long-term (developmental) change. The sole exception to this characterization is part of Berlyne's (1965) formulation of stable and dynamic habit-family hierarchies, as described in his recent book. However, this is more of an apparent than a real exception. Insofar as Berlyne's exposition involves equilibration between habit structures, it is due to nothing more than (as he himself puts it) a reinterpretation into behavioristic terminology of some of Piaget's organismic ideas on the equilibration process. Berlyne's hypotheses are not direct or necessary outgrowths of a mechanistic stimulus-response psychology of development.

The major reason why a mechanistic theory of development would not typically concern itself with an equilibration process is that it usually assumes that psychological growth is *nothing but* the increasing quantitative and continuous accumulation of behavior. A basic presumption of this type of approach is that there is no qualitative discontinuity—structural or functional—in development. Even such atypical mechanistic, mediation theorists as Vygotsky (1962) and Luria (1961), who

---

[1] Expanded version of paper originally presented for a symposium on *"Acceleration" of Logical Operations* at meetings of the Society for Research in Child Development, New York City, April 1967.

JONAS LANGER

University of California, Berkeley, California

coupled their basically stimulus-response psychology with the idea that there are discontinuous stages of thinking, did not introduce the concept of equilibrium in order to explain progressive development. As a consequence, one is at a total loss to understand what the process of development from one stage to the other may be, according to these theorists, if there are truly discontinuous stages. The problem clearly does not arise for typical mechanistic, mediation theorists, such as Kendler and Kendler (1962), who subscribe to the notion that the mediational mechanism is nothing but overt conditioning mechanisms that have become covert, and mediators are merely nonobservable responses that act as self-stimulation.

Equilibration is a central concept of the two other developmental perspectives; their basic differences lie in their conceptualization of the equilibration process and in the focus of their concern. Psychoanalytic theory is concerned with the health of personal-emotional development. A core hypothesis is that intrapsychic conflict between id desires and ego and superego restraints, and/or conflict between the individual and society, leads to personal crises or intrapsychic disequilibrium (Erikson, 1950; 1959). Resolution of these dynamic, conflicting forces—the reestablishment of equilibrium—is the prerequisite condition for normal or healthy adjustment and eventual progress to the next stage of personality development. However, the primary definition or formal determinant of the ensuing stage is the investment of libidinal energy in a new bodily zone; the epigenetic shift in the zone of instinctual localization ensures progressive development. It is not the new equilibrium achieved due to the resolution of a crisis that causes progress; this achievement merely ensures that the development will be healthy. For example, disequilibrium at the oral stage, according to Erikson, centers on the crisis of trust versus mistrust. Adequate resolution of this crisis is the prerequisite equilibrium necessary for the

23

eventual progress to the anal stage to be healthy. Successful coping, with its associated "feelings" of competence, is the type of experience that increases the child's ability and willingness to deal with new situations and challenges. However, this is not the theoretical source of the anal stage; its most immediate cause is the epigenetic shift of instinctual investment to the anal zone.

The organismic view differs from this psychoanalytic conception of the equilibration process as a means of explaining the relative health (of development) rather than development itself, and it focuses on intellectual rather than affective development. The general organismic view is that each successive stage of development is a more equilibrated transformation of the functional structures that constitute the organization of its preceding stage. The process of equilibration, then, refers to both (a) how the developing organism uses its systems of action to control itself and direct its interaction with the environment, and (b) how the actions of the growing organism direct and regulate its own development. Two versions, a topographical and a probabilistic model, of the equilibration process have been posited.

The topographical model is most closely associated with Werner's (1948) conceptions. In particular, Werner's formulation of the orthogenetic process implies that development is directed toward the evolution of increasing differentiation, centralization, and hierarchic integration—that is, toward a more equilibrated state of adaptation. There is one domain, perceptual development, where this was directly spelled out. The so-called sensory-tonic theory assumes that the growth of compensatory forces, to balance out perturbations of the organism's sensory-tonic state, is the basis of perceptual development.[2] The consequent perceptual end product progresses from global and egocentric percepts to analytic and perspectivistic percepts and eventually to synthetic and integrated percepts (Werner, 1957).

The probabilistic model of the equilibration process is most closely associated with Piaget's (1967) conceptions. The thesis is that, when the child is in a structural state of disequilibrium, his assimilatory and accommodatory functions act to establish greater equilibrium. This can only come about by the performance of those actions that compensate for the perturbation and then feedback of the information obtained by these acts to the operative mental system. In this way the child changes his mental actions and develops.

The most direct method of studying the equilibration process of perceptual and conceptual development involves externally perturbing the child so that he may be

---

[2]A succinct statement of the equilibrial dynamics of sensory-tonic states, but not of their developmental aspects and relationship to perception, is provided by N. Wiener (1964, pp. 268–269): "Human beings stand erect . . . because they are continually resisting the tendency to fall down, either forward or backward, and manage to offset either tendency by a contraction of muscles pulling them in the opposite direction. The equilibrium which we find in life processes, is not static but results from a continuous interplay of processes which resist in an active way any tendency for them to lead to a breakdown." This formulation was, of course, anticipated by Kurt Goldstein (1939) many years ago as a consequence of his work with brain-damaged patients in World War I. It has received its most advanced treatment to date as the sensory-tonic theory of perception (e.g., Wapner and Werner, 1957).

assumed to be in a state of disequilibrium. In the study of perception, the method is designed to induce disequilibrium in his sensory-tonic state by procedures such as tilting the child's body to one side at an angle of 30 degrees. In the study of conception, the method is designed to induce disequilibrium in his cognitive state by procedures such as presenting him with apparent contradictions, examples of which will be described presently.

Two major theoretical parameters of the equilibration process exist that constitute the formal determinants of progressive and regressive mental development. One parameter is organizational, and has two important aspects: (a) the interaction of differentiated mental acts that are functionally related but have not been integrated into a structural hierarchy, and (b) the interaction of the symbolic media in which the acts and the presentational problem are embodied. The second parameter is energetic. It refers to the disequilibrium that the child must feel, whether consciously or not, if he is to recognize that something is wrong and is to be motivated to change his conceptual activity.

For expository purposes, we will begin with a discussion of the two aspects of the organizational parameter, followed by a consideration of the energetic parameter.

ORGANIZATIONAL PARAMETER: ACTIONS IN INTERACTION

This aspect is relevant to the understanding of conceptual progress when differentiated mental acts develop from global or syncretic considerations of a cognitive problem. These differentiated acts function in a segregated fashion, even though their integration may be prerequisite to adequate cognitive consideration and solution. One may therefore plausibly hypothesize that conditions designed to facilitate functional integration of such segregated mental acts will have a progressive effect. If truly effective, such conditions should lead to progressive cognitive reorganization that is attested to by transfer of this progress to other but related problems. The reverse should also be true: conditions designed to interfere with functional integration should result in regressive effects.

Consider the development of the concept of class inclusion. The paradigmatic situation is one in which children are presented with ten round beads, seven of which are red and three blue, for inspection. Then, the child is asked questions such as, "Which would make a longer necklace, one made of the round beads or one made of the red beads?"

Basic to the conceptualization of class inclusion is the ability to differentiate parts from the whole, yet consider them simultaneously and in (ascending and descending) relation to each other. Eventually this leads to the theoretical understanding of class structures as having intensive (qualitative) and extensive (quantitative) characteristics. On this basis, Inhelder and Piaget (1964) hypothesize the following developmental sequence.

Preconceptual stage (about 1½ to 4 years of age). The child begins to have some inkling of what a class is. However, he cannot differentiate between a general concept and particular instances of that concept, let alone distinguish between a whole and its part. The child does not yet clearly understand that elements in a spatial configuration are discrete units, and without such differentiation there are no elements for classification, such as belonging to a class (whole) and/or subclass (part). The child's interchangeable and fluctuating usage of the terms "all" and "some" reflect this conceptual syncresis.

Intuitive stage (about 4 to 7 years of age). The child begins to differentiate between a class (whole) and its subclasses (parts), but he still confuses quality (intension) with quantity (extension). As a consequence, his considerations are limited to intuitive reflections on the whole *or* on a part. He therefore is drawn to (stimulus bound by) the most salient feature—the seven red beads—and typically asserts that there are more red beads than round beads.

Concrete stage (about 7 to 10 years of age). The child more clearly differentiates between the quality (intension) and the quantity (extension) of the elements of a spatial configuration when classifying them into wholes and parts. The child begins to be able to *simultaneously* consider (mentally integrate) both whole and parts. As a consequence, in most instances he should come to the conclusion that there are more round beads than red beads. Mental integration is still not complete, however. He has yet to develop an integrated concept of classes that takes into account unusual possibilities and materials with which he is not well acquainted.

Formal stage (about 10 to 15 years of age). During this period the development of classificatory concepts is consolidated. The child's understanding becomes principled and he can express his understanding in the form of rules.

Now, it seems reasonable that there should be a transitional phase (intermediate stage) of cognitive functioning between the intuitive and concrete stage. It should arise when the child *successively* shifts back and forth from one salient characteristic to another. Such successive cognitive shifting from parts to the whole may be spontaneous or the child may be led to shift; here he might still concentrate on one characteristic at a time and not relate them into a class concept. However, successive shifting between parts and the whole might be just the sort of interaction between discrete mental acts that would lead to disequilibrium in the intuitively established organization that is designed only to accommodate single concentrations. Helping the child to concentrate successively upon a part and then the whole, or vice versa, should facilitate the breakdown of the child's attachment to a single intuitive concentration. In addition, successive concentrations that closely follow each other should lead to the memory of opposing judgments—more round beads *and* more red beads—that must accommodate to each other. When opposing concentrations begin to be accommodated to each other, the internal conditions are ripe for the cognitive organization to begin to change from segregated to integrated, or more equilibrated functional structures. The observable changes in cognitive behavior that may be expected are (a) fluctuation of judgments, (b) increased probability of logical judgments in conditions designed to facilitate successive judgments, and (c) positive transfer to more difficult conditions that, by themselves, do not direct the child to successive concentrations.

This theoretical hypothesis led to testing children on two conditions, which we shall call the "simultaneous" and "successive" conditions. This was part of a series of studies on classificatory behavior being conducted by Mrs. Carolyn Schwartz in our laboratory (Schwartz and Langer, 1967). In the simultaneous condition the child is presented with the beads and asked which would make a longer necklace, one made of the round beads or one made of the red beads. This inquiry does not directly suggest the possibility of first considering one aspect, then the other. In the successive condition, the child is presented with the same situation, but now the inquiry directs the child to first consider one aspect and then the other. He is told: "Pretend that I make a necklace of the round beads, then I put them back. Then pretend that you make a necklace of the red beads; then you put them back. Who had the longer necklace—you or I?"

The test group comprised 32 kindergarten, 32 third-grade, and 32 fifth-grade children. As expected, the successive condition was easier for all ages tested (Table 2.1). Of particular interest was the effect of the order of presentation. At all ages, the simultaneous condition was easier to solve if it was preceded by the successive condition. Conversely, the successive condition was more difficult to solve if it was preceded by the simultaneous condition.

Table 2.1 *Number of subjects correct in successive-simultaneous condition test.*

Age (mean)	5.6		9.0		10.6	
Order	Succ	Sim	Succ	Sim	Succ	Sim
Succ - - → Sim	5	2	9	6	15	15
Sim - - → Succ	0	0	5	5	12	6
Total	5	2	14	11	27	21

Thus, when the situation induces the child to integrate his successive mental acts, his classificatory conceptualization progresses. In addition, it has a positive transfer effect on a more difficult (simultaneous) version of the class-inclusion problem, the frequency of which effect varies with the developmental level of the children. Table 2.1 reveals that it is most effective with the oldest children; the reverse is true when the child is presented with a situation that, in effect, requires the simultaneous integration of mental considerations that he is not yet capable of performing. Not only is it more difficult but it has a negative transfer effect on dealing with the easier, successive condition.

In sum, the child's mental actions lead to some transformation of his cognitive organization. This transformation is functionally progressive when his actions result in his considerations being increasingly integrated, and functionally regressive when his actions lead to his considerations being segregated.

ORGANIZATIONAL PARAMETER: SYMBOLIC MEDIUM

The second aspect of the organizational parameter of equilibration with which we are concerned is the interaction between the media in which the problem is presented and the media in which the child is thinking. We are striving for those conditions where optimal symbolic interaction obtains, enabling the child to cope most effectively with a given problem.

It is obvious that teaching the child to use a symbolic medium in a form more advanced than his own conceptual level will not ensure progress in his thought processes. Studies performed in Geneva suggest that there is an apparent parallel progression in linguistic and conceptual development. For example, Inhelder and her coworkers report (1966, and Article 1 in this book) that the child at the intuitive stage does not conserve and at the same time uses absolute (big, small), nondifferentiated (something is both big and small), and uncoordinated (bigger or smaller, but not both) descriptive terminology. The child at the concrete stage conserves and uses relative, differentiated, and coordinated terminology. Most relevant for our purposes are studies in which children at the intuitive stage are trained to understand and use the more advanced linguistic terminology usually associated with conservation solutions of children at the concrete stage. The results are negative. Their conception does not progress at all from nonconservation to conservation.

Such findings coincide with a major organismic hypothesis of cognitive development. Words are not labels that the child passively learns (in accordance with principles of conditioning and reinforcement and via a communicative process of imitation) to associate with things and eventually concepts. Rather, the mental operations available to the child constrain the constructions that the child imposes on communicated messages. As a consequence, the same words may have different meaning—productive and comprehensive meaning—for the child at different stages of his cognitive development.

We therefore have taken another tack. Rather than attempting to teach the child to use an advanced form of symbolization in the hope that it will have a progressive effect on his cognitive competence, we have begun to systematically investigate his thought processes (a) when the conceptual problem is presented in a variety of media, and (b) when the child focally utilizes different symbolic media in which to think.

In addition to the perceptual-imaginal conditions already described, the following conditions are being investigated.

Successive practical. In the class-inclusion problem, the experimenter tells the child that he is going to make a necklace out of the round beads. After making the necklace, the experimenter replaces all the beads and tells the child to make a necklace out of the red beads. After the child has made his necklace, he is told to put the beads back together with the others. Then he is asked: "Who had the longer necklace, you or I?"

Before going on to describe the other conditions, some remarks should be made about the practical versus the imaginal conditions. When the child is practically manipulating the beads, his mental operations are not limited to the gestural symbolic medium. The practical condition is merely an attempt to ensure that he also uses gestural processes. In addition, the child might be using the variety of symbolic processes—imaginal and verbal—that are available to him. By contrast, in the imaginal condition he is not permitted to practically manipulate the objects. Therefore, he is hindered in using gestural processes but not in using the other imaginal and verbal media. The comparison, then, is between conceptualization when the child is permitted to use gestural, imaginal, and all other symbolic processes versus when he is permitted to use imaginal and all other symbolic processes except the gestural.

Drawing. Children are presented verbally with the class-inclusion problem and are asked to draw what has been described to them. Then they are asked whether there are more round beads or red beads.

Verbal. The situation is described, the question is asked orally, and the child must respond orally.

Although our work on the last two conditions, drawing and speech, is still in the exploratory stage, the results that are emerging support the expectations. In comparable situations, the child can more easily cope with class inclusion if he uses practical-gestural means of thinking as compared with when he is restricted to imaginal means. When the problem situation is presented verbally but the child is allowed to draw it before being verbally questioned, class inclusion is easier than when he is limited to the verbal medium.

Another condition is also being investigated. First, the problem situation and the question are presented verbally and the child gives his solution verbally. Then he is asked to draw the problem situation, and is questioned again. The children tested tend to (a) make their drawings conform to their previous solutions, not to the actual material presented, and (b) not change their solutions.

These exploratory findings suggest the following working hypothesis. When a solution has already been formed, the child's subsequent actions will be directed toward maintaining coherence with the schemes formed, based on that prior solution. Providing the child with the opportunity to think in a drawing medium, which is easier than the verbal medium he previously was forced to think in and in which the problem situation and the question were embodied, does not have a progressive effect. This implies that a self-regulating mechanism of coherently fitting prior schemes with present actions, is operative. A progressive effect is attained by providing the child with the opportunity to think in an easier drawing medium (in addition to any others he may spontaneously employ) than the one in which the problem situation is presented before he is questioned about class inclusion. The apparent reason for this attainment is that a solution has not yet been formulated that determines the child's scheme of class inclusion. Thus, the self-regulatory mechanism of coherence is not relevant and therefore is not operative.

ENERGETIC PARAMETER

Here the concern is with the affective character of disequilibrium between mental acts as a source of cognitive reconstruction, whether progressive or regressive. In an early work on the development of causal concepts, Piaget (1927) presents evidence that suggests the child must be cognitively "ready" to assimilate contradictory information and to feel that something is wrong, if there is to be any cognitive reorganization and development. An illustration is the case of the six- to eight-year-old child who thinks that the moon moves because it is following him around. He does not question whether or not it also follows other people and whether it therefore is possible that the moon follows anybody. Only between nine and ten years of age does the child consider the idea that if the moon follows him then it might follow other people too. He realizes that this is impossible—the moon could not follow everyone at the same time. He therefore deduces that the moon follows no one but, because it is very high up in the sky, everyone sees it as just above himself and following him.

Note the formal similarity between this type of example of the ontogenetic process of conceptual progress and the characterization of the historical process of scientific progress by Kuhn (1962):

> Discovery commences with the awareness of anomaly, i.e., with recognition that nature has somehow violated the paradigm-induced expectations that govern normal science. It then continues with a more or less extended exploration of the area of anomaly. And it closes only when the paradigm theory has been adjusted so that the anomalous has become the expected. Assimilating a new sort of fact demands a more than additive adjustment of theory, and until that adjustment is completed—until the scientist has learned to see nature in a different way—the new fact is not quite a scientific fact at all.

> The preceding remarks should suffice to show how crisis simultaneously loosens the stereotypes and provides the incremental data necessary for a fundamental paradigm shift. Sometimes the shape of the new paradigm is foreshadowed in the structure that extraordinary research has given to the anomaly. Einstein wrote that before he had any substitute for classical mechanics, he could see the inter-relation between the known anomalies of black-body radiation, the photoelectric effect, and specific heats. More often no such structure is consciously seen in advance. Instead, the new paradigm, or a sufficient hint to permit later articulation, emerges all at once, sometimes in the middle of the night, in the mind of a man deeply immersed in crisis. What the nature of that final stage is—how an individual invents (or finds he has invented) a new way of giving order to data now all assembled—must here remain inscrutable and may be permanently so.

Kuhn's pessimism with respect to the possibility of scrutinizing how the final stage of a scientific invention emerges derives from his Gestalt perspective: construction or discovery of a new paradigm or a novel hypothesis is a process of instantaneous and unconscious insight. Our own assumption that development is a process of progressive construction leads us to be more optimistic with respect to the possibilities for theoretical and empirical scrutiny of conceptual change in ontogenesis.

Our basic hypothesis is that disequilibrium is an initial source of cognitive development. Smedslund (1961) first began to investigate directly the progressive effects of introducing cognitive conflict so that the child will feel that something is wrong. He reports some limited success. To date, the most successful endeavor using direct cognitive conflict is reported by Inhelder et al. (1966, and Article 1 in this book). Their technique is designed to make the child *successively* consider different aspects and outcomes of the problem. The child is presented with two columns of three glasses. Five of these glasses are equal in size, one of the glasses in the middle row is taller and thinner. The bottoms of the top four glasses have taps that can be opened to let the liquid flow into the glasses underneath them. Equal amounts of liquid are poured into the top two glasses and the child is allowed to familiarize himself with the workings of the apparatus. Then he is asked to predict the level the liquid will achieve when it runs into the glasses in the row below. After each prediction, the liquid is let down into the row below. The child makes observations of the liquid level achieved and is confronted with the contradictions between his predictions and the outcomes. The apparent nature of the contradiction, plus the fact that the transformations are performed successively in front of him, facilitates partial progress. A few children who are at the intuitive stage (where they do not conserve at all) change to "fluctuation and uncertainty" or partial conservation. Many children who are at the transitional stage change to completely conservation answers. It is as if a partial shift is the only development possible when the child is already in a transitional phase between stages.

Here then we see the progressive conceptual consequences of a conflict condition that leads to successive consideration of different aspects of the situation. In contrast, we wanted to examine more directly the consequences of an impossible (potential conflict) condition that directs the child to simultaneous rather than successive consideration since, from our own investigation, we know that induced successive consideration—practical or imaginal—has progressive effects by itself. The following situation was used. The child was presented with the same ten beads, but this time he was instructed to place the round beads on one side of the table and the red beads on the other. As presented, this is an impossible task from the adult point of view because all of the beads are round. We will call this impossible task the *simultaneous-practical* condition.

The previously mentioned studies by other investigators seem to assume that external contradiction will lead to cognitive conflict and that this will, so to speak, energize cognitive reorganization or conceptual progress. Since we make no such assumption about the efficacy of externally introduced perturbations, our approach was to try to measure the emotional reaction to an "impossible" cognitive task. We wanted to observe whether young children would perceive the problem as having something wrong with it, and if they did, what they would do about it. Finally, we wished to determine whether it would have a positive, progressive effect or a negative, debilitating effect.

To these ends, the analysis discussed here is directed toward the child's feelings that something is wrong. It is based on the stages described 40 years ago by Brind,[3] who was concerned with the development of critical attitudes toward erroneous assertions such as "When it rains, it's dry." The first precritical period is composed of two stages.

Stage 1: Naive credulity. In our situation this means that the child blithely separates and places the beads on the opposite sides of the table without questioning the task demand. Nothing is wrong.

Stage 2: Uncertainty or diffuse distress. According to Brunswick, this is the ontogenetic and historical mark of the beginnings of independent judgment. It is indicated by puzzlement—a questioning look or frown—while separating the beads. The child is beginning to feel that something is wrong.

This precritical period is followed by three stages of criticalness proper where the child feels that something is wrong. These stages are characterized by progressive differentiation between correct and incorrect assertions.

Stage 3: Stereotyped rejection or global negativism. The child says something like "No," "Bad," and "It is an incorrect problem."

Stage 4: Specific rejection. The child gives a specific reason for his rejection of the problem: "I can't put the red beads in two places at the same time." He is, in fact, pointing to the weakness in the task.

Stage 5: Positive correction. The child points to the weakness in the task and at the same time tries to modify the task requirement so that a solution is possible. For example, one child said "I can do it but not at the same time."

The next two stages of *higher-order criticism* are the most advanced. According to Brunswick, they "transcend criticism in the narrow sense of the word."

Stage 6: Constructive interpretation. This includes responses reflecting realization of the impossibility as the problem stands, but with a change of the material so that a constructive solution is possible. For example, one child suggested painting the beads another color. Another lined the beads up so that the blues were on one side and the rest on the other; his reasoning was that he had "all" and "some" that way.

Stage 7: Amusement or disgust. An expression of superiority. The only example we had was one fifth-grader who laughed at the experimenter's request.

The reactions of all but one of the kindergarten children belonged to the precritical period. Of the test group, 19 were at the first stage—naive credulity—and 12 were at the second stage—uncertainty or diffuse distress. One child's behavior was characteristic of the fifth stage, that of positive correction. The third-grade children were not much more advanced: 19 were at the first stage, 10 at the second stage, and 3 at the fourth stage of specific rejection. The big advance took place at the fifth-grade level: 9 were still at the first stage and 1 at the second stage, but 7 were at the fourth stage of specific rejection, 5 at the fifth stage of positive

[3] A fascinating report of Brind's work is contained in an essay by Egon Brunswick, "Ontogenetic and Other Developmental Parallels to the History of Science."

correction, 9 at the sixth stage of constructive interpretation, and 1 at the seventh stage of amusement.

The older the child the more likely he is to display aspects of criticalness appropriate to several stages. Earlier forms of criticalness are not necessarily replaced but rather are integrated into the later pattern of criticalness and, in some instances, unfold in a microgenetic sequence. In this way we are able to begin to determine whether the child recognizes that something is wrong. We can also assess the cognitive aspect of his emotional reaction, namely, his criticalness if he feels that something is wrong. It should be stressed that introduction of this impossible and (particularly in the older children) conflict-producing condition does not always have a progressive effect on coping with the other conditions of classification; if anything, its effect may be regressive. Children often do more poorly in some conditions if they are preceded by the simultaneous-practical condition. Questioning of the children afterward seems to reveal that their thinking in these situations may become more rigid. When asked what their instructions had been, they sometimes describe them in accord with the solutions they gave, rather than the actual instructions; the child may say: "You told me to put the blue ones here and red ones over here."

Again, the cognitive purpose seems to be the maintenance of coherence. That is, the child seems to assimilate his memory of the instructions to accord (fit) with the scheme of his prior solution. Whether the child is consciously or unconsciously engaged in maintaining coherence requires further empirical study. The degree to which self-regulatory activity of this type is unconscious and/or conscious is probably determined by the developmental level of the child's mental operations, and particularly by his standing on the egocentrism-perspectivism dimension.

Let us now briefly consider another but related type of cognitive conflict that has been utilized in studies where the children's conceptual level of performance was initially determined. The children are exposed to an adult model who consistently gives judgments that are different from those of the subject. Some children are exposed to models who respond at levels that are theoretically higher, and others to models whose responses are lower. The children are rewarded if they change their subsequent performance to accord with the model's level of judgment. The greatest success with this technique has been reported by Bandura and McDonald (1963) in a study of moral judgment. Their study does not deal with logical concepts per se, and is limited to only one aspect of moral judgments: whether the child morally judges acts in terms of their intentions or amount of consequence.

The technique, however, has some interest for the question of disequilibrium as a source of change. In some recent work (Cowan, Langer, Heavenrich, and Nathanson, 1969), we have attempted to replicate aspects of the Bandura and McDonald study. Three findings are of particular interest.

1. It is extremely difficult to categorize some of the subjects' judgments. Actually, it is only possible to rate the children's responses by assigning assertions about amount to the category of low judgment, and assuming that the rest of the responses are high. The range of responses is vast in this latter category and almost impossible to classify.

2. The changes brought about in the children's moral judgments range in the 50 percent to 60 percent level. This means that approximately one-half of the judgments remain the same, while the other half changes to fit the model's type of judgment.

3. Some of the children are overtly distressed and may even ask the experimenter what to do.

The above suggests that the children are confused because of the apparent conflict between their own judgment or mental acts and the model's judgment. It does not mean that their cognitive organization has been transformed, but it does suggest that conflict between judgments is one type of perturbative activity that may provide the appropriate energizing conditions necessary to disequilibrium and conceptual change. However, it should be remembered that studies of conformity behavior suggest that situations such as the one used above may have two general consequences: acquiescence, and attempts at verification. In the former, the child tries to say what he thinks the model is saying and what the experimenter wants. This would hardly bespeak reorganization in the logic of the child's thinking. Attempts at verification may take place if the disparity between his own judgments and those of the model (if the child accepts him as a reference group) leads the child to doubt both his and the model's judgments. Then he may attempt to obtain some determining "proof" by mental experimentation.

Consequently, I would hypothesize that major changes in cognitive organization require additional possibilities for the child to perform mental operations directed toward obtaining verification of one or the other kind of judgment. Little opportunity is provided for this in the Bandura and McDonald study. As a matter of fact, one might plausibly hypothesize that, if used as a pedagogical method, the modeling and reinforcement technique would result at worst in confusion leading to rigid mimicry without understanding. At best, it might lead to some progress if the required intellectual jump is small. This is precisely what Turiel (1966, and Article 5 in this book) has reported in a recent study of moral judgment. In addition, Turiel finds that children are very resistant to attempts to induce both small (one-stage) backward shifts and big (two or more stages) forward shifts.

One suspects that the reason for resistance to backward shifting is different from that for resistance to forward shifting. Resistance to backward shifts of only one stage cannot be the result of the requisite cognitive structure not being available. After all, the child has presumably just passed through the stage to which the experiment is trying to shift him back. If the orthogenetic principle (Werner, 1948) is operative, then we must assume that the functional structures of the previous stage that the experiment is trying to evoke are not lost. Observations of children in cognitive situations suggest that the issue is not that the children have lost the functional usage of earlier structures and therefore cannot cognitively comprehend the theoretically more primitive position. Rather, the resistance comes from their having rejected the more primitive cognitive position as inadequate; for example, in longitudinal studies, children who are reminded of their earlier judgments of nonconservation often laugh at them and call them silly.[4]

Small (one-stage) forward progress coupled with resistance to big (two or more stages) progressive jumps suggest the converse. Functional structures requisite to the next stage of development may be present in potential or rudimentary form. Disequilibrium may trigger activation of these functional structures and their transformation from rudimentary to comprehensive configurations. However, functional structures requisite to two stages ahead cannot be activated as easily, even when they are present in rudimentary form, because those of one stage ahead must first develop and have their period of ascendancy.

As a final comment on these studies it should be added that, if we are to speak about the process(es) of cognitive development in general and not only about the development of moral concepts, we must await attempts to accelerate logical conceptualization per se with the modeling and reinforcement technique by itself. In particular, we may wonder if this technique can be used to achieve a stable change in children's logical concepts—such as from nonconservation to conservation—and whether this generalizes to other concepts, such as classification. This is the minimal requirement if one is concerned with the progressive transformation of cognitive organization in development.

An additional consideration must be emphasized at this point. The empirical generalization that children imitate a model under the conditions ("Look what I can do ... you can do anything you want.") investigated by Bandura and his associates (such as Bandura and Walters, 1963) is questionable. This basic tenet of social learning theory is questionable, even when the model's performance involves only a motoric act and not a cognitive judgment.

In some research with a student, Mrs. Deanna Kuhn, we have been inquiring into the so-called imitation situation (Kuhn and Langer, 1968). Among other results, we found that children under four years of age do not usually perform the behavior they observed when given the instructions used by Bandura and his associates. Four-year-olds do perform aspects of the observed behavior. The difference, it seems, is that children under four years old are relatively unable to decode the implicit message in the instruction to perform the behavior they have just observed. By four years of age, children develop the cognitive competence to understand that they are being implicitly instructed to take the presented behavior as a model for the performance that is desired by the experimenter. These and the other results that are emerging from our studies point to an empirical generalization that is consistent with the theory of cognitive development: *the person's level of cognitive competence informs (sets the limits to and the potentials for) the range of his conduct.*

---

[4]Apparently, similar reactions have been obtained recently when children were presented with moral judgments that were more primitive than their own (Turiel, Article 5 in this book).

CONCLUDING REMARKS

We have started a direct study of affective disequilibrium due to the introduction of external perturbations, and of its consequences for cognitive development. The developmental problem is to determine when the child's internal state of organization is capable of successfully coping with perturbations. This means that we need to know in what way he is able to assimilate a given type of perturbation at successive stages of development—to recognize that it is a perturbation and that something is wrong. This we have begun to investigate; the paradigmatic approach that I have described is the study of the development of criticalness. It also means that we need to know in what way the child is able to accommodate to a given type of perturbation at successive stages of development, for example, whether the child will passively acquiesce and mimic or actively seek to experiment and prove.

The pedagogical problem, of course, is to find the right type of perturbations for each developmental stage, so that adequate rates of progress will be obtained. A plausible hypothesis, which we are beginning to examine empirically, is that perturbations have greater significance for cognitive development—progressive or regressive—when they are internally generated and produced by the child himself than when they are externally generated and presented to him. That this is far from an easy or a solved issue is attested to by our own results, which indicate that the consequences of at least some kinds of perturbation are just as likely to be interference and debilitation instead of cognitive progress. This, of course, is to be expected. Moreover, whether the effect is progressive, regressive, or neutral, probably varies with the developmental status of the child—the cognitive functional structures that are available to him.

Our investigations reinforce the conclusion that a comprehensive theory of developmental change (qualitative progress or regress) is heavily dependent on elucidation of the equilibration process. To date, however, organismic theorists have looked on equilibration as an internal process of achieving the most balanced intellectual organization possible. They have tended to neglect the opposite side of the coin, namely, that the internal organization must be in disequilibrium for the child to perform any adaptive mental action and, therefore, for change to take place. When cognitive theorists have looked at disequilibrium, as in the cognitive conflict studies, it has been defined as an external perturbation imposed on the child.

Our own view is that the child is an active operator whose actions are the prime generator of his own psychological development. When he is in a relatively equilibrated state, he will not tend to change; he will only change if he feels, consciously or unconsciously, that something is wrong. This means that both affective and organizational disequilibrium are necessary conditions for development. When these conditions are present, the energetic or emotional force for change in action is activated, and stabilizing interactions between mental actions and the symbolic media in which they are represented can be constructed in order to generate greater equilibrium. It is this constructive activity that constitutes the force of self-development. It is this constructive mental activity—its energetic (affective) and organizational (intellectual) parameters—that we are exploring in order to more fully understand the process of psychological development.

REFERENCES

Bandura, A., & McDonald, F. J. Influence of social reinforcement and the behavior of models in shaping children's moral judgments. *Journal of Abnormal and Social Psychology*, 1963, **67**, 274–281.

Bandura, A., & Walters, R. H. *Social learning and personality development*. New York: Holt, Rinehart & Winston, 1963.

Berlyne, D. E. *Structure and direction in thinking*. New York: Wiley, 1965.

Cowan, P. A., Langer, J., Heavenrich, J., & Nathanson, J. Social learning and Piaget's cognitive theory of moral development. *Journal of Personality and Social Psychology*, in press.

Erikson, E. H. *Childhood and society*. New York: Norton, 1950.

Erikson, E. H. Identity and the life cycle. *Psychological Issues*, 1959, **1**, No. 1.

Goldstein, K. *The organism*. New York: American Book Co., 1939.

Inhelder, B., Bovet, M., Sinclair, H., & Smock, C. D. On cognitive development. *American Psychologist*, 1966, **21**, 160–164.

Inhelder, B., & Piaget, J. *Early growth of logic in the child: Classification and seriation*. New York: Harper & Row, 1964.

Kendler, H. H., & Kendler, T. S. Vertical and horizontal processes in problem-solving. *Psychological Review*, 1962, **69**, 1–16.

Kuhn, D., & Langer, J. Cognitive developmental determinants of imitation. Unpublished manuscript, University of California, 1968.

Kuhn, T. S. *The structure of scientific revolutions*. Chicago: University of Chicago Press, 1962.

Langer, J. *Theories of development*. New York: Holt, Rinehart & Winston, 1969.

Luria, I. A. *The role of speech in the regulation of normal and abnormal behavior*. New York: Liveright Publishing Corp., 1961.

Piaget, J. (1927). *The child's conception of physical causality*. London: Routledge & Kegan Paul, 1951.

Piaget, J. *Biologie et connaisance*. Paris: Gallimard, 1967.

Schwartz, C., & Langer, J. Aspects of classificatory conceptualization. Unpublished manuscript, University of California, 1967.

Smedslund, J. The acquisition of conservation of substance and weight in children. V. Practice in conflict situations without external reinforcement. *Scandinavian Journal of Psychology*, 1961, **2**, 156–160.

Turiel, E. An experimental test of the sequentiality of developmental stages in the child's moral judgments. *Journal of Personality and Social Psychology*, 1966, **3**, 611–618.

Wapner, S., & Werner, H. *Perceptual development*. Worcester: Clark University Press, 1957.

Werner, H. *Comparative psychology of mental development*. Chicago: Follet, 1948.

Werner, H. The concept of development from a comparative and organismic point of view. In D. Harris. *The concept of development*. Minneapolis: University of Minnesota Press, 1957.

Wiener, N. *I am a mathematician*. Boston: MIT Press, 1964.

3

ORGANISMIC-DEVELOPMENTAL THEORY:
SOME APPLICATIONS TO COGNITION[1]

As implied by the name, organismic-developmental theory, the approach to cognition[2] which guided the experimental studies described in this article has two facets: (1) *The organismic perspective* (as partially specified in sensory-tonic theory, for example, Werner and Wapner, 1949, 1952, 1956; Wapner and Werner, 1957) which features general analysis of organismic systems and sub-systems in holistic terms with an attempt to characterize principles that underlie perception and other cognitive processes in structural, formal terms; (2) *The developmental perspective* (as specified earlier in comparative-developmental theory e.g., Werner, 1940, 1957; Wapner and Werner, 1957; Werner and Kaplan, 1963; Kaplan, 1966) which focuses on formal, organizational analysis of progressive changes in a system undergoing transition; this perspective treats such system change by use of a principle, the orthogenetic law, which states that with development there is increasing differentiation and hierarchic integration of parts and functions.

These two perspectives should be considered briefly with respect to some of the assumptions made by the approach. First, the normal adult is assumed to be characterized by multiple intentionality or directiveness: he does not maintain an invariant intention toward the world but rather is able to adopt different intentions or attitudes with respect to self:world relations. For example, he can adopt a cognitive set orienting him toward acting, toward perceiving or toward thinking, or he can

[1]This investigation was supported in whole by Public Health Service Grant MH-00348 from the National Institute of Mental Health. This paper was presented at a lecture series on developmental psychology, Department of Psychology, University of California, Berkeley, February 20, 1967.
[2]The experimental studies and theoretical conceptualization to be presented here derived from a research program initiated in 1950 by the author and the late Heinz Werner.

SEYMOUR WAPNER

Clark University, Worcester, Massachusetts

adopt a cognitive set orienting him toward things, or toward self, or toward others. The holistic assumption suggests that differences in perception, for example, will obtain depending on the intention adopted. This capacity for differentiable intentionality has developmental significance in keeping with the orthogenetic law. Multiple intentionality does not appear full-blown in the newborn infant, but rather develops with psychological growth. Thus, the infant cannot differentiate between self and world; with development, however, these poles are differentiable and the capacity emerges to adopt an attitude of directiveness toward one or the other pole (self or world). Moreover, there is a developmental sequence with respect to intentions of acting, perceiving, and thinking, which follows the general form of a developmental shift, from motoric toward ideational behavior. Further, individual differences in normals and group differences in psychopathology are assumed concerning the degree to which individuals can flexibly adapt or to which they must rigidly adhere to particular cognitive sets with respect to the self:world polarity,[3] and the intentions of acting, perceiving, and thinking.

[3]As suggested by this broad characterization, a general assumption underlying the methodological approach of the research relates to the distinction between achievement and underlying process (Werner, 1937): wherever possible, attempts are made to focus on underlying process, with recognition that the processes underlying given achievements are not necessarily unitary (Rand, Wapner, et al., 1963). Instead of assuming that process and achievement have a one-to-one relation, it is assumed that they are characterized by a many-to-one [for example, many different processes—sensori-motor, perceptual, conceptual-symbolic (as described by Werner, 1940)—may underlie a given achievement, such as solving the embedded figures task] or one-to-many relation (for example, a particular process may be utilized in different achievements).

Another crucial assumption is that the organism, as a system which exhibits directiveness toward goals, furthers them by a multiplicity of means or cognitive operations, including sensori-motor, perceptual, and conceptual-symbolic operations. Sensori-motor operations involve direct, external motoric manipulation of objects; perceptual operations involve directiveness toward properties of objects or things in external space; conceptual-symbolic operations involve manipulation of symbols representative of objects. All three deal with cognition insofar as: they serve as means for obtaining information about the world and the self; they represent means which yield qualitatively different information concerning a given stimulus field; or they represent different means of cognitively constructing a stimulus object.

The relationships among these three categories of cognitive operations are viewed and experimentally treated from both the organismic and developmental perspectives.

From the organismic perspective, sensori-motor, perceptual, and conceptual-symbolic cognitive operations represent three strata of organismic functioning and the question is posed as to how these operations relate to one another in the psychological functioning of an individual of a given developmental status.

The developmental perspective deals with relationships among the emerging cognitive operations. Considering the progression from early to late stages of development, sensori-motor operations are assumed to emerge first, followed by perceptual operations and, finally, by conceptual-symbolic operations. An operation that emerges at later stages of development does not supplant an operation already present, but is hierarchically related to it; the mature individual is assumed to have at his disposal the early- as well as the late-appearing functions.

A final assumption to be noted in this brief review relates to the very general treatment of the notion of development. Given the proposition that development can be defined in terms of idealized progressive change in the organismic system undergoing transition, the principle of "increasing differentiation and hierarchic integration" has been applied to any series assumed to be developmentally orderable, rather than being restricted to ontogenesis (cf. Werner, 1940; Werner and Kaplan, 1963; Wapner, 1964; Kaplan, 1967). That is, the orthogenetic principle is applied to analysis of problems of *general psychology* (for example, the unfolding of a sensori-motor pattern in learning), *psychopathology*, *retarded development*, *aging*, and *individuality*, as well as to problems of ontogenesis.[4]

[4]Hence, a sensori-motor pattern, a percept, or a concept—if it develops—is expected to change progressively in keeping with the general law; the regulative principle of increasing differentiation and hierarchic integration of parts is expected to apply to a variety of modes of functioning. Similarly, the same principles may be applied to seemingly diverse groups. For example, problems of psychopathology may be treated in relation to ontogenetic change if it is assumed that psychopathological groups operate at levels in certain areas which are formally similar to early levels of development (regression hypothesis). Analogously, the effects of psychopharmacological agents, such as lysergic acid diethylamide (LSD-25), as well as aging, can be studied on the grounds that there is a developmental regression with respect to some formal, organizational

Now that some general theoretical formulations have been briefly sketched, the implications of the organismic-developmental approach for analysis of cognitive organization and its development will be exemplified. This will be done in two ways: (a) by treating some aspects of the problem of learning, and (b) by treating the role of self:object relations in perception.

RELATIONS AMONG COGNITIVE OPERATIONS IN LEARNING

A recent study on posture and memory (Rand and Wapner, 1967) illustrates one way in which organismic-developmental theory provides an approach to the analysis of learning. The holistic principle of the organismic perspective suggests that all features of organismic functioning (even such a seemingly inconsequential aspect as postural state) should play a role in the learning process. Moreover, when learning is viewed from the developmental perspective, differences are expected between early and late stages in the learning process. The assumption was made that at early stages in learning there is an interpenetration between organismic variables (posture) and verbal variables and, further, that these variables should be differentiated as learning proceeds so that the postural influences which are maximal at early stages of learning should be minimal at late stages.

A simple experiment was conducted. The role of posture in nonsense-syllable learning was assessed by testing subjects under contrasting conditions of congruent body orientation (learn erect-relearn erect; learn supine-relearn supine) and incongruent (learn erect-relearn supine; learn supine-relearn erect) body orientations in learning and relearning. It was found that under congruent postures there is a significantly greater saving in relearning, as measured by errors and trials to criterion, *but this effect held only in the early stages of recall* (with a weak criterion for relearning); the effect is not significant with a strong criterion for relearning. Thus, posture plays a significant role in recall when one is groping for the correct response, as in the early stages of relearning. Assuming that verbal language originates in a gestural medium, the basis for the relation between verbal memory and postural status is self-evident. While the results of the study suggest that organismic context variables, like posture, play a significant role in the memory for verbal material, it is also evident that under conditions of overlearning, the process of verbal learning may become relatively autonomous or independent of organismic context. It would be of considerable interest to assess the interaction between this posture-memory relationship and ontogenetic change.

features of behavior (cf. Krus and Wapner, 1959). In the same way, individual differences have been studied developmentally by assuming that the individual can be characterized by his relative developmental position in functions that undergo development, by assuming that the individual does not operate on a fixed level but rather manifests a range of operations and is characterized by "flexibility-rigidity" and "lability-stability" in regards to developmentally ordered cognitive operations. A crucial note of caution must be interjected here. The regression hypothesis is employed as an heuristic device and the analysis should not stop with the establishment of similarity among developmental series. *Similarity is not identity*. Ultimately, the problem is one of *establishing differences as well as similarities* (cf. Wapner, 1964a, 1964b; Bibace, 1966).

Another approach to analysis of the learning process from the organismic-developmental point of view focuses on the developmental perspective by stressing differences in cognitive operations at different stages of development. The focus is on the *how* or the means whereby learning takes place and its implications for *what* is learned. Thus, differences in cognitive organization at different developmental levels imply that learning is not mediated by a unitary process at all stages of development, but varies depending on the cognitive operations available.[5] Further, assuming that the nature of the means for obtaining information determines the nature of the information obtained, it is expected that there are differences in *what* is learned depending on developmental status.

A number of studies in the Clark laboratories have taken this approach. One conducted by Frank Clarkson (1961) used a method that grew out of Husband's (1931) and of Warden's (1924) studies on stylus and finger maze learning by adults.

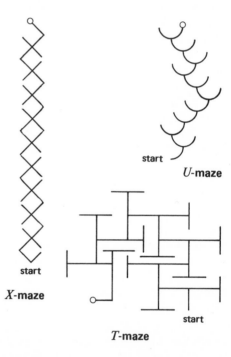

These investigators used three mazes which varied respectively from lesser to greater spatial differentiation, an *X* maze, a *U* maze, and a *T* maze, to study the methods employed by adults in learning. They reported that while subjects were learning to traverse the maze blindfolded, verbal (for example, "three turns left, two right," etc.) and motor ("follow the feel of the hand") methods were most frequent and less frequent was a perceptual-imagery method (an image is built up), which also contained verbal and motor components. Further, Husband and Warden reported that the method of learning depended to some extent on the type of maze, for example, the verbal method predominated with an *X* maze and the motor with a *T* maze. From the viewpoint of organismic-developmental theory, these individual differences in the cognitive operations parallel those categorized as sensori-motor, perceptual, and as conceptual-symbolic, and served as a basis for an ontogenetic study.

Figure 3.1 *Finger mazes (adapted from Clarkson, 1961).*

Thus, in a PhD thesis Clarkson (1961) used *T, U, X* finger mazes (Figure 3.1) with children and adults where the task was to learn the maze pattern

[5]Cf. J. Piaget's (1968) lecture in the 1967 Heinz Werner lecture series, Clark University.

while blindfolded. It was expected that children (ten to twelve years old) with conceptual-symbolic operations less readily available would have differentially greater difficulty than adults with the *X* maze, which provides a minimum of sensori-motor cues, and that such age differences would be minimal for the *T* maze which was largely learned by sensori-motoric means. These expectations were verified, suggesting (in keeping with theory) the dominance of sensori-motor operations in children as compared with adults, who are able to bring to bear such conceptual-symbolic operations as counting. Among other supportive evidence, Clarkson also found that analysis of subjects' statements describing the methods they employed revealed that conceptual operations were more frequently reported by the adults.

In another PhD thesis at Clark University, Kempler (1964) undertook a complementary study investigating developmental changes in processes underlying serial learning. Again he expected a developmental shift in the cognitive means employed in learning—from sensori-motor to conceptual-symbolic—and further that the developmental shifts in cognitive means employed would be paralleled by changes in intraserial organization. Three age groups—a seven-year-old, a nine-year-old, and a thirteen-year-old group—were required to learn a sequence task consisting of eight choices, each involving four possible alternatives (Figure 3.2). The choices were

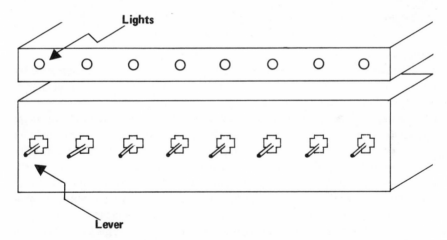

Figure 3.2 *Serial learning apparatus (adapted from Kempler, 1964).*

arranged in keeping with a pattern: the sequence of correct responses followed a principle of clockwise rotation—light on when first lever moved left, second up, etc.

While success in learning the serial task, as measured by errors, was found to increase with age, the more crucial findings did not pertain to the increased efficiency with increase in age, but rather to the linkage between the nature of the modes of solution employed by subjects and their developmental status. There were striking differences in the serial error curves for the different age groups (Figure 3.3). The youngest group largely learned the extreme ends of the total sequence, the nine-year-old group showed the classic bowshaped curve, and the thirteen-year-

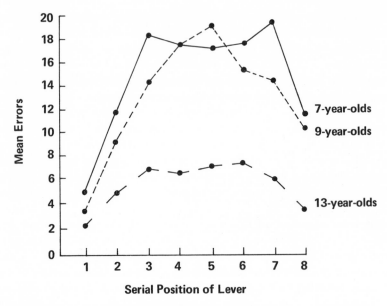

Figure 3.3 *Number of errors made by each age group with each lever on the sequence task (adapted from Kempler, 1964).*

old group had a relatively equal number of errors at all serial positions (elimination of the bow-shaped curve). These findings represented one line of evidence used by Kempler to indicate developmental shifts in the cognitive operations employed in achieving intraserial organization.

In addition to these age differences in manner of achieving the criterion, there was evidence from what the subjects were able to do following performance to an identical criterion—two errorless trials—that suggested further differences in what had been learned. One task tested for *reversibility*: subjects were required to perform the sequence in a reverse direction from that of the original sequence. Since the nine-year-olds performed more poorly than the oldest and the youngest children, it was assumed that the nine-year-olds organized the sequence as a unidirectional chain; in contrast the thirteen-year-olds organized it in terms of a conceptual principle that was reversible. The second task involved *extension* of the series; that is, the subjects were required to indicate correct choices for imaginary units added to the series. It is striking that only the oldest group was able to extrapolate from the concrete series to the required extension series.

This study has significance for two reasons: (a) it demonstrates that subjects of different age groups learn the sequence in different ways dependent on the cognitive operations available to them, and (b) there is evidence that the nature of the cognitive operations available to them sets limits on the type of learning or information they obtain from the situation. Extension and reversibility of the sequence were possible for the oldest age group because they organized the materials according to conceptual-symbolic operations; this is a very different and more powerful kind of learning than obtains in the youngest age group, who master it mainly in terms of a sensori-motor sequence or a concrete verbal sequence. It is clear that the means of obtaining information determines markedly the nature of the information that is obtained.

Another study carried out by Switzer as a PhD thesis (1961) provides support for these generalizations and opens other important problems. Switzer used groups ordered developmentally in terms of chronological age (eight-year-old versus twelve-year-old children) as well as in terms of psychopathology. Given the principle that with development there is a shift from motoric to internal, ideational behavior, clinically deviant, hyperactive children were assumed to exhibit developmentally less mature cognitive behavior than clinically deviant, hypoactive children. Accordingly, eight-year olds were compared with twelve-year olds, and hyperactive children were compared with hypoactive children on learning tasks presumed to favor use of different cognitive operations. One task required learning a sequence of positions by a sensori-motor organization (a series of white lights flashed in boxes located at different positions on a table in front of the subject—place task). In another task, a series of colors flashed successively in one light box and the subject was required to learn the sequence of color names, presumably through verbal-conceptual organization (name task). In addition, a task was employed that could be organized in either of these ways [a series of different colors also located in different places—place-name task (Figure 3.4)]. In the latter place-name task, a

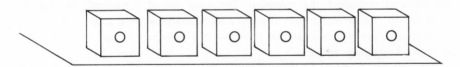

Figure 3.4 *Serial learning apparatus (adapted from Switzer, 1961).*

higher proportion of the two groups of subjects functioning at earlier developmental levels (eight-year-old; hyperactives) spontaneously indicated the stimulus in terms of "place" whereas a higher proportion of the subjects operating at a later developmental level (twelve-year-olds; hypoactives) indicated the stimulus in terms of color name, thus suggesting that different modes of organization were employed by the developmentally ordered groups. In addition, observations of the subjects' behavior during learning showed more external activity (whispering, pointing, nodding, etc.) was exhibited by the younger than by the older children.

In addition, differential performance on the place and name tasks was found in normal and pathological groups. The normal children showed flexibility insofar as they could handle optimally both place and name tasks; the hypoactive children performed relatively poorly on the place task; and the hyperactive children performed relatively poorly on the name task.

Thus, the organismic-developmental approach in distinguishing between levels of cognitive operations leads to the finding that the older children spontaneously organize the learning task in conceptual terms, whereas the younger children spontaneously organize the task in sensori-motor or perceptual terms. In addition, there are parallel findings for the developmentally ordered pathological groups clinically defined as hyperactive and hypoactive.

One variation of Switzer's experimental procedure involved forcing the subjects to use externalized sensori-motor operations—pointing—while learning the task in order to determine whether these operations could function supportively. Externalized sensori-motor operations under these forced conditions functioned to disrupt performance in contrast to such operations when they occurred spontaneously. A suggestion from this finding was that there is a relationship between developmental status and capacity to profit from superimposed sensori-motor operations in learning a task: the subject must be at a high enough level in development to be able hierarchically to integrate operations of different kinds.[6]

While Switzer's study is provocative and informative it is limited by the ages of children studied, by the incomplete categorization of the subjects' behavior, and by omission of a set of data found to be very useful in studies such as that of Clarkson—the subjects' own reports of the mnemonic devices they employ. Accordingly, a more complete analysis of this situation was carried out recently in a replication and extension of Switzer's place-name task by Wapner and Rand (1967). Two hundred and forty subjects between eight and eighteen years of age were presented with a horizontally arranged series of six colored lights in boxes, which flashed on in a fixed random order (see Figure 3.4), and left to their own devices to find ways to reproduce the sequence. The main aim of the experiment was to categorize the behavioral means employed in establishing serial order, with an attempt to decipher age changes, the nature of the means employed, and the interrelations among these means.

Here, as in other experiments on learning, we found overall ontogenetic changes in learning efficiency assessed by both trials and errors to criterion; more specifically, trials and errors showed a decreasing exponential function with increase in age (Figure 3.5). However, from our view the main findings once again pertain to the analyses of the observable aspects of the subjects' behavior accompanying learning and their introspections concerning the mnemonic devices they utilized in carrying out the task.

First of all, observation of the subjects while they were learning the sequence showed that they used a number of complex ways of indicating the stimuli comprising the series. We grouped these into three classes which respectively parallel sensori-motor, perceptual and conceptual-cognitive operations.

---

[6]There is evidence in keeping with this notion in a study (Wapner and Rand, 1967) which shows that meaning loss under repetition of a word is retarded with motoric-gestural support in an eighteen-year-old but not in younger subjects, and in a study by Dowling (1962) who had difficulty in obtaining a supportive relation between motoric-gestural activity and word recognition when a conceptual-symbolic task—forced guessing—was required along with the motoric and perceptual task.

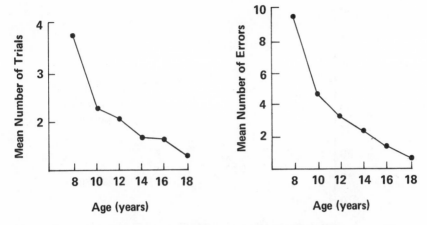

Figure 3.5 *Age differences in achievement of criterial performance with serially presented material (adapted from Wapner and Rand, 1967).*

Location. The stimuli of the sequence were indicated by referring to the spatial position of the individual light boxes by pointing with the hand or index finger. This behavior was often accompanied by verbal forms of pointing—"this one"—and/or verbal reference to ordinal position of the item in the series— "this is the first one."

Color. The sequence was indicated by "calling off" color names, disregarding differences in spatial position of the flashing lights.

Numerical position. A number was assigned to each box (from 1 through 6), thus indicating the position of each from left to right as positioned on a table in front of the subject. When the lights were flashed in a random sequence the order was recalled as a series of numbers then translatable into location.

Inspection of the frequency count of the subjects falling into the various categories in Figure 3.6 showed that (a) indicating with respect to location (the most primitive response) was most frequent in the youngest groups and tended to decrease in the oldest groups, (b) dealing with the stimulus event as an ordinal series of colors was most frequent in the youngest age group and tended to decrease in frequency with increase in age, and (c) translation into a series of numerical positions was characteristic of the performance of almost 50 percent of the older subjects, but was absent in the youngest age groups. Designation of item by location or color showed no significant differences in frequency depending on age, whereas the increase with age in frequency of designation by numerical position was significant.

The second set of data concerned the reports by the subjects, after exposure to the learning task, of the mnemonic devices they used. These fell into three general classes.

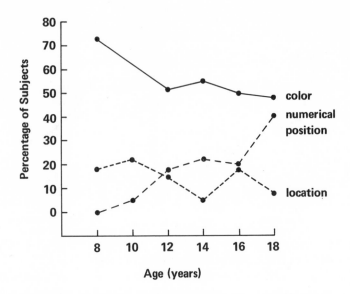

Figure 3.6 *Age differences in manner of designating stimuli
(adapted from Wapner and Rand, 1967).*

Unit designating devices (Figure 3.7). There were two examples of this type of device: *iteration*, which tended to decline with age, in which the subjects said they repeated each unit to themselves as the unit appeared, labeling it according to color and ordinal position, and *deiction*, where subjects reported pointing to the individual boxes as a mnemonic device to help them learn; deiction or pointing again was found primarily in the reports of the youngest age group and significantly decreased with increase in age.

Ordering devices (Figure 3.8). The first device in this class was *cumulative repetition*, where the subjects said they repeated all prior units in the series following the appearance of the current unit (for example, red, blue; red, blue, white; red, blue, white, green). It was found that cumulative repetition increases significantly and regularly with age. The second ordering mnemonic device was *recapitulation*, where the subjects reported recapitulation of the order of the series between presentations; this essentially involved implicit rehearsal—peculiarly enough there was a relative paucity of this response in all age groups.

Organizational devices (Figure 3.9). The first device in this developmentally ad-vanced class of mnemonic devices was *grouping*, where the subject divided a series into subgroups varying in length (first third versus last third, first fourth versus last fourth), which was employed mainly by the oldest subjects. The second subgroup was *pattern recognition*, where the subjects said they perceived a spatio-temporal pattern governing the order of flashes. For example, they alternated from "outside

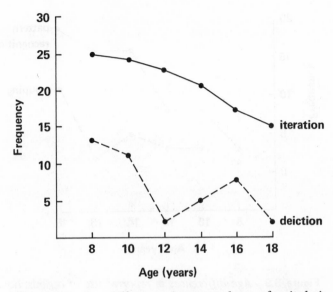

Figure 3.7 *Age differences in reported use of unit designating mnemonic devices (iteration and deiction) (adapted from Wapner and Rand, 1967).*

to inside" or "odds versus evens." This mnemonic device was infrequently employed by children less than fourteen years of age and was found to be very common in adults—an ontogenetic change that is significant.

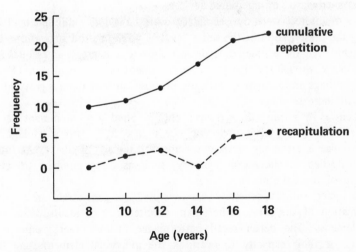

Figure 3.8 *Age differences in reported use of ordering devices (cumulative repetition and recapitulation) (adapted from Wapner and Rand, 1967).*

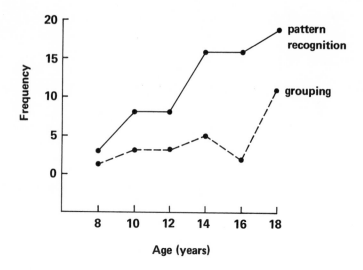

Figure 3.9   *Age differences in reported use of organizational mnemonic devices (grouping and pattern recognition) (adapted from Wapner and Rand, 1967).*

An interesting part of the analysis concerns the relationship between age and mnemonic devices. It was found that the younger subjects were restricted to one mnemonic device, whereas in the adult group there was a higher number of reports of combined classes of mnemonic devices.

Also of interest were the secondary overt behaviors exhibited by the subjects during the presentation of the series, such as pointing, nodding, whispering and lip movement. All these mnemonic devices showed a decrease in frequency with increase in age, though the change for lip movement was not significant (Figure 3.10). These findings are in keeping with the proposition that there is greater internalization with increase in age.

Taken as a group, the younger children had a predominant tendency to focus on the color series; with increase in age there was a tendency for subjects to use a rationally devised scheme for translating the event into a form easily handled in short-term memory, such as using numbers to refer to the location of the light boxes.

The older subject generally was inclined to give attention to the overall organization of the series rather than to reiteration or identification of individual elements. The better recall performance in the older groups is partly a product of their capacity to overlook the individual elements and to see the pattern in the series as a whole. For the younger groups, it is quite clear that the opposite is true—the event is seen and organized as a series of independently defined, nominally designated units. The findings of these studies on learning may be summarized as follows:

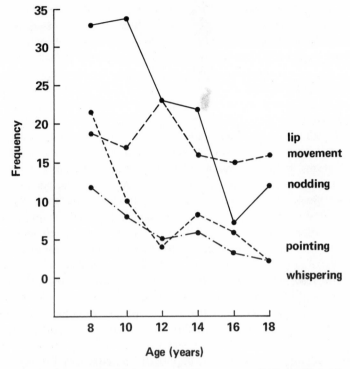

Figure 3.10   *Age differences in frequency of occurrence of secondary behaviors (pointing, nodding, whispering and lip movement) (adapted from Wapner and Rand, 1967).*

1. The cognitive operations available to subjects differing in developmental status—both in terms of age and pathology—are linked to the different processes underlying seemingly (as judged on the superficial grounds of errors and trials to learn) identical achievement.

2. The means of processing information sets limits on the nature of the information gleaned from the world of objects.

3. Simultaneous consideration of developmentally ordered cognitive operations and the nature of the task leads to predictions that cannot be obtained by assuming that a unitary process underlies a given achievement, such as learning a serial task.

4. The organismic-developmental approach has heuristic value in analyzing some characteristics (the "how" and the "what") of the learning process.

SELF:OBJECT RELATIONS

The second general problem to be discussed deals with the implications of the organismic-developmental approach—in particular with the implications of the relations between self and object—for cognitive organization with special reference to perception. Self:object relations are intimately tied to the problem of interrelations among cognitive operations. To understand this linkage, it is necessary to note that the organismic-developmental framework assumes a reciprocal relationship between organism and environment, in analyzing the role of perceptual and other forms of cognitive functioning as the means whereby the organism comes to terms with the environment.

As noted earlier, means and ends are differentiated and a given goal is assumed to be achievable by more than one means or cognitive operation. The linkage of these operations to self:object relationships is evident when the cognitive operations are characterized in terms of degree of differentiation between self and world: sensorimotor operations represent minimal differentiation between self and world, since they involve concrete motoric manipulation of objects; perceptual operations involve greater differentiation between self and world since they require directedness toward properties of objects "out there"; and finally, conceptual-symbolic operations involve greatest differentiation between self and world because they involve manipulation of symbols which are differentiated from, but representative of, objects. A critical concept in this analysis of cognitive functioning is the recognition that "self" and "environment" stand in a polar relationship; one pole does not exist to the exclusion of the other. Another feature of the analysis derives from the assumption of "multiple intentionality"— that is, that the organism can adopt different intentions, cognitive sets, or cognitive attitudes with respect to self:object relations—and the further assumption that these different intentions have important consequences for the nature of cognitive organization. There are two quasi-quantitative aspects of polar self: object relations which may be distinguished.

The first aspect is degree of distance or differentiation between the poles, which at one extreme is relative de-differentiation (fusion or linkage) between self and world and, at the other, is relative differentiation (separation or articulation) of self and world.

The second aspect is directedness toward one or the other of these poles. Directedness involves a relative emphasis on either self or world—"self-directedness" versus "object-directedness."

While these two aspects of self:object relations—degree of differentiation and pole-emphasized—are distinguished, they are recognized as not being completely independent. It is assumed that emphasis on the self pole is related to relatively less differentiation, and emphasis on the object pole is related to a relatively higher degree of differentiation between self and object.

Further, the conditions affecting degree of differentiation of self and object are interdependent with developmental factors, such as ontogenetic level, psychopathological status and other developmentally orderable conditions. The feature of separateness, oppositeness, distance or differentiation between self and object is characteristic of the organism at the more "mature" pole of the developmentally orderable series. This polarity is assumed to be lacking in early childhood and to develop during the course of ontogenesis. In parallel fashion, for the normal adult under primitivizing drugs like LSD-25 where there is a condition of stress, or for those cases of pathology where more primitive behavior is evident, the differentiation between self and world (which exists for the optimally functioning adult) breaks down. Further, when the normally functioning adult is experimentally put into a situation where the world is distorted by use of such media as prisms, the relations between body perception and thing perception which obtain under normal circumstances are disturbed and the subject is required to cope with these changes by developing new relationships between self and object.

How do these different self:object relations affect perceptual organization and developmental change in perceptual organization? A variety of experiments conducted during the past few years in the Clark laboratories demonstrates that their effects are pervasive in cognitive organization. This is evident from the multiple ways in which self:object relations have been approached. The studies completed have utilized a wide range of situations, tasks, and conditions. They included: variation in the self:object cognitive set induced by instructions and by physical arrangements between subject and object; ongoing individual differences in self:object cognitive set, including comparison among developmentally ordered groups (ontogenetically ordered as well as in terms of neuropathology and psychopathology); such tasks as space localization, discrimination and identification; the tactual-kinaesthetic modality as well as the visual; light room and dark room conditions; and such abnormal conditions as obtain when the subject is exposed to the distorting effects of lenses which rotate the visual field, and under water in the condition of neutral buoyancy (Sziklai, 1966; Wapner, 1964a, 1964b).

First, consider some studies which demonstrate that there are changes in cognitive organization dependent on *transient variation of "self:object" cognitive set, induced by instructions.* Using perception of the median plane (or straight-ahead) as the experimental situation, Glick (1964) found differences in localization dependent on self:object cognitive set induced by instructions. In this situation the task was to adjust the fixated edge of a luminous rectangle in the dark to a position in which the edge appeared straight ahead. With a set of looking at objects as separate from or independent of self,[7] the apparent median plane

---

[7]Our current procedure in inducing cognitive set of differentiation and de-differentiation is as follows: first, we point out that there are two different ways of experiencing the relation between a person and a thing, one which we call an attitude or set of differentiation, or independence of person and object; the other we call an attitude of de-differentiation, fusion or linkage, or feeling of being part of an object. These are exemplified by a variety of illustrations; e.g., the subject is told "Some people, when they go bowling, demonstrate this attitude of differentiation. When they release the ball from their hand they behave as if they have no control over it or connection with it. They feel that the ball is completely separate from them. This is the attitude of differentiation from the object. Other people experience an attitude of fusion. You can see this from their behavior. After they release the ball they use so-called 'body English,' meaning they try to change the course of the ball as it is rolling, by moving their bodies." These and other instructions are being assesssed in current experimentation.

shifts in the direction to which a figure extends from fixation; with a de-differentiated self:object set—experiencing objects as fused, tied, or linked to self—the apparent median plane shifts opposite the direction to which the figure extends from fixation (Figure 3.11).

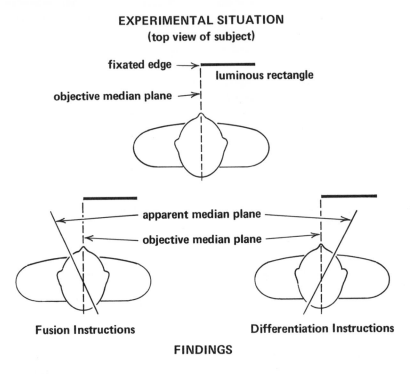

EXPERIMENTAL SITUATION
(top view of subject)

fixated edge →
luminous rectangle

objective median plane →

apparent median plane
objective median plane

Fusion Instructions   Differentiation Instructions

FINDINGS

Figure 3.11   *Shifts in position of apparent median plane under instructional variation of self:object cognitive set.*

In another study (Porzemsky, Wapner, and Glick, 1965), cognitive sets of de-differentiation and differentiation of self and object induced by instructions significantly affected apparent location of fingertip (body perception) and apparent location of target (object perception) when the subject was instrumentally related to a target-object by pointing. In the dark, by means of a luminous indicator, the subject indicated where he experienced his fingertip to be and where he experienced the target to be. It was found that both apparent fingertip and apparent target location shifted relatively toward each other under the de-differentiated as compared with the differentiated self:object set (Figure 3.12).

Another study, showing that instruction induced variation of self:object cognitive set plays a role in perceptual organization, utilized tactual discrimination threshold. The task was that of selecting sandpaper from a graded series that matched a grade of sandpaper which served as a standard. This was done with instructions to be object-directed—when subjects were told to attend or direct themselves to the nature of the surface of the object—and when they were instructed to be body-directed—when they were told to attend to the experience on the skin of their fingertips. The stimulus conditions on the sensory surface were identical, yet the threshold was significantly lower (finer discrimination) when subjects operated under an object-directed set than under a body-directed set (Mahrabian, Werner, and Wapner, 1964).

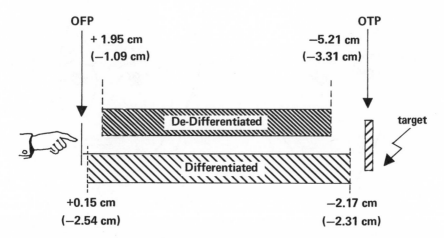

Figure 3.12 *Shifts in position of apparent fingertip and apparent target location under instructional variation of self:object cognitive set. [Deviations of mean position of apparent fingertip location and apparent target location are given with respect to objective fingertip position (OFP) and objective target position (OTP), respectively: deviations toward subject are designated by "−"; deviations away from subject are designated by "+". Findings are given for an experiment and its replication.]*

I might add, very briefly, that we have been breaking ground in the study of perception of persons by use of the median plane methodology mentioned earlier. Based on the general proposition that eye-gaze has a potent role in interpersonal relationships, face-forms representing an "other" person ambiguous with respect to eye-gaze have been used in a dark room as stimuli instead of a luminous rectangle (Figure 3.13). Three conditions of set concerning experience of eye-gaze are employed: the eyes of the face-form look toward the subject's left, look straight at the subject, and look toward the subject's right. Under each of these conditions, the subject has the task of adjusting the face-form either to the left or right so that it appears to be located straight-ahead. Evidence is available that these sets concerning eye-gaze affect perceived location of the drawing of a person. Under the set suggesting presence of eye contact (eyes of face-form are looking straight at you), the range of physical positions accepted as straight-ahead is significantly narrower than under the conditions of instructional set suggesting absence of eye contact. Thus, de-differentiated self:other relations as obtain under presence of eye contact with "other" have significantly different effects than differentiated self:other relations as obtain under absence of eye contact with "other" (Nachshon and Wapner, 1967).

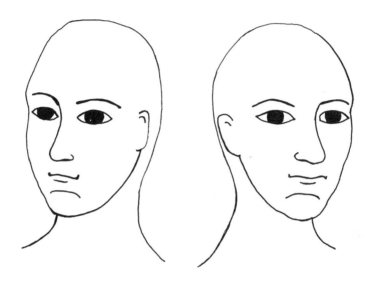

Figure 3.13   *Ambiguous face-forms.*

Studies on changes in perceived body:object relations during the course of adaption to prisms (monocular) rotating the visual field $20°$ clockwise under two cognitive sets and stimulus conditions have been conducted by Rierdan and Wapner (1966, 1967). In one experiment, the subject wore a prism that rotated the field $20°$ clockwise. Both visual and tactual-kinaesthetic verticality (object perception) and perceived position of the longitudinal axis of the body (body perception) were assessed at different points in time: prior to wearing prisms, 0 minutes, 20 minutes, 40 minutes, and 60 minutes after wearing prisms, and following removal of the distorting media. Two conditions were employed: (a) object-directed, in which the subject was directed toward looking at objects in the room and was not given any direct visual information on his own position, and (b) body-directed, in which the subject was directed toward experience of his own body—in addition to having available a view of objects in the room, a mirror on the wall permitted him to see a mirror image of himself (tilted $20°$, of course). It is assumed that in directing the subject toward objects without a mirror field, an attitude of differentiation, or separation of self and world, is fostered, and that in directing the subject toward his body (that is, in viewing a mirror image of himself along with objects in the field) an attitude of de-differentiation or fusion between self and world is fostered.

It was found that there were significant visual changes in both perception of body (apparent body position) and perception of objects (apparent vertical) while wearing the prisms. This can be seen in Figure 3.14, where the overall mean location of apparent vertical and apparent body position shifted systematically in the direction (clockwise) in which the prisms rotated the visual field.

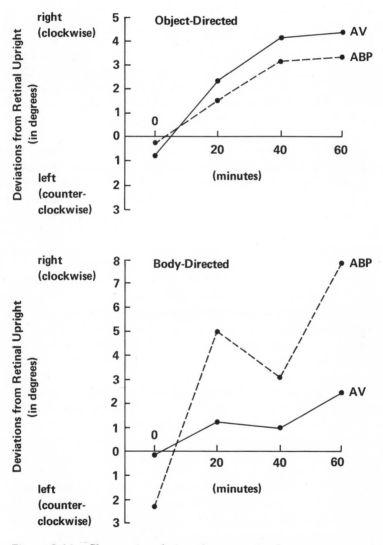

Figure 3.14 *Changes in relations between visual apparent vertical (AV) and visual indication of apparent body position (ABP) during adaptation to prism rotation of the visual field 20° clockwise under object-directed and body-directed conditions.*

Opposite locations of apparent body position relative to apparent vertical occur dependent on body-directed versus object-directed adaptation conditions. Examination of Figure 3.14 indicates that, under the object-directed condition, apparent body position is located increasingly counterclockwise of apparent verticality, while under the body-directed condition the opposite obtains.

With exposure to a distorted visual field there is general adaptation in tactual-kinaesthetic perception, that is, a shift systematically in the direction to which the prisms rotate the visual field. However, the interactive effects depending on task and directedness that obtain in the visual do not obtain to a significant degree in the tactual-kinaesthetic modality. That general changes do occur emphasizes that the theoretical models for treating figural adaptation should be of an organismic character, with concepts that handle interaction among sensory systems.

Since the form of adaptation varies dependent on conceptual set introduced along with the nature of visual stimuli and sensori-motor activity permitted, it is evident that in adaptation to visual rearrangement, as in cognition in general, there are available alternative means for coming to terms with the world. This suggests that a comprehensive treatment of adaptation to prismatic rearrangement requires consideration of sensori-motor, perceptual (of both body and object), and conceptual activity; and thereby stands in contrast to other interpretations that have considered adaptation in terms of the operation of only one of these factors—for instance, Held and Hein (1958) and Held and Schlank (1959), who focused on changes in sensori-motor behavior, and Harris (1965), who considered adaptation in terms of changes in proprioceptive awareness of body position.

The study also illustrated that the change that occurs during adaptation is progressive and systematic and manifests different resolutions by the organism of the discrepancy between body perception and object, as dependent on cognitive set and/or visual input.

A second set of studies demonstrated that there are changes in cognitive organization dependent on changes of an *environmental arrangement between subject and object*, which are assumed to make for variation of self:object relations. One study within this group deals with the physical distance between the subject and the object, the properties of which the subject is required to perceive. Utilizing the same situation described earlier—effect of asymmetrical extent on position of the apparent median plane or straight ahead—it was expected that longer physical distance between subject and object (eight feet) would operate in a manner analogous to differentiated self:object set, relative to a shorter physical distance between subject and object (two feet). As expected, under longer physical distance between subject and object, the apparent median plane shifted relatively in the direction of asymmetrical extension of the figure from fixation; under shorter physical distance, the apparent median plane shifted relatively opposite the direction of asymmetrical extent (Glick and Wapner, 1966).

Recently, the problem was pursued further by variation of stimulus and physical arrangement. The stimulus employed consisted of two luminous lines placed at right angles to each other with centers intersecting: an x-shaped object (or a plus sign, rotated 45°). Thus, with a restriction imposed by instructions, namely,"What algebraic symbol is this?"—the stimulus could be interpreted as a plus sign, when viewed in one orientation, or a multiplication sign, when viewed in another orientation. It was assumed that physical arrangement in terms of size-distance would operate analogous to variation in self:object cognitive set, which in turn was expected to affect the meaning attributed to the stimulus. Two conditions were employed: a large stimulus was placed close to the subject (two feet) and a small stimulus was placed far from the subject (eight feet). The large-near stimulus was expected to induce an attitude of de-differentiation, and the small-far stimulus an attitude of differentiation between self and object. The person was tilted 45° right and the stimulus was arranged so that one axis of the plus sign was in line with the longitudinal axis of the body, or, stated another way, the main axes of the multiplication sign were 45° off true vertical. In keeping with expectation, with the large-near stimulus, the initial reports by the subjects were plus sign, whereas with the small-far stimulus subjects for the most part reported that they saw a multiplication sign. Not only were the reports of the subjects in keeping with this expectation but, in addition, when they were later asked to make a drawing of what they saw on a piece of paper placed in front of them on a desk, those subjects who were exposed to the large-near stimulus predominantly drew a picture of a plus, whereas those presented with a small-far stimulus drew a multiplication sign. These findings were statistically significant.

Another study showed that perceptual organization depends on physical arrangements between subject and environmental context and also suggested that there are *differences among individuals with respect to ongoing self:object set*, which interact in a complex way with physical subject-object arrangements (Clate, 1965). This study was initiated on the hypothesis that variation of self:object conditions would make for changes in degree of differentiation between self and object which, in turn, would affect object perception as measured by localization of the apparent median plane. Under one set of conditions, the subject sat in a hard chair in which articulation of the body boundaries was enhanced; in a contrasting condition the subject sat in a chair lined with a six-inch foam rubber mattress, which in turn presumably de-emphasized articulation of the body boundaries. The critical point, and this was obtained in two further replications of the study, was that no significant findings emerged when the data were analyzed in terms of the environmental subject-object variable alone, but that significant findings were evident when the subject's ongoing self:object set was assessed and introduced as an axis of classification in the analysis.

That individual differences in ongoing self:world cognitive sets play a role parallel to those transiently induced is supported by another experiment conducted by Glick (1964). While subjects were presented with asymmetrical auditory stimulation—sound to left or right ear—they were required to adjust a luminous line to the straight-ahead position in a dark room. This was done under neutral instructions and, after assessments of the location of the apparent median plane were made, the subjects were questioned to determine whether they characteristically held a relatively de-differentiated or relatively differentiated self:object cognitive set. It was found that for individuals characterized by the differentiated self:object set, the straight-ahead shifted opposite the side of auditory stimulation and, in contrast, those characterized by the de-differentiated set shifted the straight ahead toward the side of stimulation.

In addition to perceptual-cognitive organization being affected by self:object relations in terms of transient variation of attitude induced through instructions, induced through environmental arrangement between subject and object, and dependent on ongoing individual differences, a number of studies have shown parallel effects dependent on comparison of *developmentally ordered groups presumed to manifest different ongoing self:object cognitive sets* with respect to "distancing" and "pole-emphasized." As noted earlier, the conditions affecting degree of differentiation of self and object are interdependent with genetic factors such as onto-genetic level, psychopathological status, and other developmentally orderable conditions. Thus, groups ordered developmentally in these terms are expected to show differences in perceptual organization that parallel those findings obtained by the other ways of inducing changes in self:object relations.

Given the assumption that there is increased polarization of body space and object space with development, a study was conducted to investigate ontogenetic change in the relationship between apparent body position and apparent object position (Wapner, 1964a, 1964b, 1968; Wapner and Werner, 1965). In keeping with the assumption that there is an ontogenetic shift from lesser to greater differentiation between self and world, it was expected that object perception, body perception, and the relation between them—known to vary depending on self:object cognitive attitudes—will show parallel shifts in the course of ontogenesis. Angular separation between apparent vertical (adjusting a rod to a position in which it appears vertical) and apparent body position (adjusting a rod so that it appears aligned with the longitudinal axis of the body) was measured in these experiments. It was assumed that such angular separation between thing and body position under body tilt can serve as an index of degree of differentiation of perceived body and perceived object position. In keeping with expectation that there would be differences in the degree of angular separation depending on age, it was found (a) that the angular discrepancy between apparent vertical and apparent body position is somewhat greater than the angular discrepancy between true vertical and true body position for the young child (six years), (b) that this difference is approximately the same until about thirteen years of age, and (c) that following the age of thirteen there is a sharp increase in the angular discrepancy between apparent vertical and apparent body position. Thus, there is evidence of increasing differentiation between perceived body and perceived object position with increase in age (Figures 3.15 and 3.16).

In an ontogenetic study testing boys and girls from six to eighteen years of age, data also have been collected under neutral self:object instructions on the apparent median plane situation described earlier, that is, with luminous rectangular figures extending to left and right of a fixated edge. As shown in Figure 3.17, at the earliest age levels, just as with the transiently induced set of de-differentiation between self and object in the adult, the apparent median plane shifts opposite the side of asymmetrical extent; with the exception of the fourteen to fifteen age group, the apparent median plane shifts in the direction of asymmetrical extent, as

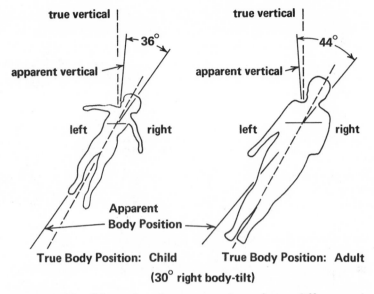

Figure 3.15 *Schematic of representation of age differences in angular disparity between apparent vertical and apparent body position under 30° body-tilt.*

in the other studies with adults.[8] Thus, during ontogenesis we find cognitive organization following a course that corresponds to set variation from lesser to greater differentiation between self and object, or from lesser to greater objectification. The exception in the curve—the shift back to a de-differentiated self:object relation

---

[8]These results are consistent with those reported above on variation in physical distance between subject and object (Glick and Wapner, 1966), on variation in cognitive set by instructions (Glick, 1964), as well as with those to be reported below on hemiplegics (Barton, 1964); however, they are inconsistent with findings from an earlier developmental study (Wapner and Werner, 1957), which showed that with children from six to nineteen years old the apparent median plane was located markedly toward asymmetrical extent, with a sharp decrease at eighteen to nineteen years of age. The basis for this discrepancy is being examined. The procedures in the recent group of studies and that of the earlier study (Wapner and Werner, 1957) differed: straight ahead was defined with respect to a body part (the nose) and stepwise adjustment was used in the earlier study, whereas straight ahead was defined without reference to a body part and continuous adjustment of the stimulus was used in the recent studies. It has already been ascertained that such procedural differences are, at least in part, the basis for the discrepancy (Baker and Wapner, 1968). The further hypothesis is being explored that the shift of AMP opposite the direction of extent does in fact obtain with preschool subjects even when stepwise adjustment and body-oriented instructions are employed; this appears to be a lively possibility since Pollack and Carter (1967), using procedures similar to Wapner and Werner (1957), found the smallest magnitude of shift of the AMP toward asymmetrical extent in kindergarten as compared with grade-school children. If the studies in progress produce the expected findings, they will have two important consequences: first, they will resolve the apparent discrepancy; second, they will advance our understanding of the interaction of the variety of factors pertinent to self:object relations in perception and perceptual development (cf. Bauermeister, Wapner, and Werner, 1967; Baker, 1968; Baker and Wapner, 1968).

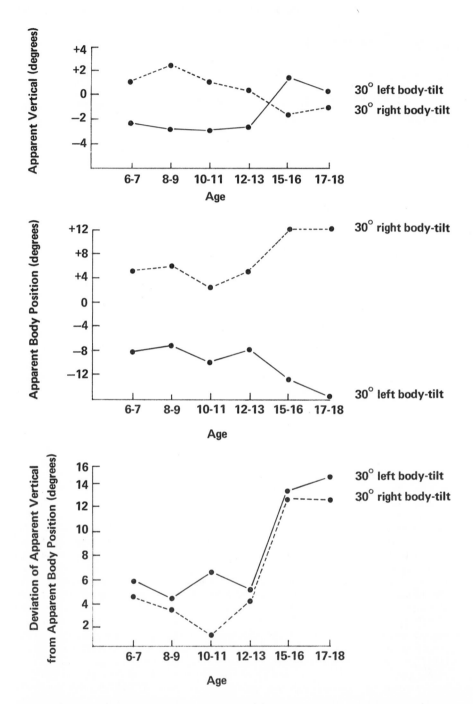

Figure 3.16 *Age differences in angular disparity between apparent vertical and apparent body position under 30° body-tilt.*

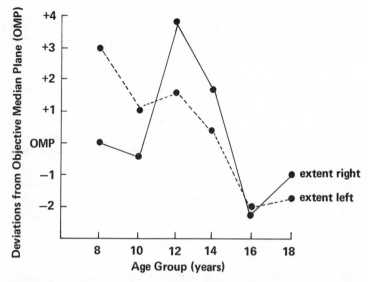

Figure 3.17 *Developmental changes in location of apparent median plane (AMP) with figures extending asymmetrically from fixation.*

in the adolescent period—parallels other findings we have obtained with adolescents, and it might be added, with people in the forty to fifty age range.

Recently, an ontogenetic study was conducted utilizing the situation involving dependency of meaning (multiplication sign versus plus sign), on physical arrangement between self and stimulus (Sister Clare Walsh and Wapner, 1967). Again, the stimulus consisted of two luminous lines placed at right angles to each other, with centers intersecting, that is, an x-shaped object (or a plus sign rotated 45°). This stimulus object was presented in a dark room to children tilted 45° and located at three physical distances from the stimulus: eight inches, three feet, and nine feet. The children were drawn from the third, fourth, fifth, and sixth grades of a local elementary school, with 10 subjects placed at each of the three distances for each of the four grades, making a total of 120 subjects. In keeping with the earlier study, it was expected that the greater the distance of the stimulus from the subject, the more likely that it would be interpreted as an "x" (in keeping with the external framework), and the shorter the distance, the more likely that it would be interpreted as a plus sign (in keeping with the egocentric framework). Similar differences were expected depending on the age of the subject, in particular, greater frequency of reports of "plus" for the younger children than the older. A preliminary analysis indicates that the findings are in the expected direction. The greatest frequency of the "plus" response occurred in the youngest age groups at the closest physical distance. Thus, there is evidence in this study of interaction of two factors presumed to affect self:object relations—developmental status and physical arrangement between self and object (distance).[9]

[9]More systematic studies must be conducted (such as one separating the factors of retinal size and distance) to assess the nature of the factors operative in this situation, and to be certain of these ontogenetic changes.

In keeping with both the developmental perspective and the organismic perspective as well, a study of neuropathology was undertaken in the Clark laboratories by Barton (1964) using hemiplegics. Barton took into account the dual characteristics of hemiplegic subjects (neuromuscular asymmetry and cortical injury) in attempting to study perceptual organization in these groups. He assumed that the neuromuscular asymmetry in the hemiplegic group would be manifest in systematic left-right differences in space localization; he further assumed by virtue of signs other than neuromuscular asymmetry (such as increased concern with body, language disturbances) that a right hemiplegic group would be relatively more regressed in cognitive functioning than a nonhemiplegic group. An illustration of the manner in which Barton sought findings in keeping with organismic-developmental theory is his experimental situation dealing with left-right localization: the location of the apparent median plane under conditions where the figure extends to the left of fixation for half of the trials and to the right of fixation for the other half.

The results of his study (Figure 3.18) indicate three effects worth noting: (a) independent of conditions, the overall shift of the apparent median plane is relatively to the right (to the side of muscular weakness) in the right hemiplegics as compared

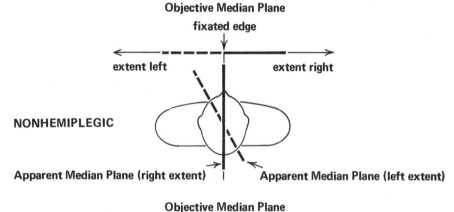

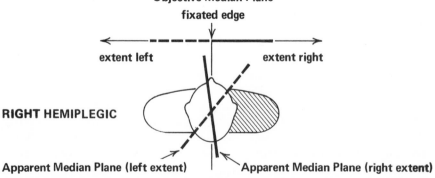

Figure 3.18 *Position of apparent median plane with asymmetrically extended figures, in hemiplegic and nonhemiplegic subjects.*

with the nonhemiplegics; (b) there are relatively opposite shifts of the apparent median plane, depending on the direction of asymmetrical extent, for the right hemiplegic and the nonhemiplegic group; (c) further, the direction of these differences are in keeping with developmental expectation—for the hemiplegics, the apparent median plane shifts relatively opposite asymmetrical extent as compared with the nonhemiplegics. Over and above the perceptual asymmetries dependent on asymmetry of neuromuscular involvement, there are findings pertinent to self:object relations in the hemiplegic brain-injured patient group that parallel those obtained from normals under instruction-induced lower-level congnitive attitudes and those obtained with younger children.

A final illustration is of the application of a parallel analysis to some preliminary data collected a number of years ago on a small group of schizophrenics. They were tested on perception of verticality and perception of body position under body tilt, and there was evidence that there was a shrinkage of this angular discrepancy between apparent vertical and apparent body position in the schizophrenics as compared with normal adults. Thus, some limited evidence was available that for schizophrenics, just as for younger children, there is decreased differentiation of body and object space.

It seems appropriate to conclude that this analysis of self:object relations in cognitive organization has marked significance. Considering the studies that have been presented, there is ample evidence that the theoretical approach has power in economically making coherent a diversity of data. The data sample such subject groups as normal children and adults, psychopathological children and adults, and adults with neuropathology; they sample such psychological functions as postural orientation, cognitive set, discrimination, identification, and space localization; and on the methodological side, they sample such experimental conditions as instructions, physical arrangements between subject and object, and use of distorting media (lenses). In the presentation, the center of focus was on the nature of the coherence among this variety of data and the linkage between theory and problem formulation. However, one aspect of significance to the studies has not yet been mentioned: the problem of the relationship between methodology and theory. It would appear that any theory must not only adequately account for the empirical data to which it addresses itself, but also must account for the linkage between those data and the methods by which they were generated. Theory, problem formulation, and method are not and should not be encapsulated.

REFERENCES

Baker, A. H. Perception under active and passive attitudes of self in relation to world. Microfilmed PhD thesis, Clark University, 1968.

Baker, A. H., and Wapner, S. Effect of task instructions and psychophysical method on space localization in children. Unpublished paper, Clark University, 1968.

Barton, M. I. Aspects of object and body perception in hemiplegics: An organismic-developmental approach. Microfilmed PhD thesis, Clark University, 1964.

Bauermeister, M., Wapner, S., & Werner, H. Method of stimulus presentation and apparent body position under lateral body tilt. *Perceptual and Motor Skills*, 1967, 24, 43–50.

Bibace, R. Applications of Werner's developmental psychology to clinical problems. In S. Wapner and B. Kaplan (Eds.) *Heinz Werner (1890-1964)*. Worcester, Mass.: Clark University Press, 1966.

Clarkson, F. E. A developmental analysis of the performance of children and adults on a maze learning and an embedded figures task. Microfilmed PhD thesis, Clark University, 1961.

Clate, Suzanne B. Effects of articulation of body on object perception. Unpublished Master's thesis, Clark University, 1965.

Dowling, R. M. Effect of sensorimotor conceptual activity on perceptual functioning. Microfilmed PhD thesis, Clark University, 1962.

Glick, J. A. An experimental analysis of subject-object relationships in perception. Microfilmed PhD thesis, Clark University, 1964.

Glick, J. A., & Wapner, S. Effect of variation in distance between subject and object on space localization. *Perceptual and Motor Skills,* 1966, 23, 438.

Harris, C. Perceptual adaptation to inverted, reversed, and displaced vision. *Psychological Review,* 1965, 72, 419-444.

Held, R., & Hein, A. Adaptation of disarranged hand-eye coordination contingent upon re-afferent stimulation. *Perceptual and Motor Skills,* 1958, 8, 87-90.

Held, R., & Schlank, M. Adaptation to disarranged eye-hand coordination in the distance dimension. *American Journal of Psychology,* 1959, 72, 603-605.

Husband, R. W. Comparative behavior on different types of mazes. *Journal of Genetic Psychology,* 1931, 5, 234-244.

Kaplan, B. The study of language in psychiatry: The comparative developmental approach and its application to symbolization and language in psychopathology. In S. Arieti (Ed.), *American Handbook of Psychiatry*. New York: Basic Books, 1966, 3, 659-688.

Kaplan, B. Meditations on genesis. *Human Development,* 1967, 10, 65-87.

Kempler, B. Developmental level and serial learning. Microfilmed PhD thesis, Clark University, 1964.

Krus, D. M. & Wapner, S. Effect of lysergic acid diethylamide (LSD-25) on perception of part-whole relationships. *Journal of Psychology,* 1959, 48, 87-95.

Mehrabian, A., Wapner, S., & Werner, H. Tactual recognition under polarized versus depolarized self-object cognitive attitudes. *Acta Psychologica,* 1964, 22, 162-168.

Nachshon, I. & Wapner, S. Effect of eye-contact and physiognomy on perceived location of other person. *Journal of Personality and Social Psychology,* 1967, 7, 87-89.

Piaget, J. *On the development of memory and identity*. Worcester, Mass.: Clark University Press, 1968.

Pollack, R. H., & Carter, D. J. Subjective median plane as a function of age and source of stimulation. *Perceptual and Motor Skills,* 1967, 25, 691-692.

Porzemsky, J., Wapner, S., & Glick, J. A. Effect of experimentally induced self-object cognitive attitudes on body and object perception. *Perceptual and Motor Skills,* 1965, 21, 187-195.

Rand, G., & Wapner, S. Postural status as a factor in memory. *Journal of Verbal Learning and Verbal Behavior,* 1967, 6, 268-271.

Rand, G., Wapner, S., Werner, H., & McFarland, J. H. Age differences in performance on the Stroop Color-Word Test. *Journal of Personality,* 1963, 31, 534-558.

Rierdan, J., & Wapner, S. Experimental study of adaptation to visual rearrangement deriving from an organismic-developmental approach to cognition. *Perceptual and Motor Skills*, 1966, 23, 903–916.

Rierdan, J., & Wapner, S. Adaptive changes in the relationship between visual and tactual-kinesthetic perception. *Psychonomic Science*, 1967, 7, 61–62.

Switzer, J. Developmental differences in place and name sequence learning in normal, hyperactive, and hypoactive eight- and twelve-year-old boys. Microfilmed PhD thesis, Clark University, 1961.

Sziklai, C. Underwater studies of space orientation. Microfilmed PhD thesis, Clark University, 1966.

Walsh, Sister Clare D., & Wapner, S. A developmental study of the dependency of "meaning" on physical arrangement between self and stimulus. Paper presented at Eastern Psychological Association Meetings, 1967, Boston, Massachusetts.

Wapner, S. An organismic-developmental approach to the study of perceptual and other cognitive operations. In C. Scheerer (Ed.) *Cognition: theory, research, promise*. New York: Harper & Row, 1964a.

Wapner, S. Some aspects of a research program based on an organismic-developmental approach to cognition: Experiments and theory. *Journal of the American Academy of Child Psychiatry*, 1964b, 3, 193–230.

Wapner, S. Age changes in perception of verticality and of the longitudinal body axis under body tilt. *Journal of Experimental Child Psychology*, 1968 (in press).

Wapner, S., & Rand, G. Age changes in verbal satiation. *Psychonomic Science*, 1967, 9, 93–94.

Wapner, S., & Rand, G. Ontogenetic differences in the nature of organization underlying serial learning. *Human Development*, 1968 (in press).

Wapner, S., & Werner, H. *Perceptual Development*. Worcester, Mass.: Clark University Press, 1957.

Wapner, S., & Werner, H. An experimental approach to body perception from the organismic-developmental point of view. In S. Wapner and H. Werner (Eds.) *The body percept*. New York: Random House, March, 1965.

Warden, C. J. The relative economy of various modes of attack on the mastery of a stylus maze. *Journal of Experimental Psychology*, 1924, 7, 243–275.

Werner, H. Process and achievement. *The Harvard Educational Review*, 1937, 353–368.

Werner, H. *Comparative psychology of mental development*. New York: Harper, 1940; (2nd ed.) Chicago: Follett, 1948; (3rd ed.) New York: International Universities Press, 1957.

Werner, H. The concept of development from a comparative and organismic point of view. In D.B. Harris (Ed.) *The concept of development: An issue in the study of human behavior*. Minneapolis: University of Minnesota Press, 1957.

Werner, H., & Kaplan, B. *Symbol formation: An organismic-developmental approach to language and the expression of thought*. New York: Wiley, 1963.

Werner, H., & Wapner, S. Sensory-tonic field theory of perception. *Journal of Personality*, 1949, 18, 88–107.

Werner, H., & Wapner, S. Toward a general theory of perception. *Psychological Review*, 1952, 59, 324–338.

Werner, H., & Wapner, S. Sensory-tonic field theory of perception: basic concepts and experiments. *Revista di psicologia*, 1956, 50, 315–337.

4

DEVELOPING THE SKILLS
OF PRODUCTIVE THINKING[1]

Cognitive development of the individual proceeds in gradual, sequential stages—from the emergence of the most elementary perceptual functions in the young child through the elaboration of the most complex processes of productive thinking in the adult. Whether or not this cognitive growth can be accelerated appreciably by providing specific training of the various functions at appropriate stages is still a moot question. Most of the research on this issue has dealt with attempts to train the simpler processes in the young child, such as efforts to produce earlier acquisition of the concept of conservation. Relatively little has been done with the training of the more complex thought processes as these develop in the older child.

However, regardless of whether or not specific training can significantly speed up the time at which the various cognitive capacities *emerge*, it seems clear to us that the ability and readiness to *use* these capacities efficiently and effectively at any given stage of development can benefit substantially from direct training. This appears to be particularly true of the higher-level functions central to productive thinking and problem solving—our observations convince us that, for most individuals and at all age levels from the child to the adult, there exists a pronounced gap between productive thinking *potential* and productive thinking *performance*. To close this gap and to achieve a level of highly skilled productive thinking, the

[1]The study reported here was made possible by a grant from the Carnegie Corporation of New York to the Institute of Personality Assessment and Research in support of a project directed by Dr. Richard S. Crutchfield and Dr. Martin V. Covington. This study was carried out at Cragmont School in the Berkeley (California) Unified School District. We wish to express our great appreciation to those whose cooperation made this study possible—Dr. Harold J. Maves, Assistant Superintendent for Instruction; Miss Glena Crumal, Principal of Cragmont School; and particularly the fifth- and sixth-grade teachers at Cragmont, who played an indispensable role.

ROBERT M. OLTON

RICHARD S. CRUTCHFIELD

University of California, Berkeley, California

simpler cognitive functions must first be organized and integrated into appropriate skills. Since the development of any kind of skills (motor or mental) requires specific training, we believe that appropriate training can produce significant increments in the skills of productive thinking. In this article results from a recent school study are presented to confirm this view. Such results have both theoretical importance for the light they shed on the developmental stages of high-level cognitive processes, and practical significance in their implications for educational aims and methods.

THE NEED TO END "THOUGHTLESS" EDUCATION

Systematic programs for teaching the student how to think should be one of the central concerns of education at all levels and for all types of pupils. An education without such instruction will produce adults who are destined eventually to become crippled by their own obsolete patterns of thought and by knowledge that is no longer relevant, to become confused and then overwhelmed by a vastly changed future society in which they will no longer know how to participate.

Since today's education emphasizes mastery of the *known*, it does very little to prepare an individual to cope effectively with the *unknown*. Yet many of today's school children will be spending more than half their lifetime in the unknown world of the twenty-first century. To cope effectively with the unknown, an individual must have a well-developed ability to think. Thus, an education that will prepare today's student for a useful, fulfilling life in the twenty-first century must provide him with extensive, systematic instruction in the skills required for original, independent thinking and problem solving.

This coming century will present man with enormously complex and urgent problems: how to limit population size, so that the "human" qualities of life will not be suffocated by the cruelly impersonal demands of life in an overcrowded world; how to cope in the coming computer age so that man, and not the machine, will be the master; how to find fulfillment, rather than an aimless boredom, in the leisure that will result from a three-day (or shorter) work week; how to deal with the consequences of man's awesome ability to change his capabilities and perhaps his very nature through the use of powerful new biochemical techniques; how to construct an urban environment that will bring out the best rather than the worst qualities of its citizens and make urban life a source of profound human satisfaction rather than of destructive frustration.

It is sobering to realize that it is *today's* students—not some comfortably distant generation—who are going to have to deal with these staggering problems. It is today's students who must be prepared for a world in which their ability to function will not depend on their mastery of the facts and principles now taught in school, but rather on their ability to deal with new facts and principles that have not yet even been imagined. It is today's students whose search for personal satisfaction and fulfillment will require them to re-evaluate and restructure their beliefs and actions in accord with a vastly different and constantly changing world where many of today's beliefs and customs will seem irrelevant or even absurd. Thus it is today's students who should be receiving extensive, systematic instruction in how to think. This should be the very center of their education, for a "thoughtless" education makes the student an ultimate prisoner—rather than master—of his own knowledge and beliefs.

Fortunately, recognition of the need for teaching the student *how* to think, rather than *what* to think, is one of the central themes of the innovative movements now taking place in American education. Several recent noteworthy books by educators and researchers have stressed the importance of productive thinking in the schools (Aschner and Bish, 1965; Torrance, 1965; Fair and Shaftel, 1967) and this emphasis is reflected in the new curricula in mathematics, science, and social studies.

When parents in a recent nationwide Gallup survey were asked to rate the importance of some 48 possible goals of public school education, they gave a particularly high rating to "the ability to figure things out for oneself" as contrasted with relatively low ratings for many of the traditional educational goals. A similar note was recently sounded by a blue-ribbon citizens' committee in California which made the following recommendation to that state's Board of Education: "Let the schools concentrate on the heart of the matter, which is training pupils to think for themselves. Education should center around the ability to solve problems."

It seems clear that the kind of problem solving that these educators and citizens are talking about is not that of the cut-and-dried arithmetic problem or the exercise in formal logic. Their concern is with the kind of problem solving that requires the individual to do independent thinking and to strive to achieve his own solutions to complex problems. Such productive thinking involves generating original ideas, looking at a problem in a new or different way if one gets "stuck," asking insightful questions, and seeing the implications of crucial facts or events. It involves working in an organized, planned manner on problems that seem to resist solution, formulating and evaluating new possibilities, and developing a sensitivity to odd or unusual circumstances that may lead to a discovery or fresh insight.

This is the kind of thinking that will better equip an individual to cope with the unknowns of life in the year 2000. This is the kind of thinking that enables a person to deal intelligently and effectively with his own problems and opportunities, and that will provide him with an increasing sense of enjoyment in the use of his mind. And it is this kind of thinking in which today's student should (but does not) receive extensive, systematic instruction.

A PROGRAM FOR THE DEVELOPMENT
OF PRODUCTIVE THINKING SKILLS

In order to help meet the need for instructional materials that will increase the student's ability to do this kind of thinking, *The Productive Thinking Program* (Covington, Crutchfield, and Davies, 1966) has recently been developed. This set of booklet materials, designed primarily for fifth- and sixth-grade students, provides systematic instruction and carefully guided practice in the skills of productive thinking and problem solving. The 16 programmed booklets are individually self-administered and self-paced, each requiring approximately one hour.

These materials have been used in a series of school studies (e.g., Covington and Crutchfield, 1965; Crutchfield, 1966; Olton, Wardrop, et al., 1967) and have consistently been found to produce significant gains in student performance on a variety of tests of productive thinking. Specifically, the trained students have demonstrated strengthened skills in such cognitive functions as generating ideas of high quality, asking relevant questions, being sensitive to crucial clues, making effective use of information, and achieving solutions to problems. These gains have been found to occur across a wide spectrum of ability levels—among low achievers as well as high, among the culturally disadvantaged as well as the advantaged.

These consistently positive outcomes support our view that properly directed training can bring about a measurable improvement in the individual's skilled *use* of his gradually developing capacities for productive thought. It is noteworthy that the amount of training we have employed in these studies is relatively modest (16 hours total) and that the conditions of training have been far short of optimal. For example, in the largest of the studies, that of 47 fifth-grade classes in Racine, Wisconsin (Olton, Wardrop, et al., 1967), the training was severely compressed into a four-week period, thus losing the advantages of distributed practice, and the materials were taken by each student entirely alone, without the support of teacher help or class discussion. Yet even under these restrictive conditions, the training produced an appreciable improvement in the students' thinking ability.

THE PRESENT STUDY

The school study reported in this article was carried out under conditions designed to maximize the impact of the training and hence to prove the upper limits of effectiveness of this instructional program.

This study went beyond the previous ones in four principal ways. First, the training period was extended from four weeks to eight weeks. Second, the teacher was brought into an active role in the instructional program, stimulating and guiding class discussions of the materials. Third, the basic 16-lesson series was augmented by a set of supplementary problem exercises that gave the student considerably more practice in using the productive thinking skills and strategies taught in the basic lessons. Finally, to enhance the transfer of these skills and strategies to a broad spectrum of problems representative of the several main school curriculum areas, the contents of these supplementary practice exercises were widely diversified, touching on social studies, science, human relations, and current affairs. A comparable variety of educationally relevant thinking tasks was included in the criterion battery of tests used to assess the effectiveness of the instructional program.

A total of 280 students, comprising 5 fifth-grade and 5 sixth-grade classes, participated in this study. These students were generally above average in intellectual ability. The mean IQ of the group was 115, with a range of IQs from 80 to 150. The mean level of performance on six subtests of the Stanford Achievement Battery was approximately one and one-half school years ahead of the students' current grade level.

Most of the detailed results reported in this paper will focus on a comparison of two groups of fifth-grade students drawn from the total group, for whom the fullest test information is available. In order to equate these two groups for the influence of a particular teacher and a particular classroom climate, a split-class technique was used. Half the students from each of 2 fifth-grade classrooms were selected to receive instruction in productive thinking (Instruction group), while the other half of each class served as a noninstructed Control group. These two groups, of 25 students each, were matched as closely as possible with respect to IQ and achievement. Although the Instruction group showed a slight superiority and somewhat greater variance on both measures, these differences were far short of statistical significance (Table 4.1).

Table 4.1 *IQ and achievement scores of Instruction and Control groups.*

Measure	Instruction		Control	
	Mean	S.D.	Mean	S.D.
IQ	117.50	17.00	113.50	14.00
Achievement	6.88	1.64	6.60	1.36

Both groups were given a pretest battery of productive thinking problems to determine the extent to which any differences in productive thinking proficiency existed before instruction began. Then during the next eight weeks the Instruction group devoted approximately one hour per school day to instruction in productive thinking, while the Control group spent this same daily hour in an activities program consisting of stories, movies, and various projects chosen to interest the children and to have general educational value, but not to relate to productive thinking. At the end of the eight-week period, performance of the two groups was compared on an extensive posttest battery of thinking problems. Six months later their performance was again compared on a follow-up battery of thinking tests.

THE INSTRUCTIONAL MATERIALS

The augmented version of *The Productive Thinking Program* used in this study contained two types of self-instructional material: (a) a set of 16 programmed lessons that provided direct instruction and a certain amount of guided practice in productive thinking and problem solving; (b) a set of supplementary exercises intended to strengthen the skills taught in the programmed lessons by giving the student extensive practice in using these general skills on productive thinking tasks representative of a variety of subject-matter areas.

The Basic Lessons

Each of the 16 programmed lessons is an individual booklet that features an engaging detective-type mystery problem that the student is called on to solve. As the mystery unfolds, the student is given instruction in appropriate productive thinking skills: how to generate many ideas, particularly clever and unusual ones; how to evaluate his ideas with respect to relevant facts and conditions of the problem; how to look at the problem in a different and more fruitful way if he gets "stuck"; how to clarify the essentials of a problem and work on it in an organized and planful way. At various points in the booklet lessons, the student practices using such skills and writes down his ideas, questions, or suggestions for what should be done next. Feedback or confirmation of his efforts is then provided on the succeeding pages in the form of a set of responses illustrative of those that would be appropriate at that point in the problem. Through such repeated guided practice of basic thinking skills in a variety of problem contexts, the student is led to understand what constitute relevant and original ideas, how to proceed fruitfully when faced with a challenging problem, and what effective strategies to use when one encounters difficulties.

Each of these lessons is self-administering, permitting the student to progress through the problem at his own pace and in accord with his particular reading level and intellectual capacity. The major points taught in each lesson are summarized for the student at the end of the booklet.

Student interest is readily engaged by the mystery theme and cartoon-text format of the lessons, and also by a continuous storyline that features two children of the student's age, Jim and Lila Cannon. Jim and Lila are intended to serve as stimulating "companions" for the reader as he pursues these intellectual adventures, and they are presented as typical children with whom the reader can identify— likable, human, and quite capable of making mistakes. As the series develops, a number of constructive changes occur in Jim's and Lila's attitudes toward thinking and in their sense of confidence in their own abilities. At the same time, a subtle but sustained attempt is made to increase the student's own interest in and liking for activities that involve the use of the mind, and to build up his willingness to work on thinking tasks in a persistent and concentrated way. Each lesson is so designed that, as the student works through the problem, he is led eventually to discover the solution for himself, thus giving him the thrill of discovery and helping him develop a sense of confidence in his ability to cope with difficult and challeng- ing intellectual tasks. A brief segment of one of these lessons is illustrated on pages 88 through 91.

The detective-mystery content of these programmed lessons captures student interest and serves as an excellent vehicle for teaching productive thinking skills, but such content does not give the student direct practice in applying these skills to the types of problems found in the subject matter of the usual school curriculum. That function is fulfilled by the supplementary exercises.

The Supplementary Exercises

These exercises reinforce and strengthen the skills taught by the basic lessons and give the student repeated, guided practice in using these skills on curriculum- relevant tasks.

One of the exercises, shown in Figure 4.1, concerns the currently pressing prob- lem of how to dispose of the ever-growing quantities of waste materials produced by our society—a problem clearly relevant to social studies and science. This exer- cise was administered to the student the day after he had worked on a lesson that showed him how to *look at a problem in a new and different way if one approach to solving it does not work.*

The students first worked on this exercise individually and then shared their ideas in a class discussion. During this discussion, the teacher sought to guide and clarify the students' understanding of what it means to look at a problem in a new and different way (as opposed to thinking only of new variations of a single ap- proach). The teacher was assisted by a Teacher's Guide that suggested some new ways of looking at the waste disposal problem. One new way might be to ask the question: "What could be done to *produce less waste in the first place?*" (For example, packaging foods by spraying them with a specially developed plastic coat- ing that would dissolve in warm water, thus eliminating the trash produced by containers.)

Another way of looking at the problem might be to ask: "What could be done to *transform waste materials into useful products?*" (For example, chemically con- verting the waste into fertilizers, fuel, insulation, or other building materials.) Yet another way of looking at the problem is to ask: "How could the waste materials be *used as a filler material?*" (For example, filling in gullies in eroded land and

Thinking about waste is not wasted thinking:

All cities and towns today are faced with the problem of what to do about the huge and constantly increasing amounts of trash, garbage, and other waste materials produced in homes and industries.

Experts have been working on various ways of destroying this waste material. They have thought of many methods for doing this—such as burning it so it makes little smoke, dissolving it with special chemicals, crushing it under high pressure, etc. But they are still searching for better methods of destroying the waste materials, and they need more ideas.

Now you try to look *in a new and different way* at this problem of what the cities can do about the huge and constantly increasing amounts of waste material. The experts have been asking themselves, "How can we *destroy* the waste material?" But a new way to look at the problem would be to ask the question:

_____

_____

_____

_____

_____

Another new and different way of looking at this problem would be to ask the question:

_____

_____

_____

_____

_____

_____

Figure 4.1 *Sample page from a supplementary exercise of* The Productive Thinking Program.

swamps.) These suggestions are, of course, by no means exhaustive, and the class discussions that took place in our study yielded additional ways of looking at this problem.

The basic lessons and the supplementary exercises were used in a carefully coordinated instructional schedule occupying approximately one hour per day for four days of each school week (the fifth day was used for individual make-ups) over a period of eight weeks. Typically, a basic lesson was given one day, followed on the next day by a brief class discussion and by a set of supplementary exercises related to that prior lesson. Two basic lessons and two sessions of supplementary exercises plus discussions were covered each week; thus the total instructional program occupied approximately 32 hours.

The intent was to give the student the materials under practical conditions approaching those of regular, large-scale school use, yet without providing any special teacher training in productive thinking. Accordingly, the only preparation for the teacher was that supplied by a Teacher's Guide, which gave background information on the pedagogical aims and methods of *The Productive Thinking Program* and suggestions for administering the materials and conducting class discussions.

CRITERION MEASURES OF PRODUCTIVE THINKING

The effects of the eight-week instructional program were assessed by comparing the performance of Instruction and Control groups on three batteries of specially created productive thinking tasks. These tasks are unlike most regular school tests in that they are not primarily concerned with how much the student *knows*, but rather with how well he *thinks*. In the construction of these tasks, particular effort was made to minimize the importance of specific knowledge, and to design tasks that the student would find novel and challenging and that would tap his ability to perform a variety of productive thinking functions on problems having educational relevance.

For example, in one task the student read an account of the migratory behavior of a hypothetical flock of birds, including facts about variations in the size of the flock at different points on the route. Embedded in the account were several puzzling and unexplained circumstances in the birds' behavior (such as the fact that the size of the flock dropped sharply during one portion of the flight and never recovered). The student was asked to write down anything about the behavior of this flock that struck him as odd or puzzling, and later, after having had the several puzzling facts pointed out to him, to try to devise an explanation that could account for these facts. The student's responses were scored for the total number of puzzling facts noticed and for the total number of puzzling facts satisfactorily explained.

In another of the tasks, the student was told that during his lifetime, medical science will have made it possible to transplant various organs of the body from one person to another. He was then asked to consider the many possible consequences of such a technological advance and to list as many different such consequences as he could, both medical and nonmedical.[2] The student's responses were scored on three variables: number of acceptable ideas generated; number of main categories of ideas reflected in this list (cognitive breadth); number of relevant information-seeking questions asked.

In still another task (Figure 4.2) the student was asked to write an essay about

[2]When we gave this problem it was intended to evoke thinking about a purely hypothetical medical possibility of the future. Eight months later came the first successful transplant of a human heart by Dr. Christian Barnard in South Africa. Thus the future overtook the present, and the productive thinking skills intended for the world of tomorrow had to be pressed into service to deal with the world of today. No doubt this pattern of future developments that suddenly and unexpectedly become present realities is an occurrence that will be repeated often during the lives of these students; hence the necessity of providing them with appropriate thinking skills now.

the urgent social problem of poverty. The number of causes of poverty mentioned and the number of suggestions made about how to end poverty were scored as indices of productive thinking in this task.

A problem of poverty in a land of plenty:

When Americans travel abroad, they are sometimes asked how can it be that the United States, the richest nation in the world, is faced with such a great problem of poverty among many of its people.

Some people in other nations say they are puzzled by the fact that in spite of the great wealth of our nation, many of our cities have great slum areas, many of our people are dependent for their support on relief and welfare funds, and many of our people do not share in the American dream of enjoying a high standard of living.

Now, suppose that you and your family are visiting a foreign country this summer. Some children your age in that country ask you about why the United States is faced with such a problem of poverty. What would you say?

Take time to think about this; then write below what you would say to them about this puzzling problem of poverty in a land of plenty. (There are several additional blank pages attached to this page, so you may write as much as you wish.)

Figure 4.2 *A sample productive thinking test item.*

As a final example, the student worked on a hypothetical problem in archeology, in which he was asked to discover which one of ten possible persons was buried in a nameless ancient tomb. He was scored on the number of appropriate strategic steps that he could specify for attacking the problem, on correct elimination of suspects who did not fit the facts, and on achievement of final solution of the problem—successful identification of the person who was buried in the tomb. The total set of tasks making up the three test batteries is as follows.

Pretests:

Controlling the weather	Student thinks of various consequences of man's future ability to change the weather.
Project for a village	Student puts himself in the shoes of a Peace Corps volunteer who must first acquaint himself with the customs and mores of a tribal village. Then, without offending such customs, he must figure out ways the inhabitants can earn money for their village needs.

Posttests:

Transplanting organs	Student thinks of various consequences of man's future medical ability to transplant bodily organs from one person to another.

"Black House" problem	Student attempts to solve a puzzling mystery problem in which he must make an insightful reorganization of the elements of the problem.
A visit to Karam	Student puts himself in the shoes of a diplomat who is the first outsider in 50 years allowed into a small country. He sees many puzzling things on his short visit. Student attempts to explain what is going on in this country.
Conflict among tribes	Student attempts to generate new and more fruitful ways of looking at an intertribal problem faced by many newly independent African nations.
Bird migration	Student reads an account of the migratory behavior of a hypothetical flock of birds. He is asked to note anything about the behavior of the flock that seems puzzling, and to try to account for these puzzling facts.
Poverty essay	Student writes an essay in which he has the opportunity to demonstrate his thinking ability in connection with the problem of poverty.

Follow-up Tests:

The missing jewel problem	Student attempts to solve a puzzling mystery problem in which he must make an insightful reorganization of the elements of the problem.
The nameless tomb	Student works on a hypothetical problem in archeology in which he must discover which of ten possible suspects is buried in a nameless ancient tomb.
The lost colony	Student reacts to the challenge of a problem that requires thinking about the puzzling failure of the first attempted English colony in the New World.
Understanding thinking	Student indicates what thinking strategies are useful at various stages of work on a complex problem.
Natural resources essay	Student writes an essay in which he has the opportunity to demonstrate his thinking ability in connection with the problem of conserving natural resources.

Several points about this set of tasks should be underlined. First, it is obvious that the tasks are highly diverse in content. Second, the tasks vary widely along a convergent-divergent dimension of thinking—from those that are fairly well *structured*, permitting only a limited range of acceptable responses (for example, the bird migration problem) to those that are open-ended, permitting much greater scope for creativity in responses (for example, the poverty essay). Third, the tasks are chosen so as to reflect in some degree virtually all the important components of productive thinking.

Composite Performance Scores

All the Instruction and Control students took the three different batteries of productive thinking tests. The pretest battery was administered one week before the instructional program began; the posttest battery was administered just after the eight-week instructional period had ended; the follow-up battery was given six months after the posttest.

In each of the three batteries, a given student's performance was summarized in a single composite score that reflected his overall productive thinking skill, based on the various measures in that battery. The composite score was compiled in the following manner. For each variable, the scores of all students (both Instruction and Control) were pooled and arranged in a frequency distribution. Any student whose score fell above the median of this distribution was given one point on the variable, while any student scoring at or below the median received no credit on the variable. The composite score was the sum of points earned on all the variables of the test battery. For example, five variables were scored in the pretest, so the maximum composite score possible for that battery was five (indicating that such a student had scored above the median on all five variables) and the lowest possible score was zero. Similarly, 13 variables were scored in the posttest battery, permitting a maximum composite score of 13, while a maximum score of 10 was possible on the 10-variable follow-up battery.

The use of such composite scores as summary indices of over-all productive thinking skill adds considerable stability and generality to the following analyses of results.

RESULTS

Table 4.2 compares the composite productive thinking scores of the Instruction and Control groups on each of the three test batteries. The findings may be summarized as follows:

1. Performances of the Instruction and Control groups were nearly identical on the pretest battery, indicating that they were well matched in productive thinking proficiency before instruction began. Indeed, the small difference that did exist favored the Control group.

2. After the instructional program had been completed, a clear and substantial superiority in thinking was shown by the students who had received instruction.

3. On the follow-up battery, performance of the Instruction group continued to surpass that of the Control group by a significant margin. Thus the gain in thinking skills produced by the eight weeks of instruction was still evident more than six months after instruction had ended.

The most comprehensive measure of thinking performance was obtained by combining each student's scores on the posttest and follow-up test batteries. This measure reflected his over-all performance based on 23 different indices of productive thinking, and hence was a measure of considerable scope. The clear superiority of

Table 4.2 *Composite performance scores of Instruction and Control groups on productive thinking test batteries.*

Test Battery	Instruction		Control			
	Mean	S.D.	Mean	S.D.	*t**	*p*
Pretest	2.36	1.47	2.52	1.36	0.39	n.s.
Posttest	7.12	2.78	4.76	2.69	2.69	<.01
Follow-up	5.20	1.77	3.40	1.68	3.15	<.005

**df* = 48

the instructed students on this measure is graphically demonstrated in Figure 4.3, which shows the distributions of scores for the Control and the Instruction groups.

Note that the entire distribution of scores for the Instruction group of students is shifted more or less uniformly upward as compared with the distribution of the Control group. This implies that the positive effect of training was not limited to only a few of the instructed students but was evident across the board regardless of whether a student was initially low or high in thinking proficiency. The sheer magnitude of this effect can be appreciated by noting the point at which the median of scores for all the students cuts the two distributions. The fact is that 72 percent of the Instruction group fall above this midpoint, while only 24 percent of the Control group do so.

Specific Examples of Training Effects

The preceding results are based on composite performance scores which, although valuable for summary purposes, give no information about the effects of the training on specific tests or specific functions of productive thinking. We will present a few such specific data now.

In the posttest "bird migration" problem, the student was asked to try to explain three puzzling facts about the migratory behavior of a hypothetical flock of birds. Students in the Control group managed to explain an average of 1.08 of these facts, while students in the Instruction group were able to account for an average of 1.90—nearly twice as many. Moreover, if we consider only those students who were able to account for all three puzzling facts, it is found that 38 percent of the Instruction students were able to do so, as compared with only 12 percent of the Control students—a superiority of three-to-one.

Another example of the increased thinking skill of the Instruction group can be seen in performance on the "nameless tomb" problem of the follow-up test battery. In this hypothetical archeology problem, the student's task was to figure out which one of ten possible personages was buried in a nameless ancient tomb. Seven of these suspects could easily be eliminated on the basis of a few simple facts contained in the problem that made it impossible for any of those individuals to be buried there. Of the three remaining suspects, one was rendered the most likely by a clue that was obvious, but the significance of which was apparent only if the student was able to break free of one line of thought and to entertain another main possibility. Throughout the problem, the student was given a great deal of prompting in the form of suggestions, hints, and leading questions; the intent was to present him with a problem in which the strategic plan of attack had already been worked out for him, so that his task would be straightforward and relatively easy. With such careful guidance, the Control students demonstrated a respectable level of performance; for example, 37 percent of them correctly eliminated the seven suspects who could not have been buried in the tomb. However, they were far surpassed by the Instruction students, of whom 69 percent made the correct eliminations. Moreover, while 91 percent of the Instruction students were able to grasp the significance of the final clue and hence solved the problem, only 58 percent of the Control students were able to do so. Differences of this magnitude, obtained some six months after the instructional program had ended,

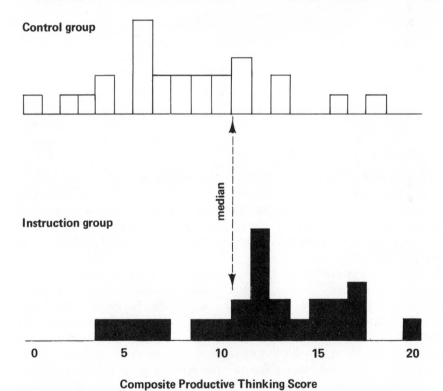

Composite Productive Thinking Score

Figure 4.3 *Distributions of 23-item productive thinking composite scores for Instruction and Control groups, showing the median of the combined groups. A significantly higher proportion of Instruction than of Control students scored above this median ($\chi^2 = 22.09$, $p < .001$).*

indicate significant and enduring facilitation of the skills required in insightful use of data in problem solving.

A final example can be seen in quite a different type of thinking task, the "poverty essay" (Figure 4.2). As we have said, this task was entirely open-ended, the student being left completely free to write whatever he wished about this important social problem. His essay was scored on three variables: (a) the number of *descriptions* of poverty included in the essay (e.g., "The people don't have any money"; "Their houses are broken down"); (b) the number of *causes* of poverty mentioned (e.g., "They got replaced by machines"; "Some of them are black and there's discrimination"); (c) the number of suggestions made about *how poverty might be ended*. The mean scores of Instruction and Control groups on the first two of these variables are presented in Table 4.3.

Table 4.3 *Performance of Instruction and Control groups on posttest poverty essay task.*

Variables	Instruction		Control		Significance Test	p
	Mean	S.D.	Mean	S.D.		
Number of Descriptions	2.20	2.63	1.68	1.55	$t = 0.82*$	n.s.
Number of Causes	4.72	3.98	1.50	1.44	$\chi^2 = 9.63\dagger$	$<.002$

*$df = 45$

†The nonparametric median test was used here because of the large difference in the variances of Instruction and Control groups.

Note first that the Instruction and Control groups did not differ significantly in the number of purely descriptive statements about poverty they offered. Such descriptive statements require no productive thinking on the problem; they represent at best some nominal grasp by the student of the concept of poverty. Thus, we can infer that the two groups were roughly equivalent in basic *knowledge* about poverty.

In terms of the amount of *thinking* demonstrated in the essays, however, the two groups differed considerably. One evidence of this is given by the greater number of causes of poverty mentioned by the Instruction students. This variable differs from most of the other performance variables in that it is not so much a measure of the student's *ability* to think as it is an index of his actual *readiness* to do so. The student was not specifically directed or urged to mention causes of poverty in this open-ended essay; he was entirely free to write whatever he wished. Hence, choosing to consider causes of poverty is a step toward self-initiated productive thinking on this problem. In light of this consideration, it is impressive that students in the Instruction group mentioned an average of nearly five causes per essay, more than three times the Control students' average of 1.5 (Table 4.3). An additional step toward creative thinking was taken by those few students who went on to suggest ways that poverty might be ended. Of the five students who did so, four were in the Instruction group. Taken together, these findings indicate that one of the results of the instructional program was to strengthen the student's readiness to think even when not required to do so by the specific task. Such a positive set toward productive use of the mind is, of course, a prime goal of education.

IQ and the Effects of Instruction

The results presented so far show that the Instruction group as a whole demonstrated substantial and enduring gains in productive thinking skills from having participated in the instructional program. Beyond this, however, it is important to know whether these gains occurred for students throughout a wide range of intellectual ability, or whether the effectiveness of instruction was limited primarily to students of a particular IQ level—for instance, to the gifted. To investigate this question, the Instruction and Control groups were each subdivided: students with IQs above 115 were placed in the so-called high-IQ subgroup, while all other students were placed in the so-called average-IQ subgroup. The IQ means and ranges of the subgroups, presented in Table 4.4, indicate that the subgroups were appropriately named.

Table 4.4 *IQ and composite productive thinking score for average-IQ and high-IQ subgroups.*

	Instruction			Control		
Subgroup	IQ Mean	IQ Range	Composite Score	IQ Mean	IQ Range	Composite Score
Average-IQ	99.0	(80-110)	10.0	102.8	(86-114)	5.9
High-IQ	129.4	(116-148)	13.6	124.2	(116-140)	10.6

The mean performance score of each subgroup on the 23-item productive thinking composite is also presented in Table 4.4. Two of the findings are noteworthy:

1. At both high and average intelligence levels, the Instruction students outperformed the Control students by a sizable margin. This finding indicates that students at *both* levels of ability demonstrated significant instructional benefits, and confirms similar results in earlier studies with the program (Covington and Crutchfield, 1965; Olton, et al., 1967).

2. The performance of the high-IQ groups surpassed that of the average-IQ groups, both trained and untrained. Thus there is a positive relationship between IQ and performance on productive thinking tasks. Despite this relationship, the instructional effects were great enough that the performance score of the average-IQ students after training (10.0) was virtually as high as that of the high-IQ students

who were not trained (10.6). In other words, the program raised the level of thinking skill shown by an "average" student to the level typical of a student with an IQ some 25 points higher. Similar gains have been reported in a previous study using an earlier version of these materials (Covington and Crutchfield, 1965).

Gains of this magnitude imply that existing school programs are doing less than they should in teaching students how to think, because if the schools were being more effective in this regard, one would not expect to be able to produce these appreciable gains in thinking ability with a program of such modest proportions. Such gains produced in a relatively short period of time also imply that the instructional program did not achieve its effects by changing the basic cognitive *capacities* of the student. Rather, it seems likely that the program showed the student how to make far more effective *use* of the cognitive capacities he already had. Perhaps this point can be made best by citing the comment of one Instruction student on an end-of-the-study questionnaire. The student wrote: "Now I see that I'm not dumb; I just didn't know how to use my mind."

Change in Attitudes

The progressive development of a skill, such as skill in productive thinking, is likely to be associated with positive attitudes toward that skill. On the one hand, the effectiveness of training in the skill may be reinforced by building up positive attitudes about it; on the other hand, the very growth of the successful skill may result in positive attitudes toward its use. An essential part of the process of developing productive thinking skills, therefore, is the promotion of positive attitudes toward productive thinking. Accordingly, *The Productive Thinking Program* includes not only direct instruction and practice in thinking performance but also some carefully interwoven material intended to influence the student's attitudes toward thinking. Considerable stress is placed on building up the student's positive evaluation of productive use of the mind and his confidence in his own abilities and potential as a thinker.

For these reasons an attempt was made in this study to measure some of the student's opinions and beliefs about productive thinking activities and to assess changes occurring in these opinions and beliefs as a result of the instructional program. This was done by means of an objective questionnaire, similar to the *Children's Attitude Inventory for Problem Solving* (Covington, 1966). The questionnaire consisted of 20 statements about productive thinking activities in the school setting, the student being asked to indicate the extent of his agreement or disagreement with each statement on a five-point scale. An over-all index of positive attitudes toward productive thinking was obtained by summing the scale values for the 20 items. Sample statements (scored "plus" for agreement): "I am often curious about unexplained things around me and want to try to understand them"; "I think I have the makings of a really creative thinker." Sample statements (scored "plus" for disagreement): "Some students are just naturally poorer thinkers than others and there is nothing they can do about it"; "I often keep my ideas to myself because I think others may laugh at them."

This questionnaire was administered as part of all three test batteries (pretest, posttest, and follow-up) thus permitting an analysis of changes that occurred throughout the nine-month time period encompassed by the complete study. The pretest index score was found to be equivalent for the Control and the Instruction groups. On the posttest and the six-month follow-up, the students who had gone through the instructional program tended to change toward higher scores on the index, that is, tended to express beliefs and opinions more favorable to productive thinking activities and toward themselves as thinkers.

The greatest shift occurred between the pretest and the follow-up test, some nine months later. Of the Instruction students, 68 percent showed an increase in their favorability index over this period as compared with 42 percent of the Control students. However, the variance in individual scores was very large and the obtained differences were only marginally significant.

Much stronger evidence of the favorable impact of the instructional program on the attitudes of the students is given by their answers on a questionnaire evaluating the program, which was filled out at the end of the eight-week instructional period. Table 4.5 presents the results of this survey made of all 202 fifth-grade and sixth-grade students who went through the thinking program. Clearly, the majority of the students felt that they had improved in thinking skills, had come to enjoy using their minds more than before, and were favorably inclined toward further instruction in productive thinking.

SUMMARY AND CONCLUSIONS

The instructional program described in this study produced substantial and enduring gains in the productive thinking skills of fifth- and sixth-grade students. These gains were evident on a broad variety of educationally relevant thinking tasks that involved many different aspects of productive thinking and varied widely in form and content. Students of a wide range of intellectual ability demonstrated such gains and many also developed somewhat more positive attitudes toward productive thinking as a result of the program.

The fact that these substantial and enduring gains could be produced by a program of modest proportions suggests that existing school programs are doing less than they should in teaching students how to think because, as already observed, if the schools were being more effective in this regard, it is unlikely that such a modest program would have had such impressive effects. Therefore, if the schools intend to make effective progress toward the newly emphasized goal of teaching the student *how* to think rather than merely teaching him *what* to think, there must be new educational programs designed to provide extensive, systematic instruction in productive thinking skills for all students and at all grade levels.

The results of this study also suggest that considerable increments in thinking proficiency can be produced by showing the student how to make more effective use of the basic cognitive capacities he already possesses, rather than by attempting to accelerate the emergence of basic capacities that normally develop at a later age. Since most current studies of developmental cognition are concerned with the

Table 4.5 *Number of students choosing each alternative on an end-of-instruction questionnaire.* *

1. Do you feel that *your thinking has improved* since you began working with the lessons in productive thinking?

1	14	87	86	11
became poorer	no change	improved slightly	improved quite a lot	improved greatly

2. Do you now *enjoy using your mind* more than you did before you began the lessons in productive thinking?

7	50	55	62	28
less than before	about the same as before	a little bit more than before	quite a bit more than before	very much more than before

3. Do you feel that the lessons and exercises in productive thinking have *helped you in your regular school work*?

3	61	96	27	11
have made me poorer in my regular school work	have not helped my regular school work	have helped slightly in my regular school work	have helped quite a bit in my regular school work	have helped a great deal in my regular school work

4. Do you feel that the lessons in productive thinking have made your *school work more interesting*?

4	95	48	39	13
have made it less interesting	have made it neither more nor less interesting	have made it slightly more interesting	have made it quite a bit more interesting	have made it a great deal more interesting

5. Do you think it would be a good idea for the students who are coming into this same grade next year to be given these lessons in productive thinking?

19	183
NO	YES

6. Would you like to have some new lessons in productive thinking as part of your school work next year?

89	106
NO	YES

* Total number of respondents was 202; a few of the questionnaires were incomplete.

emergence of basic capacities, we believe that far too little attention is being paid to the extent to which important gains in thinking ability might be achieved by providing appropriate instruction in the use of cognitive capacities that are naturally present at each successive stage of development. The results of the present study suggest that this latter aspect of cognitive development is an important area for future research.

REFERENCES

Aschner, Mary Jane, & Bish, C. F. (Eds.). *Productive thinking in education.* Washington, D. C.: National Education Association, 1965.

Covington, M. V. A childhood attitude inventory for problem solving. *Journal of Educational Measurement,* 1966, 3, 234.

Covington, M. V., & Crutchfield, R. S. Facilitation of creative problem solving. *Programmed Instruction,* 1965, 4 (4), 3–5, 10.

Covington, M. V., Crutchfield, R. S., & Davies, L. B. *The productive thinking program.* (Revised edition, by Covington, M. V., Crutchfield, R. S., Davies, L. B., & Olton, R. M., to be published by Charles E. Merrill Publishing Co., Columbus, Ohio.)

Crutchfield, R. S. Creative thinking in children: Its teaching and testing. Brim, H., Crutchfield, R. S., & Holtzman, W. *Intelligence: Perspective 1965.* New York: Harcourt, Brace & World, 1966, 33–64.

Fair, Jean, & Shaftel, Fannie R. *Effective thinking in the social studies.* Washington, D.C.: National Council for the Social Studies (A Department of the National Education Association), 1967.

Olton, R. M., Wardrop, J. L., Covington, M. V., Goodwin, W. L., Crutchfield, R. S., Klausmeier, H. J., & Ronda, T. *The development of productive thinking skills in fifth-grade children.* Technical Report, Research and Development Center for Cognitive Learning. Madison, Wisconsin: University of Wisconsin, 1967.

Torrance, E. P. *Rewarding creative behavior: Experiments in classroom creativity.* Englewood Cliffs, N. J.: Prentice-Hall, Inc., 1965.

Segment of a Lesson
from *The Productive Thinking Program*
(Copyright 1966 by Martin V. Covington,
Richard S. Crutchfield, and Lillian B. Davies)

Uncle John notices Jim's silence:

Here's another thinking guide that will give you a method for discovering many of the different ideas about this problem.

What is it?

Pick out each of the important things in the story--each object and person. Then take each of these things one at a time, and try to figure out how it might have had something to do with the disappearance of the water.

This method will make sure that you don't miss any important part of the problem that could give you ideas.

Now, what will happen as Jim and Lila take Uncle John's advice? Turn the page to find out.

You try making a list, too. Go back to pages 8 and 9 and read the story
again. Then pick out each of the main things in the story and write it
down:

_____

_____

_____

_____

_____

_____

5

DEVELOPMENTAL PROCESSES
IN THE CHILD'S MORAL THINKING

Students of moral development have found difficulty in defining the term "moral" and in deciding what are to be labeled "moral responses." Very young children manifest behavior and attitudes that give the appearance of being in the realm of the moral, apparently indicating that the young child has developed values and conscience. An example is the following interchange between an uncle and his five-year-old nephew, as overheard by this author. While relating some of his past experiences to his nephew John, the uncle decided to tell the boy that he had once been in jail—although he never had been. John's first reaction to this news was one of disbelief and a demand for reassurance that it was not true. The uncle failed to reassure him, insisting that it was indeed true. John seemed convinced because he backed away, glared at his uncle from the other end of the room, and would not speak to him for the rest of the day—nor would John believe his uncle's later insistence that he had not been in jail.

The uncle assumed that this was an instance of a fairly strong moral response on the part of his nephew, in line with the views of some theorists who also make the assumption that such attitudes and behaviors on the part of children indicate a presence of moral values. These theorists assume that the child internalizes the rules, norms, or values of the culture, that through a passive internalization process he comes to have his own moral values and to behave morally. One theoretical approach to moral development that makes these assumptions is taken by the learning theorists, who view the development of morality as one aspect of human learning that follows the same laws as any other aspect. Eysenck (1960) has presented the simplest analysis of moral development from this point of view. Eysenck would interpret John's behavior as a "moral reaction" that, like all moral behavior, was acquired through the conditioning of anxiety responses. When the child

ELLIOT TURIEL

Department of Psychology, Columbia University, New York

behaves in a socially undesirable way he receives punishment. The association of punishment with particular situations and behaviors results in conditioned anxiety, causing the avoidance of certain behaviors. Individual differences in moral behavior are explained in terms of constitutional differences in conditionability.

Other subscribers to an internalization theory have posited more complex acquisition mechanisms than instrumental conditioning. For instance, Sears (1957) and Whiting (1960) have accepted the notion of a more global internalization of social rules, and Bandura and Walters (1963) have assumed that moral behavior is a result of reinforcement and modeling. However, these learning theorists agree with Eysenck in defining morality as conformity to cultural norms. Consequently, they all view moral development as increasing conformity to cultural standards, based on the assumption that the child directly internalizes the standards of his society. John's reaction would be interpreted by these theorists as a moral one because he reacted to an infraction of a societal rule—the rule that it is bad to be in jail.

Basing their experiments on the internalization theory, researchers have investigated the factors that lead the child to directly internalize his culture. The study of development is the study of the increasing strength and accuracy of the internalization, so moral responses are measured for their strength and for how closely they approximate society's norms. While the strength and accuracy of John's response would be studied, there would be no concern with John's conceptualization of punishment or jail as related to society's goals and institutions.

Psychoanalysts also have defined morality as conformity to cultural standards and have conceptualized the problem in internalization terms, viewing moral development as the incorporation of a set of rules and values that come from the external world (Freud, 1923). In this case, the child forms an ego-ideal consisting of his parents' standards; in turn, the parents are seen as the transmitters of cultural standards. The child is moralized when he manages to make the ego-ideal his own. The acquisition mechanism postulated by psychoanalytic theory is different than that of the learning theorists. The superego, which represents the standards (ego-ideal) and punitive functions (conscience) of the moral process, is acquired through a strong global identification with his parents that resolves the oedipal conflicts (Freud, 1923, 1924).

Although psychoanalysts do not see the incorporation of rules as being as mechanical as learning theory, they do agree with learning theorists that the process is a direct internalization and that morality is mainly a cultural imposition on the individual. Society ensures its survival by imposing restrictions on the individual's destructive impulses (Freud, 1930) and since morality represents a negative imposition on the individual, it must ultimately be viewed as a process regulated by sanction—guilt (Freud, 1928). Therefore, man's social or moral behavior is maintained through either external or internal sanction, with concepts such as guilt representing the internalization of external sanctions.

In contrast to the foregoing discussion of John's behavior, it could be maintained that the child's response was not necessarily a moral one and that it did not reflect an internal value. An alternative approach would be to examine the properties of the situation that led the five-year-old to express what appears to be moral indignation. A story told about Thoreau provides an interesting comparison. Thoreau was in jail for refusing to pay city taxes. One day his friend Emerson was walking in the street past Thoreau's window when, much to his surprise, he spotted Thoreau peering through the bars. Emerson rushed to the window and asked, "Henry, what are you doing in there?" Thoreau, taken aback by Emerson's query, replied, "Waldo, what are you doing out there?"

Thoreau's response was similar to John's in that they both expressed some form of moral indignation. John was indignant because his uncle had been in jail and Thoreau because his respected friend was not in jail. For the moment it will be assumed that the responses were of equal intensity, although the strength of each response seems difficult to measure: both expressed apparent moral indignation, but they expressed it at opposite actions. Thus the little boy made the "correct" moral response because he was indignant at something normally unacceptable in our culture. Thoreau on the other hand, was indignant in the face of an action that was normally quite acceptable in his culture. Was Thoreau making the "incorrect" moral response? Are we then to assume that the five-year-old had more stringent and better internalized values—as these are defined by society—than Thoreau? On the surface it would seem that John's behavior more strongly conformed to the cultural rules. Consequently, we would have to say that John manifested better moral development than Thoreau, if one is to regard moral development as increasing conformity to cultural rules.

An assumption that Thoreau's response reflected a more elevated morality than that of the five-year-old would be based on our wide knowledge of Thoreau's philosophy. Similarly, in the study of moral judgments and moral behavior it is essential to examine the thought structure underlying the content of moral responses in order to understand moral development. An individual's response must be examined in light of how he perceives the moral situation, what the meaning of the situation is to the person responding, and the relation of his choice to that meaning: the cognitive and emotional processes in making moral judgments. Certainly, Thoreau's reaction could be viewed as a developed moral response because it reflected a highly differentiated and integrated form of structuring the social and moral world. John's reaction, on the other hand, may not have been a moral judgment. Let us assume that this child could not make a distinction between his judgment of a person in jail and one with a contagious disease. If John's aversion to a man in jail was no different than his aversion to a person with measles, his response would not indicate he had formed moral values. It might very well be that he is yet unable to discriminate between a physical danger and a moral one.

The types of observations described above are more clearly understood when moral development is viewed as a self-constructive process, culminating in a state in which principles are followed for their own sake rather than to avoid pain, blame, or self-condemnation. The research and developmental processes to be discussed are based on the assumption that moral development is a self-constructive process involving changing conceptions and emotions. In this approach, developmental changes are considered to be the result of the growing child's interaction with a general social and moral environment. The term "moral environment" is defined here as an environment that presents rules, standards, values, and principles.

The study of moral development from this point of view requires investigation of the organism's efforts to organize and regulate social experiences. It is through active coping with a social environment and attempts to order and organize social experiences—rather than through passive incorporation—that the child comes to develop moral structures, which have both affective and cognitive components; these structures are generated through interaction with a social environment. However, the manner in which a child structures his moral world represents neither an inaccurate, incomplete copy of the structure of the environment nor a copy of parental teachings. Rather, the developing child imposes his own structure on the environment and his structure is qualitatively changing as a result of his social experiences. These changing structures represent successive transformations of ways of thinking and feeling about the social world, about right and wrong, and about the self in relation to these.

In studying the development of moral judgments or moral conduct, a distinction must be made between the content of a moral response and the structure underlying the response. We contrasted the story of John with the Thoreau incident to exemplify that the content of moral responses cannot adequately explain the nature of the moral judgment or the developmental process. The same moral responses can be made by means of different cognitive processes and consequently have different developmental significance. Some researchers (Piaget, 1932; Kohlberg, 1963a) indeed have examined developing morality from a structural point of view, focusing on an examination of the modes of thought underlying moral responses. Both Piaget and Kohlberg have maintained that the organization of a child's thought is qualitatively different from that of an adult and that the study of moral development must include a sequential stage analysis of developmental changes.

Kohlberg's (1958, 1963a, 1968) concern was not so much with the content of moral responses as with the thought structure behind that content. To study moral thought, Kohlberg developed an interview containing stories posing hypothetical moral dilemmas. The following story is an example.

> In Europe, a woman was near death from a special kind of cancer. There was one drug that the doctors thought might save her. It was a form of radium that a druggist in the same town had recently discovered. The drug was expensive to make, but the druggist was charging ten times what the drug cost him to make. He paid $200 for the radium and charged $2,000 for a small dose of the drug. The sick woman's husband, Heinz, went to everyone he knew to borrow the money, but he could only get together about $1,000 which is half of what it cost. He told the druggist that his wife was dying and asked him to sell it cheaper or let him pay later. But the druggist said: "No, I discovered the drug and I'm going to make money from it." So Heinz got desperate and broke into the man's store to steal the drug for his wife. Should the husband have done that?

As in all of Kohlberg's stories, this one poses a conflict between two culturally unacceptable (or acceptable) alternatives. It is culturally unacceptable to steal, but it is also culturally unacceptable to allow one's wife to die if it can be prevented. By designing stories that do not have a culturally correct answer it is possible to partially circumvent the normative problem and elicit moral reasoning rather than moral knowledge or opinion. The reasoning used in judging right and wrong in these situations reflects a child's internally organized mode of structuring the social and moral world. Kohlberg identified six qualitatively different modes of thought successively passed through in the moralization process by cross-sectionally and longitudinally studying a large number of children between the ages of ten and seventeen. Kohlberg postulated the following six stages, which can be conceptually encompassed within three levels.

Level I. Value resides in external quasi-physical happenings, in bad acts, or in quasi-physical needs rather than in persons and standards.

Stage 1: *Obedience and punishment orientation.* Egocentric deference to superior power or prestige, or a trouble-avoiding set. Objective responsibility.

Stage 2: *Naively egoistic orientation.* Right action is that of instrumentally satisfying the self's needs and occasionally the needs of others. Awareness of relativism of value to each actor's needs and perspective. Naive egalitarianism and orientation to exchange and reciprocity.

Level II. Moral value resides in performing good or right roles, in maintaining the conventional order and the expectancies of others.

Stage 3: *Good boy orientation.* Orientation to approval and to pleasing and helping others. Conformity to stereotypical images of majority or natural role behavior, and judgment by intentions.

Stage 4: *Authority and social order maintaining orientation.* Orientation to "doing duty" and to showing respect for authority and maintaining the given social order for its own sake. Regard for earned expectations of others.

Level III. Moral value resides in conformity by the self to shared or shareable standards, rights, or duties.

Stage 5: *Contractual legalistic orientation.* Recognition of an arbitrary element or starting point in rules or expectations for the sake of agreement. Duty defined in terms of contract, general avoidance of violation of the will or rights of others, and majority will and welfare.

Stage 6: *Conscience or principle orientation.* Orientation not only to actually ordained social rules but also to principles of choice involving appeal to logical universality and consistency. Orientation to conscience as a directing agent and to mutual respect and trust.

Kohlberg's research indicates that the process of moral development is more gradual and long-term than has been theorized (Freud, 1923; Sears, 1957). Examining the structures underlying the moral response showed that, even at the late ages of eight or nine, children are at a premoral level in which right and wrong are defined in terms of punishment and in terms of conformity to power figures. While many of Kohlberg's young subjects made responses that looked like moral responses, investigatory techniques probing into the judgmental process showed that the children's thoughts were premoral, as defined by stages 1 and 2. Further probing of John's moral thought probably would have indicated that John had not developed moral values and was only at the early developmental phases of a long process. Thoreau's responses probably reflected the mature thinking of level III, which usually does not begin to appear till about the age of sixteen.

Just as cognitive structures are not copies of reality (Piaget, 1947), these moral stages do not represent successive acquisitions of patterns presented to the child by the culture. Instead, they represent qualitatively different modes of organizing the social and moral world through which the child passes. Kohlberg views the series of stages as forming an invariant sequence in which the attainment of a stage is dependent on the attainment of the preceding stages. Each child normally must pass through one stage before moving on to the next one. However, movement from one stage to the next does not involve an addition to the earlier stage, but is a reorganization displacing the less advanced stage.

The stage approach (Piaget, 1954; Kohlberg, 1968) assumes that each individual must pass through the stages in the prescribed sequence, if the sequence is correct. This implies that the child cannot skip stages and that he cannot proceed in a different order. However, it is the order of the stages that is constant, while the age at which a stage appears is not fixed. The age of the emergence of a structure is largely dependent on the environment, which can provoke or impede development. The ages related to the stages should vary from culture to culture as well as from individual to individual.

Within this theoretical framework, development is a function of the child's interaction with his environment. The existing mental structure is seen as influencing how the environment is experienced and new experiences are seen as leading to reorganization of structure. While this theoretical approach is interactional regarding the influence of innate and experiential factors, it can be said that almost all theories are interactional. For instance, even Eysenck's (1960) strongly associationistic view considers such constitutional factors as conditionability and innately determined learning capabilities. Maturational stage theories (Gesell, 1954) assume that genetically determined stages unfold in a series of age-specific patterns. However, the importance of experience is recognized as an influence on the way the structures unfold.

The important theoretical differences on the issue of interaction lie in identification of the source of developing structures. The maturationalist considers that the source is located entirely in the innately determined structures. For the associationistic theorist, moral thought is located entirely in the environment since the cultural norms are directly internalized. From the developmental viewpoint, moral thought is neither wired-in to the organism nor a copy of reality; the development of moral thought involves assimilating and integrating the external world to the structure of the organism. Thought is a result of the organism's attempts to organize reality rather than the unfolding of innate patterns or the internalization of environmental patterns.

The developmental approach is interactional in that biological characteristics combine with experience in forming structures. The way in which the organism deals with reality is in part determined by the biological principles of organization, adaptation, and equilibration (Piaget, 1947). However, the problem is more complex because the theory considers multiple interactions. At any given developmental phase, change is due to an interaction of experience and the functioning stage of the child. The existing structure influences how the environment is experienced and it is an interaction of that structure and new experience that leads to a reorganization of structure. The effect of experience can be analyzed in terms of how it is dealt with by a child with a particular structure. The child's structure has been acquired in the developmental process and has been determined by an interaction of organismic tendencies and his previous experiences. The interactions must be conceived as multiple since, in a sense, new experiences are interacting with previous experiences, as these are represented in the existing structure.

The remainder of this article discusses stages of moral development that define qualitatively different forms of moral thought. Description of some of the characteristics of developmental stages is followed by discussion of a series of experiments designed to investigate hypotheses about moral development.

Three classes of empirical work will be discussed: (a) the findings from two experiments that dealt with the sequentiality of stages by investigating the ways children interact with new moral concepts, (b) an examination of the role that earlier stages play in an individual's functioning after he has attained a more advanced stage, presenting both theoretical and methodological criteria for use in determining the functions of earlier stages in a hierarchical organization, and (c) the general finding that most individuals function on more than one moral stage. Data are presented supporting hypotheses about the interaction of stage mixture and modal stage in the process of development.

An understanding of developmental change must include theoretical as well as empirical analyses of sequentiality, stage mixture, and the equilibration process. Therefore, this article concludes with a discussion of research on the ways in which disequilibrium may affect change from one stage to the next.

CHARACTERISTICS OF DEVELOPMENTAL STAGES

One of the characteristics of stages of development, as defined by Piaget (1954), is that they are "structured wholes." Therefore, a moral stage defines how moral judgments are made rather than how well they approximate the culturally correct responses—the differences between the stages are qualitative rather than quantitative. Another characteristic is that the stages form an invariant sequence in which each stage must be passed through in the prescribed order.

The stage concept is not solely a descriptive concept as used within this framework. While the stages describe the nature of the child's thought at a given time, their most important function is as explanatory concepts. Knowledge of the organism's structure is indispensable for an explanation of how development occurs. A given stage helps explain how the individual interacts with the environment and how the environment affects the individual, and also provides understanding of how the subsequent stage develops because each stage builds on the previous ones. The state of the organism and the transitional factors in development are interrelated and inseparable in explanations of change.

In the developmental process, which is a function of an interaction of the existing mental structure and experience, the child encounters a large variety of stimuli and deals with a broad environment. However, the child responds more to some aspects of the environment than to others. It thus is necessary to consider what the child responds to in the environment as well as the nature of interaction with environment that leads to change. The effectiveness of environmental influence largely depends on the match between the level of concepts being encountered and the developmental level of the individual. Some aspects of the environment will be below the individual's level, other aspects will be at his level, and still others will be above his level. However, environmental aspects can be a little above a person's level or they can be far above. We are suggesting here that a child constantly is encountering a range of environmental influences, but that these influences are best understood if defined in relation to the child's own structure.

At the earlier stages, much of the child's environment that is structurally higher will have a minimal influence on his structural development. The child is able to deal only with aspects of the environment that are closest to his own level. It must be noted, however, that this way of representing the environment is in part artifactual because the environment influences the developing child in general, as well as in specific, ways. Although our discussion tends to highlight the specific influences, the fact that general environment also greatly influences development should be remembered.

Accompanying development to the subsequent stage is a change in the environ-ment influencing the child. Some of the aspects of the environment that previously were too advanced are now closer to his level, possibly close enough for him to assimilate. It is not the environment that has changed, but its relation to the child's structure. Concepts too far above the stage 1 child, although they remain the same, are close enough to influence the stage 2 child's development. On the other hand, some aspects of the environment that are beyond the stage 1 child's grasp and, therefore, ineffective in causing developmental change, are also beyond the stage 2 child. These may be aspects that influence the more advanced stage 3 or 4 child.

Having stressed the changes in the way constant environmental events affect development as the child moves from stage to stage, consideration should now be given to the fact that as the child develops chronologically and structurally there are also changes in the environment itself. We assume that there is a combination of constancy and age-grading in the environmental influences: the younger child does not encounter all of the experiences of the older child. For instance, the level of a child's education is constantly changing; the nature of his social interactions, the responsibilities he is forced to assume, and the roles in which he must participate also vary with age. More new influences above the child's structural level are en-countered as he advances, while many influences below the child's stage tend to drop out of his field.

EXPERIMENTAL INVESTIGATIONS OF THE
HIERARCHICAL ORGANIZATION OF MORAL STAGES

We have conducted experimental studies designed to both validate and further explore some of the developmental processes discussed here. The first study under-taken (Turiel, 1966) was an attempt to experimentally test some developmental hypotheses regarding Kohlberg's moral stages. As mentioned previously, Kohlberg (1963a, 1968) postulates that his stages form an invariant sequence in which the attainment of a stage is dependent on the attainment of the preceding stages. He bases his theory on (a) evidence of age trends in various cultures that conform to the postulated sequence (Kohlberg, 1968), (b) more direct evidence of an invariant sequence that comes from the finding that the stages fit a "Guttman quasi-simplex" correlational pattern, a pattern expected from stages forming a developmental order (Kohlberg, 1963a, pp. 16-17), and (c) longitudinal studies that have also supported the sequence (Kohlberg, 1968).

Experimental evidence for these hypotheses comes from one of our studies, which tested the following two developmental hypotheses.

That the six moral stages form an invariant sequence. Since moral development involves an organismic self-constructive process of organizing the environment, there is a logical necessity to the order of the structures.

That the movement from one stage to the next is a restructuring and displacement of the preceding stage. The concept of restructuring implies that development involves one structure changing into a new structure, with the earlier structure becoming part of the next structure (Piaget, 1954). However, such change is not simply an addition of elements to one stage to form another stage, but rather, there is a reorganization so that the new stage is qualitatively different from the previous one.

An implication of our first hypothesis is that a child who is exposed to moral concepts that are above his own stage could assimilate only those concepts that are slightly above his level; concepts that are further above could not be assimilated because that would involve skipping stages. The implication of our second hypothesis is that children tend to reject thinking that is at stages below their own. If developmental change does involve reorganization, then the lower stages are displaced for higher modes of thought. In such a case, the child who is exposed to a displaced mode of thought will not accept it into his own thinking.

These hypotheses were examined by exposing subjects to either the stage one above, the stage two above, or the stage one below their own stage. Three steps were involved in the experimental procedure. First, subjects were administered a pretest containing six situations from the Kohlberg moral judgment interview. Using standardized coding forms (Kohlberg, 1958), the subjects' stages were determined and those in stages 2, 3, and 4 were retained for the remainder of the experiment. Then an experimental treatment, which comprised exposure to new moral concepts, was administered two weeks after the pretest to all but a group of control subjects. One group of subjects was exposed to the stage directly below its own (−1 condition), a second group was exposed to the stage directly above (+1 condition), and a third group was exposed to the stage two above its own (+2 condition).

The experimental condition involved role-playing of three of Kohlberg's situations not used in the pretest. The subject was instructed to play the role of the actor in the situation and to seek "advice" from two friends. The roles of the "friends" were played by the experimenter. In each situation, the friends gave advice at the appropriate stage of exposure: one friend supported one side of the conflict while the other friend supported the opposing side. For example, a stage 2 subject being exposed to stage 3 concepts in the +1 condition would be advised by one friend to steal the drug (see the Kohlberg situation described previously in this article) and by the second friend not to steal the drug, with both friends' arguments containing stage 3 statements. All the sets of advice used in the experimental treatment were constructed from Kohlberg's (1958) coding forms.

To assess the influence of the treatment, all subjects were administered a posttest one week after the experimental treatment. The posttest, containing nine moral judgment situations, included the six situations of the pretest and the three that had been used in the experimental treatment, making it possible to obtain two measures of influence of the stage of moral judgment exposure. One measure, which came from the responses to the three treatment situations, represented the *direct* influence of the experimental exposure. The posttest responses to the other six situations represented the degree to which the subjects could generalize any learning to different situations (*indirect* influence).

The clearest and most significant findings came from the direct influence. As expected, the most successful condition was the +1 exposure. Subjects exposed to the stage directly above their own showed a significant use of that stage, exposure to the stage two above had no effect, and exposure to the stage below had significantly less effect than exposure to the stage one above. The trends for the indirect scores were in the expected directions and similar to those of the direct scores, but the amount of indirect influence was not as great as that of the direct influence.

The findings of this study indicate that the moral stages form a developmental continuum in which change involves a series of restructurings through an invariant sequence. That the +2 condition did not influence subjects to use +2 thinking in their own judgments, while the +1 condition did influence subjects to use +1 thinking, indicated that a fixed sequence is followed by each individual and that stages cannot be skipped. That the −1 condition did not influence subjects to use −1 thinking as much as the +1 condition influenced them to +1 thinking, supports the idea that the attainment of a stage of thought involves restructuring and displacement of the previous stages.

In some ways this latter finding of rejection of −1 thinking is perplexing. Even if an earlier stage is displaced and therefore no longer part of the child's functioning, that earlier stage does represent a simpler, less cognitively difficult mode of thought for the child. Why then should he not use that mode of thought when an adult "teacher" presents it to him? For most subjects the stages one below and one above were more or less quantitatively equal in relation to the assigned stage. Subjects were classified at their most used (dominant) stage but they also showed some usage of other stages, particularly the ones directly below and directly above. Nevertheless, the children attempted to deal with the concepts of the stage above more than they did with the concepts of the stage below, despite the fact that it would be easier for them to comprehend and reiterate concepts of the stage below.[1]

If moral learning was primarily a function of social reinforcement, subjects would have at least mimicked the −1 thinking in order to obtain approval from the adult experimenter. If modeling and imitation were the acquisition mechanisms for moral learning, subjects would have imitated the more easily imitatable experimenter—that is, the one presenting the stage below. The concept of competence motivation (White, 1959) can aid us in understanding why children reject thinking that is easier to comprehend while they cope with more difficult thinking. According to White, organism-environment interactions are directed toward a more effective understanding of the environment. Developmental progress is caused by attempts at more adaptive assimilation of environmental events (Piaget, 1947; Werner, 1948). Thus, within a developmental sequence each stage represents a more adaptive and equilibrated state than the preceding stage. This principle implies that the child's primary motivation is

[1] A study to be discussed later in this article (Rest, Turiel, and Kohlberg, in press) has presented evidence supporting the notion that children can more easily comprehend moral thinking below their dominant stage than thinking above.

competence rather than approval—being motivated to use a higher form of thought the child rejects a "worse" mode of thought.[2]

When the child is dealing with structural material, the basic motivation is to be correct rather than to meet adult expectancies. Consequently, his attempt to reach a more equilibrated state leads to more assimilation of a higher stage that is close enough to be understood (+1). It is likely that competence motivation applies to the acquisition of modes of thought and not necessarily to specific response learnings. If Kohlberg's stages did represent a series of culturally transmitted patterns, the adult presenting the −1 responses should have been a more effective influence; he was not effective because the competence motive applies to structural change. Other studies (Bandura and McDonald, 1963) have used some aspects of Piaget's moral stages in such a way that specific responses could be learned without concept attainment. Indeed, Bandura and McDonald obtained results contrary to ours.

The interpretation of our findings in terms of competence motivation and successively higher, more adaptive forms of equilibration is based on the assumptions that the stage below the child's dominant stage is more easily understood than the stages above, and that the stages above are viewed as being better than the stages below. Another of our studies (Rest, Turiel, and Kohlberg, in press), designed to replicate and examine implications of the first study (Turiel, 1966), provided direct evidence supporting these assumptions. The Rest, Turiel, and Kohlberg study hypothesized (a) that subjects would judge statements above their dominant stages to be better than statements below, and (b) that stages above the dominant stage would be increasingly more difficult to comprehend than stages below.

In this study, the subjects' initial moral stages were determined by means of a pretest interview. The study included 45 fifth- and eighth-grade boys and girls with a range of dominant stages from 1 through 4. The subjects were grouped according to initial stage and were seen within those groups in a second session held one week after the pretest. In this second session, subjects were given two booklets, each containing a moral judgment situation. (Situations II and III were used, situation III being the above described story about Heinz's decision to steal the drug for his dying wife.) The first part of each booklet contained a somewhat altered form of the situation. For instance, the end of situation III read: "Heinz was not sure what he should do in this difficult situation. So he went to some of his friends and asked them for advice. Listed on the next page are the names of the six friends Heinz went to and next to each name you will find the advice given by that friend."

The next part of the booklet contained the "advice" given by the six friends. Each of these statements, which were similar to those used in the treatment condition of the previous study, corresponded to one of the moral stages. For any given subject, the six statements were at three different stages in relation to the subject's

[2]The Rest, Turiel, and Kohlberg study demonstrated that subjects view stages above their own level as being better than stages below.

dominant stage. Two statements advocating opposing courses of action were at the stage below the subject's stage (−1), two statements were at the stage one above (+1), and two statements were at the stage two above (+2).[3]

The subjects were told to examine the advice statements and then were presented with several written questions about these statements.

    a. They were asked to choose two friends who gave the best advice and to state why they chose those two.

    b. They were asked to choose the two friends giving the worst advice—and why.

    c. They were asked several questions regarding which advice was the "smartest" and the "most good." Each of these questions also asked why.

    d. They were also told to pretend that they were one of the actor's (e.g., Heinz) friends and to give their own advice to the actor.

One booklet (situation III) also contained a question asking the subjects for recall of the advice.

The responses to these questions made it possible to determine whether or not subjects preferred statements above their stage more than statements below. The frequencies of choice of −1, +1, and +2 statements as best and worst, are summarized in Table 5.1. These results strongly indicated that the subjects considered

Table 5.1 *Percentage choice of advice at different stages by all subjects.* *

Stage of Advice†	General Preference‡	Selected as "Worst" Advice
−1	15	51
+1	43	23
+2	42	26

*From Rest, Turiel, and Kohlberg study, in press.
†Relative to pretest dominant stage.
‡Includes data from all questions asking for best, smart, and good advice.

statements above their own stage to be better than statements below. The −1 statements were chosen as the worst advice with significantly more frequency than either the +1 or +2 statements ($p < .01$). The +1 and +2 statements were also judged as being better than the −1 statements ($p < .01$), and the results indicate also that these two statements were equally preferred.

The subject's discussion of why he preferred a statement usually included a

[3]Stage 1 subjects could not be presented with −1 advice, so they were presented with advice corresponding to their own stage.

restatement or a recapitulation of the statement presented to him. These recapitulations and the responses to the recall question, which were scored for stage level, could be used as a measure of the degree of comprehension. Table 5.2 shows that the accuracy of recapitulation decreased as the stage increased. Subjects attempting to recapitulate the −1 statements did so with a fairly high degree of accuracy, attempted recapitulation of the +1 statements yielded a moderate degree of accuracy, while recapitulations of the +2 statements were the least accurate. These findings ($p < .001$), along with the finding that more −1 statements were recalled than any others, indicate that the stage below is more easily understood than the stages above.

Table 5.2 *Percentage of recapitulations of advice at each stage.* *

Stage of Advice Recapitulated†	Stage of Recapitulation						
	-3	-2	-1	0	+1	+2	+3
-1 as "preferred advice"	06	03	64‡	14	11	02	00
-1 as "worst advice"	02	06	79	11	02	00	00
+1 as "preferred advice"	03	05	27	18	43	03	00
+1 as "worst advice"	04	06	34	16	36	04	00
+2 as "preferred advice"	02	07	18	19	26	28	00
+2 as "worst advice"	05	05	57	05	00	30	00
Advice on Recall	05	08	38	15	25	09	00

*From Rest, Turiel, and Kohlberg study, in press.
†Relative to pretest dominant stage.
‡Underlined figures indicate "correct" recapitulations of the original statement of advice.

Table 5.2, which also contains the inaccurate recapitulations, provides further evidence that subjects find the higher stages more difficult to comprehend than lower stages. Inaccurate recapitulations of higher level (+1 or +2) advice were generally distorted to either the subject's own level (0) or to the stage below (−1), with a strong tendency existing for subjects to distort preferred advice to their own stage. This finding further clarifies the nature of the organism's interaction with the environment. At any developmental stage, the child is encountering a variety of environmental inputs at several levels. Some environmental aspects are too far above an individual's level to cause structural change. Yet, as in our +2 exposure, the individual does encounter advanced concepts in his environment. Unable to comprehend the higher level concepts, he distorts the concepts to make them manageable—interprets them in terms of his own stage.

An example from the Rest, Turiel, and Kohlberg study shows what a child does with concepts that are too advanced for his level of functioning. In this case, a stage 2 child chose a stage 4 statement as one of his preferences. The advice statement presented to the subject was:

You shouldn't steal the drug. Even though you are desperate, it is still always wrong to steal. The druggist is wrong—he should let you have it for less, but two wrongs don't make a right. The druggist does have a right to the drug since he worked hard to invent it. You are going against the druggist's rights if you steal it like that.

The stage 2 subject's reason for preferring this statement was:

Karen gave the smartest advice because she was thinking that if Hilda would steal the drug it wouldn't help her any. If she waited, the druggist might sell it for less.

While the presented advice contains stage 4 concepts of categorical wrongness and property rights, this subject interpreted the statement entirely in his own stage 2 hedonistic terms. This assimilation process of changing higher level statements to one's own stage is not likely to result in structural change: The stage 4 concepts will not change this stage 2 child's thinking if these concepts are "experienced" in stage 2 terms.

Exposure to −1, +1, and +2 statements should lead to an increase in +1 thinking rather than any other, since the stages form an invariant sequence. To assess the effects of the exposure, the recapitulation scores and the "own advice" scores were subtracted from the pretest scores. The resulting "change" scores for each measure showed that there was significantly more use of +1 thinking than either −1 or +2 ($p < .01$). If the mechanisms for moral learning were modeling and reinforcement, we would expect children to accept the more easily understood statements presented by adults. The finding that subjects assimilate thought that is somewhat less understood yet judged better is congruent with views of equilibration (Piaget, 1947; Kohlberg, 1963a) and competence motivation (White, 1959).

THE FUNCTION OF EARLIER STAGES IN A DEVELOPMENTAL HIERARCHY

An important developmental issue is the role a structure plays in an individual's functioning after he has passed through the stage. The hierarchical model of stage organization (Rest, Turiel, and Kohlberg, in press; Werner, 1937, 1948) assumes that each stage passed through is retained and accessible, although lower stages are subordinated to the higher stages. The hierarchical model implies that the lower stages of functioning are available for utilization under special conditions, such as frustration, stress (Barker, Dembo, and Lewin, 1943), pathological states, or experimental conditions of primitivization (Werner and Kaplan, 1963). However, the full theoretical importance of the accessibility of an earlier mode of thought is not yet clearly understood. Some findings of our study (Rest, Turiel, and Kohlberg, in press), which show that lower stages are not readily used, indicate that the implications of the hierarchical view require further elaboration.

The ability of subjects in the study to recapitulate statements at the stage below their dominant stage indicates that earlier stages are comprehensible. These same subjects also rejected the advice of a developmentally lower level (Table 5.1) and did not assimilate it into their own thinking. An examination of the reasons subjects gave for rejecting lower stage advice evidences that lower levels are not always readily accessible. Subjects judged lower level statements to be inadequate reasoning, yet displayed understanding of the lower level reasoning. For instance, a stage 2 subject in rejecting two stage 1 statements said the following:

> Albert says that you should tell so that you can keep out of trouble with your father. Robert says that you should not tell because if you do Joe will beat you up. He is putting wrong things into Alex's mind by telling him that his brother will beat him up.

Like other stage 2 subjects whose orientation is one of instrumental need and exchange, this subject understood the punishment and obedience orientation of stage 1 but could not accept it as a form of defining right and wrong.

This process can be followed throughout the developmental scale. In the same fashion, a stage 3 subject whose orientation is to social approval does not accept stage 2 definitions of right and wrong. A stage 2 statement advised that one should keep quiet for a brother because one might want a favor from him one day. The stage 3 subject characteristically thought this was bad advice because:

> I don't like the idea that "if you do this, then I'll do that." You should not make a decision because you'll be paid off.

Stage 3 statements in turn are judged wrong by rule- and authority-oriented stage 4 subjects, who say that morality should not be based on approval. These judgments of lower level statements show that the lower levels are not a self-accepted part of the individual's functioning. A mode of thought that can be cogently refuted as inadequate and false is perhaps one that has been displaced.

These results indicate that there is a progressive tendency in development and that regression does not occur under normal conditions. Theoretical and methodological confusion regarding content and structure can lead to the impression that earlier modes of thought are being used when they are not. This can be clarified by referring to some cross-cultural research on the dream concept (Kohlberg, 1966a). Using a standardized interview procedure to study children's conceptions of dreams, Kohlberg, like Piaget (1929), found that young children believe that dreams are external, real events. According to Piaget, these children believe dreams are external because they are in a stage of realism—a stage in which the child cannot differentiate the objective from the subjective. Kohlberg also found a gradual process of conceptualizing the dream as internal that involved movement through the six sequential steps, as presented below. On the average the last step is reached by American children at about age seven.

Step 1 *Not real.* Recognizes that objects or actions in the dream are not really there in the room.

Step 2 *Invisible.* Recognizes that other people cannot see his dream.

Step 3 *Internal origin.* Recognizes that the dream *comes from* inside him.

Step 4 *Internal location.* Recognizes that the dream *goes on* inside him.

Step 5 *Immaterial.* Recognizes that the dream is not a material substance but is a thought.

Step 6 *Self-caused.* Recognizes that dreams are not caused by God or other agencies, but rather are caused by the self's thought processes.

A similar dream interview was used with boys between the ages of eight and twenty who belonged to a preliterate, aboriginal group in Formosa, the Atayal. The Atayal tribe is one that believes in the reality of dreams—that dreams are due to ghosts who cause the soul to leave the body during the dream and have actual experiences. The younger boys in the Atayal tribe responded to the questions in the dream interview in the same manner as younger American children. Up to the age of eleven, the Atayal boys were developing through the same steps in the sequence (although more slowly than American children) toward a subjective conception of the dream. The average eleven-year-old Atayal believes that the dream is a thought and not a material substance (step 5). However, the pattern deviated after the age of eleven. The average Atayal twelve-year-old was at step 4 instead of step 6 and the average twenty-year-old had regressed even further, to step 3.

One interesting aspect of these findings was that the Atayal children developed toward a subjective view of dreams just as American or Swiss (Piaget, 1929) children did. Since the American and Swiss adult cultures have a subjective view of dreams, it may seem that the developing child internalizes the cultural teachings. However, the Atayal children, who live in a culture that does not teach a subjective view of dreams, nevertheless were found to develop toward a subjective conception. Kohlberg (1966a) correctly points out that these findings indicate that a child's conceptions are not a direct product of cultural teaching. The Atayal children's conceptions of the dream were due to cognitive judgments about the nature of dreams.

However, the cultural view of dreams does play a significant role in developing conceptions. After the age of eleven, Atayal children began to display responses characteristic of earlier stages and more in accordance with the cultural view of dreams; therefore, the twenty-year-old reverted to a view of the dream he had at about the age of eight. But had he regressed? Does this mean that the thinking of the twenty-year-old Atayal was similar to that of a five- or six-year-old American child or of the younger Atayal? If the thinking was similar, it would mean that the thinking of the twenty-year-old Atayal contained a large degree of realism. The younger child views a dream as external because he does not distinguish the subjective from the objective. The older Atayal's thinking appears similar to the child's if a distinction is not made between content and cognitive structure. Clearly, the content of the responses are the same—both see the dream as being caused by something external—but the processes may be different. While the child's response is a function of realism, it may be that the adult thinks dreams are external because he has been told and believes that ghosts exist and have certain powers, which include causing dreams to occur externally. In such a case, the cognitive structure and the mental operations utilized in arriving at the same conclusions would be different.

Another example, related to a child's egocentric thought (Piaget, 1929), will illustrate how the failure to distinguish between content and structure can lead to the false impression that regression is occurring. According to Piaget, the child's thought is animistic and he believes that events can cause other (unrelated) events. Therefore, the young child, whose moral judgments are influenced by realism, believes that automatic punishments emanate directly from objects (Piaget, 1932)—defined by Piaget as "immanent justice." Piaget's studies showed that younger children believe that an accident occurring after a misdeed is a direct punishment for the misdeed. For example, in one of Piaget's (1932) stories a boy on his way home after having stolen apples from an orchard fell into a river when the bridge he was crossing broke. Children of about six or seven say that the boy fell into the water because he stole the apples and that it would not have happened if he had not stolen. On the other hand, older children generally do not believe in immanent justice and say that the boy's fall had nothing to do with his misdeed.

Now let us consider the example of an adult who believes in the existence of a god with certain powers over human beings. This man believes that his god has the power and the inclination to punish wrongdoings, and so may well believe that a god can observe a misdeed and cause a bridge to fall when the culprit is crossing. Like Piaget's seven-year-olds, this man may also say that the boy fell into the water because he stole the apples. Again, is the adult functioning at a lower stage? Has he regressed to an earlier mode of thought which is available to him? While the content of this adult's response to Piaget's story is the same as the young child's, we cannot say the structure is similar. If the adult's thought is not animistic, the concept of immanent justice does not apply to his thinking.

The distinction between the two responses is provided by the mechanism that the individual believes is operating in this form of justice. Piaget makes it clear that, if an individual tries to place intermediate links between the misdeed and the punishment, he is not to be categorized as believing in immanent justice. Children were asked by Piaget (1932, pp. 254–255) how the punishment occurred. Those who said "God did it" were not considered to have a belief in immanent justice. The "question of the how" does not exist for the child who believes in immanent justice. That child does not look for any intermediate steps since he assumes the misdeed automatically results in a punishment. The man who thinks God did it is not using a lower mode of thought, but rather is taking into account what he believes to be the "data" and using a different process to come to a seemingly similar conclusion. To understand cognitive development, it is necessary to examine the operations rather than the content of the response. Analyses of regression tend to ignore this distinction and assume that responses resembling earlier modes of thought do indeed reflect use of that earlier mode of thought.

Making a proper distinction between content and structure is an important methodological problem in the consideration of how a developmental hierarchy functions. Another problem is determining the criteria to identify whether or not an individual is actually using an earlier mode of thought. We will try to show that these two problems—a proper distinction between content and structure and adequate criteria—are very much interrelated in the problem of the accessibility of earlier stages.

While the rejection of lower stages observed in our experiments indicated that the lower stage is not part of the individual's functioning, it is necessary to see if children would accept lower stage thinking as their own under pressure to do so.[4] We have undertaken two studies which we hope will shed some light on these issues. The first study is designed to determine whether, under some pressure, there is the inclination to move forward in the developmental sequence and strong resistance to moving back. Subjects will be pretested, using part of the Kohlberg moral judgment interview in order to assess their initial stages. Then two additional moral judgment situations will be used in a second experimental session. The subject first will be asked to discuss whether the actor's behavior in the hypothetical situation was right or wrong, and then to support the opposite position. After he has done so, he will be asked to once again support his original choice and to give new reasons for that position.

Reference to situation III provides a more concrete description of the procedure. The subject is asked if Heinz was right or wrong in stealing the drug to save his wife. Let us say the subject thinks Heinz was right in stealing. He first explains why he thinks that Heinz should have stolen. Then the subject is instructed to support the position that Heinz was wrong in stealing the drug, and is told to assume that it is like a debate and he must defend a position as best he can. Finally, the subject is requested to once again support his original position that Heinz was right in stealing the drug. However, he is told to use reasons he did not use in his original statements and to avoid using reasons he previously used. The subject's responses under these "pressuring" conditions will be scored for moral level to ascertain which stages were used.

Such a procedure may force a subject to resort to a structure he did not use spontaneously. As we know (Turiel, 1966; Rest, Turiel, and Kohlberg, in press), children are inclined to use some higher level thought when it is presented to them. In this instance no new reasoning is presented. Since there is an inclination to move forward in the sequence, we expect subjects to attempt some higher level arguments. If they exhaust these higher level arguments, will they restrict themselves to their own level or will they use lower modes of thought as well? If subjects use the lower stage under these conditions, it would indicate that earlier modes are accessible. On the other hand, if lower stages have been displaced, then subjects would strongly avoid using lower modes of thought. If the latter is correct, subjects would use much more of their own stage or resort to nonmoral judgments. We expect more usage of the level one above than the levels below because children are motivated by competence considerations to use the higher, more equilibrated stage.

A second study we have undertaken is directly related to the issue of accessibility of lower modes of thought. The procedure to be described is designed to pressure the subject to accept a lower stage. As in the other studies, subjects are pretested to

---

[4]If an individual's mode of thought does change under pressure, it is important to carefully examine the change to determine whether or not it is actually a regression. The temporary change may involve thought that resembles an earlier mode but is not really the same in structure.

ascertain initial moral stages. Then, in other moral judgment situations, the subject is presented with alternative arguments from which he must choose the most correct. Again taking situation III as an example, the situation is read to the subject and, without giving his reasons, he is asked to choose between the conflicting alternatives—whether or not Heinz should steal. He then is presented with the advice that two other people gave to Heinz. One advice statement agrees with the subject's choice (such as, Heinz should steal) but the arguments supporting that choice are at the stage below the subject's stage (−1). The second person's advice disagrees with the subject's choice but presents arguments that are at the stage above the subject's stage (+1). In another condition, the argument opposing the subject's choice is at the subject's own level (0).[5]

In these experimental situations, the subject will be asked to choose the most correct advice and to explain why he thinks that advice is most correct. Subjects may not choose the −1 advice—even though most agree with it—as frequently as the disagreeing 0 or +1 advice. Rejection of −1 advice would indicate that earlier modes of thought are not part of an individual's functioning; we theorize that lower modes of thought are not used because these are judged to be incorrect or invalid. For instance, one does not accept the notion that dreams are external and objective because his thought processes lead him to make that judgment about reality. A child's mode of thought is normally not used by an adult because he rejects it as inadequate or false logic. In some cases the −1 advice may be preferred because the subject agrees with the choice. However, it is probable that subjects will change the −1 statements to better fit their own stage in their explanations for the preference. It also is possible that some subjects will voice disagreement with the reasoning involved while agreeing with the choice.

Earlier we said that a consideration of the role played by lower levels must include the interrelated problems of adequate criteria and content-structure distinction. Individuals can understand and reiterate modes of thought below their own, but that may not be a sufficient criterion for attributing that mode of thought to an individual. Other criteria to consider are whether the earlier mode of thought is judged good or correct and whether an individual accepts that mode as his own (does not reject it). To know if the cognitive structure has been accepted as one's own, it is essential that there be a clear distinction between content and structure. In many cases, it appears that a given structure is being used because the observed response generally reflects that structure. A verbal response may be used by a child in order to obtain social reinforcement without accepting the lower (or higher) mode of thought that generally underlies the response.

One reason stricter criteria are necessary is that an individual is capable of imposing on himself responses that are not part of his functioning. If a child imposes the verbal responses of a lower mode of thought on himself, we cannot say the earlier mode is part of his hierarchy of stages. Since lower stage thinking is more comprehensible than higher stage thinking, lower modes are more easily imposed on

[5]Other conditions included in this study pit an agreeing argument at the subject's own stage against a disagreeing argument at the stage above, as well as the reverse.

oneself. A distinction between stages below and stages above may be that one can impose a previous level on oneself with much more facility than a higher stage. Still, it has been demonstrated by Smedslund (1961a, 1961b) that even a higher mode can appear to be attained through an imposition involving only verbal response learning. Smedslund found that children who did not have the concept of conservation consistently displayed conserving responses after two training sessions involving reinforcement of conservation responses. Smedslund hypothesized that such training did not result in the attainment of the concept of conservation but only in response learning. He then tried to extinguish experimentally the conservation responses of trained subjects and of children who had acquired conservation normally. His assumptions were that conservation in the trained subjects would be easily extinguished because they did not really have a grasp of the concept, while those who had acquired the concept would not extinguish readily.

All of the children who had acquired the concept in the experimental situation quite readily had their responses extinguished. On the other hand, several of the other subjects resisted the extinction efforts of the experimenter. Smedslund's study demonstrated that responses can appear to reflect the attainment of a concept when the concept has not been acquired. The same may occur when an individual displays responses reflecting an earlier structure. Such responses may be temporary and unstable, as were the conservation responses of Smedslund's subjects. The extinction Smedslund produced indicated that, although the response was learned, the concept had not really been acquired. The children who had acquired the concept were resistant to extinction because the concept was understood and seen as a logical necessity, regardless of what the experimental situation demanded. Smedslund's procedure, which adhered to the criteria we have proposed, showed that children do resist regression when a lower structure is judged to be incorrect.

Some of Smedslund's normal conservers gave nonconservation responses as a result of the extinction procedures. These regressing subjects could have been carefully studied to determine the exact nature of their nonconserving responses. A replication of this study, with a focus on those children whose genuine conservation is extinguished, would yield valuable information on the developmental issues we are considering. It would be of interest to examine the nonconserving responses in depth in order to see in what ways they resemble normal nonconservation responses.

An experimental study by Bandura and McDonald (1963) using Piaget's (1932) moral stages further reflects the conceptual ambiguity that exists regarding structural change. The position of Bandura and McDonald was that moral judgments are culturally correct responses acquired through imitation. Working with only one of the eleven dimensions of Piaget's moral sequence, Bandura and McDonald pretested subjects to determine if their initial judgments were objective (moral judgment in terms of material damage or consequences) or subjective (moral judgment in terms of intention). Then the higher level subjective children were exposed to adult models' objective responses. Conversely, lower level subjects were exposed to models responding on the subjective level. Their two measures of learning—amount of learning during the experimental treatment and posttest responses to new stories—showed that children initially responding on the basis of consequences could be influenced to the higher level and that those initially responding on intentions could be influenced to respond on the lower level. On the posttest there was more change to the lower level by the higher level subjects than change to the higher level by the lower level subjects.

Bandura and McDonald viewed these findings as indicating that what Piaget considers structural development in reality follows the laws of response learning. Indeed, elements of Piaget's moral stages may not meet his own stage criteria (Kohlberg, 1963b). Nevertheless, the Bandura and McDonald study did not make the necessary distinctions between content and structure. By using an experimental treatment that reinforced one of two possible answers, Bandura and McDonald induced changes that were not necessarily representative of change in underlying conceptualizations. A pattern could have been detected by allowing subjects to give the answer they thought was expected by the experimenter. Langer (1947) reports a replication of the Bandura and McDonald study that supports this contention.

Our view is that the expression of verbal responses related to stages above or below an individual's level can be a function of reinforcement and modeling. Thus, responses related to lower stage thinking should be more easily used since lower stages are more easily comprehended than higher stages. A finding of the Bandura and McDonald study was that responses related to the stage below were more easily imitated than responses related to higher stage thinking. The findings of studies that more adequately make the distinction between content and structure (Smedslund, 1961b, 1961c; Rest, Turiel, and Kohlberg, in press; Turiel, 1966) are contrary to those of Bandura and McDonald. While some small structural advances have been induced, attempts to move subjects backward have been unsuccessful. As we have been stressing, structural changes to a lower level are difficult to obtain.

It must be realized that the conditions causing regressive change may not be the same as those causing progressive change. While certain environmental and organismic conditions may cause regressive effects, many have assumed (as did Bandura and McDonald, 1963) that progressive and regressive changes can be induced in similar ways. Research is needed to determine the conditions leading to regressive change and the nature of such change. As Langer (1969) pointed out, regression is change to an earlier stage as it exists in the individual's present functioning, not to a structure as it existed earlier.

STAGE MIXTURE AS A FORM
OF DEVELOPMENTAL TRANSITION

The criterion of a developmental stage as a "structured whole" (Piaget, 1954) can give the impression that, at any given time, a child functions entirely on one stage and that change involves movement from one such discrete stage to another. If this was the case, the measurement problems would involve ascertaining the child's stage and distinguishing phases within a stage. The data do not conform to this interpretation of consistent stage usage by individuals. Virtually all subjects given the moral judgment interview obtained scores on several stages rather than on only one. Normally, a child's profile of scores contains a dominant stage having the largest score while its adjacent stages have the next largest scores, with the more distant stages from the dominant stage having smaller scores. A good example of the typical profile of stage usage is presented in Figure 5.1, which is based on the pretest scores of the 45 subjects in the Rest, Turiel, and Kohlberg study. The figure clearly shows that stage mixture, including dominance of one stage, is a characteristic mode of functioning.

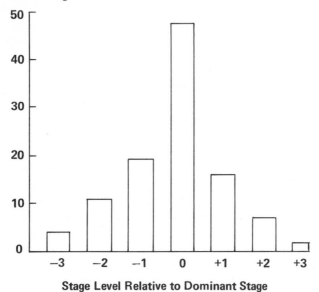

Stage Level Relative to Dominant Stage

Figure 5.1   *Profile of moral stage usage on Kohlberg moral judgment interview (from Rest, Turiel, and Kohlberg study, in press).*

Part of the stage mixture observed in individuals probably is due to some imprecision in the measuring instruments. Both the interviewing techniques and the scoring methods are not yet precise enough to yield an errorless measure of a person's moral structures. A possible source of imprecision lies in nonmoral responses made in the interview. The stages refer to thought structures used in moral judgments, as distinguished from other kinds of judgments. Some responses that are not meant to be moral judgments or definitions of right and wrong are scored as moral judgments. For instance, a higher level child may invoke the issue of punishment as a reason for choosing one of the conflicting alternatives. Punishment for this child may not be a determinant of wrongness in the situation; instead, his judgment could be based on the practical feasibility of an action. In a genuine stage 1 response, punishment is a decisive determinant and definer of wrongness.

We have argued that responses can appear to be reflective of thought structure when the appropriate verbal response, and not the concept, has been learned. In similar fashion, children sometimes give responses that coincide with structural responses, even though they have not attained the structure. This is another source of imprecision since there is still some difficulty in distinguishing between the truly structural responses and the learned verbal responses.

Methodological refinements might reduce the amount of stage mixture, but measurement imprecision does not account for all the variation. Variation exists because individuals actually do use more than one stage in making moral judgments. Such usage of various stages does not contradict the idea that development is to be described in terms of stages that meet the structured whole criterion. Stages are structured wholes not so much because they reflect a unitary form of individual functioning but because they refer to qualitatively different forms of thought. Consequently, the stages define "ideal types" which are representative of forms of thought rather than people (Kohlberg, 1968).

Some of the variation can be explained by Piaget's concept of "decalage" (Flavell, 1963). Both in the cognitive realm and in the moral realm, a child can conceptualize some issues at a higher level than others. Decalage exists because some concepts are more difficult than others and because a child has had more experience in some realms than in others (Piaget, 1932). Nevertheless, the stage concept requires a degree of trans-situational consistency. Kohlberg (1968) does report high intercorrelations among his nine situations.

In some cases, stage mixture is regarded as problematic for developmental theory. It is thought that the postulation of sequential stages of development implies that a child uses only one mode of thought. However, inability to pinpoint one stage in a child should not be regarded as a contradiction to structural theory. Rather, we propose that mixture is in itself a necessary part of development through successive structures and, in fact, will attempt to demonstrate later, in a discussion of transitional mechanisms, how stage mixture is consonant with the restructuring hypotheses. Our position is that an adequate theory of development must include both the concept of discrete structures and the concept of mixture. Instead of viewing development as discrete movement through each step of the sequence, it should be seen as upward movement within the sequence, leading to a relatively stable structure in adulthood. The childhood and adolescent years, which generally involve fairly rapid change, should be characterized by flux rather than stability. Perhaps it is during the adult years, when developmental change is minimal, that individuals function on stable structures.

To understand the role of stage mixture in development, a distinction must be made between mental structures and the structuring process. *Mental structures* refer to forms of thought that may function in more or less cohesive patterns. The *structuring process* refers to the mode of transition from primitive to more advanced forms of functioning. Piaget (1967, p. 4) defines it as follows.

We must, however, introduce an important distinction between two complementary aspects of the process of equilibration. This is the distinction between the variable structures that define the successive states of equilibrium and a certain constant functioning that assures the transition from any one state to the following one.

It may be that the pattern of stage mixture in a developing child is directly related to the structuring process. If this premise is correct, periods of change should be characterized by extensive stage variation, while periods of fixity would be characterized by consistency. Children who are progressing at slow rates would thus display somewhat cohesive structures. Consistency would also be expected in adults who have attained the more advanced stages. The highest stages, when solidified, should denote the greatest structural stability because each stage is more equilibrated and adaptive than the previous stages. Thus it becomes evident that both stage variation and consistency signify different processes at different phases of development. Variation can typify an active process of change; consistency may reflect either fixity at the less equilibrated stages or stable equilibrated functioning.

On the basis of the theoretical model thus far outlined regarding stage mixture, we assert the general hypothesis that amount of stage mixture is an important measure which, when considered with modal stage, reflects the nature of the developmental process. More precisely, there are several parts to this hypothesis, which can be stated with separate reference to the lower and higher stages. Our hypotheses regarding the lower moral stages are as follows.

1. At first, the child progresses slowly through the very early stages and is not in a truly active ongoing process of moral development. At this point there should be relatively little mixture since mixture is related to change.

2. After the initial phase, the child is in an ongoing process of substantial developmental change, at which time there would be increased mixture since mixture is necessary for restructuring.

3. Individuals who do not attain the higher stages by adulthood should display a moderate leveling off of mixture, resulting in somewhat less mixture than for individuals in the process of development (hypothesis 2) but more than those at the earliest phases of development (hypothesis 1).

Our hypotheses regarding the higher moral stages are somewhat different.

4. When first achieving the higher stages, there is much stage variability. At this point, unstable use of the higher stages (represented by high mixture) yields even higher mixture than that of hypothesis 2.

5. Then there is an ongoing process of development in the higher stages characterized by high mixture, which is about equal to that of hypothesis 2 but lower than that of hypothesis 4.

6. Stabilization of the higher stages occurs at a late age, usually in adulthood, and is characterized by low mixture. The mixture is lower than that of hypothesis 5 since a stable structure exists rather than developmental flux. The mixture at this point is also lower than that of hypothesis 3 because the advanced stages are more equilibrated and adaptive structures than the earlier ones.

A test of these hypotheses requires a systematic study examining the stage sequence and degree of stage mixture of comparable samples ranging from about ten to forty years of age. In the meantime, we have undertaken an analysis of the stage mixture of several groups of subjects already interviewed. An examination of the data to be described strongly suggests that the hypotheses outlined are valid.

Groups of subjects from seven different sources were used for the analysis described here. One group originated from a study we are presently conducting on sex differences in moral judgments. This group, which will be referred to as the "Turiel M-C" group, contains 148 upper middle class children at three ages: ten, thirteen, and sixteen. The next two groups consist of Kohlberg's (1958) original subjects. There are 36 middle class and 36 lower class children, equally divided between the same three ages: ten, thirteen, and sixteen (referred to as "Kohlberg M-C" and "Kohlberg L-C" groups). Two additional groups participated in a cross-cultural study (Owen, 1968) on moral development. One group comprises 36 American farm children (referred to as the "Rural USA" group) aged ten, thirteen, and sixteen, and the other group has 18 subjects, aged ten, thirteen, and sixteen, from an isolated Mexican village. A sixth group of ten-, thirteen-, and sixteen-year-old children, who were interviewed by the writer, come from a rural village in Turkey. The Turkish village is less isolated and primitive than the Mexican village. Finally, the last group consists of 50 subjects (from Kramer, 1968) ranging in age from fourteen to twenty-six years (to be referred to as the "Kramer" group).[6]

All of the subjects in our seven groups were administered very similar Kohlberg moral judgment interviews, and the same coding forms (Kohlberg, 1968) were used in scoring the interviews.[7] Each subject had a profile of percentage stage scores approximating the distribution shown in Figure 5.1. To provide a measure of stage mixture displayed by the subjects, a "variation score" was computed for each subject by multiplying the percentage of his responses on a stage by the number of stages separating that stage from the modal stage and then summing these products. The variation score reflects the degree of mixture; the higher the score, the greater the mixture.

Since our hypotheses regarding mixture differ on the basis of stage attained, all of the samples were divided into lower stage and higher stage groups. The lower stage group included subjects whose modal stage was either 1, 2, or 3. The higher

---

[6] Appreciation is expressed to Mrs. Constance Owen, Lawrence Kohlberg, and Richard Kramer for so generously making their data available to us.

[7] The interviews were similar enough to be used in our comparisons. However, stage mixture is probably influenced somewhat by the interviewer, the interview procedures, and the scorer. A more precise analysis of patterns in stage mixture requires a study controlling all these sources of variance.

stage group contained subjects with modal stages 4, 5, or 6. We decided to include stage 4 in the higher stage group because only a small number of subjects in all the samples were modally at stage 5 or 6. In general, very few subjects attain these two highest stages. For the ages represented in our samples, stage 4 is an advanced one and thus, for our purposes, can be regarded as a higher stage.

We will begin the analysis by looking at three American samples, the Turiel M-C group, the Kohlberg M-C group, and the Kohlberg L-C group. Figure 5.2*a* presents the mean variation scores for lower stage subjects at ages ten, thirteen, and sixteen. At age ten, children in the Turiel M-C group had significantly higher variation scores than the other two groups ($p < .05$). Hypotheses 1 and 2 indicate that the Turiel M-C group variation scores were higher because the ten-year-old subjects were more advanced in an ongoing process of development. Figure 5.3*a* presents the percentage of the ten-year-old subjects in each group at each moral stage, showing that the Turiel M-C group was indeed further advanced than the Kohlberg M-C group, which in turn was a little more advanced than the Kohlberg L-C group.

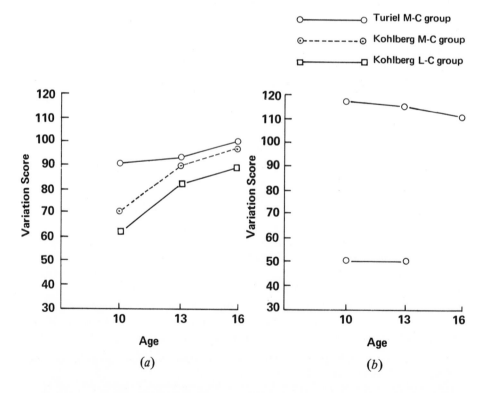

Figure 5.2 *Analysis of stage mixture: Mean variation scores for (a) lower stage (stages 1, 2, and 3) subjects in three city groups; and (b) higher stage (stages 4, 5, and 6) subjects in the Turiel M-C group.*

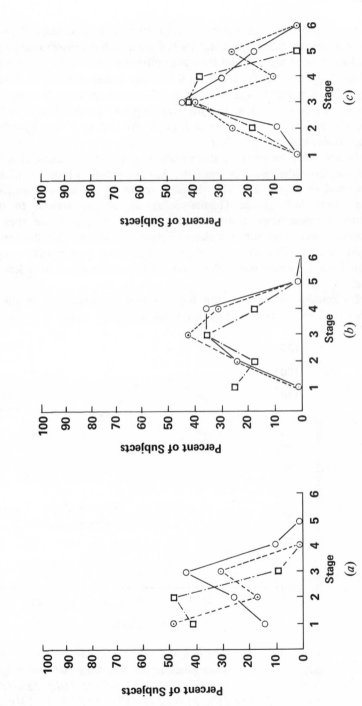

Figure 5.3 Percent of three city subject groups at each moral stage: (a) at age 10; (b) at age 13; (c) at age 16.

Turiel M-C group
Kohlberg M-C group
Kohlberg L-C group

At age thirteen, both Kohlberg groups showed a rise in stage (Figure 5.3*b*) and mixture (Figure 5.2*a*). The Kohlberg M-C subjects had higher variation scores at age thirteen than at age ten, and they were further along in the developmental process. Thus, at age thirteen the Kohlberg M-C group closely approximated the Turiel M-C group; both in variation score (Figure 5.2*a*) and stage usage (Figure 5.3*b*), while it did not do so at age ten. For the Kohlberg L-C group, mixture is higher at age thirteen than it was at age ten and, as we would expect from hypothesis 2, stage usage is also higher (Figure 5.3*b*).

To see what happens to the variation scores at later ages, it is necessary to include the older subjects from the Kramer group, whose variation scores are presented in Figure 5.4. The variation scores of the lower stage Kohlberg M-C and Turiel M-C groups (Figure 5.2*a*) rise at age sixteen to the level of Kramer's lower stage fourteen- to eighteen-year-olds. If we then follow the Kramer lower stage subjects along (Figure 5.4) we see that the variation scores begin to level off during the early twenties. Such leveling off is expected from hypothesis 3, which states that lower stage adults fixate at a less equilibrated stage.

To examine mixture in the higher stages we must rely on the Turiel M-C group and the Kramer group, since the Kohlberg groups had very few higher

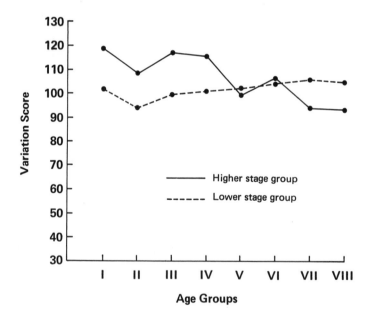

Figure 5.4 *Mean variation scores for higher and lower stage subjects in the Kramer group at the following eight age ranges: 14.0-15.11 (I); 16.0-16.11 (II); 17.0-17.11 (III); 18.0-18.11 (IV); 19.0-20.11 (V); 21.0-22.11 (VI); 23.0-23.11 (VII); and 24.0-26.11 (VIII).*

stage subjects.[8] Figure 5.2*b* shows the mean variation scores for the higher stage Turiel M-C subjects at ages ten, thirteen, and sixteen. While there are only 5 ten-year-old subjects in the higher stage group, there are a substantial number of thirteen-year-olds (20) and sixteen-year-olds (24). According to hypothesis 4, there should be more instability and mixture in early phases of the higher stages than at any other time, which is substantiated by the finding that the variation means for the higher stage subjects at each age (Figure 5.2*b*) are larger than the variation means for lower stage subjects (Figure 5.2*a*). These differences are highly significant at ages ten ($p < .005$) and thirteen ($p < .001$) and reach borderline significance at age sixteen ($p < .10$).

During the ongoing process of development through higher stages we expect the variation score to drop somewhat (hypothesis 4) so that it is approximately at the level of variation scores for lower stage subjects. Figure 5.4, containing the scores for older subjects, shows that mixture in higher stage subjects decreases with increasing age, first to the level of lower stage subjects and then even further. We expect mixture in adulthood to be less at the higher stages than at lower stages because the higher stages are more equilibrated structures (hypothesis 6).

These results can be presented more clearly by dividing the Kramer subjects into two age ranges: fourteen–eighteen and nineteen–twenty-six (Table 5.3). At the younger ages, the higher stage group has a mean variation score (113) that is significantly larger than that (98) of the lower stage group ($p < .01$). The reverse occurs at the older ages; the higher stage group's variation mean is now smaller than that of the lower stage group, and the difference reaches a borderline level of significance ($p < .10$).[9] The variation of the older higher stage group is significantly smaller than that of the younger higher stage group ($p < .001$). The difference between the lower stage groups is not significant.

Table 5.3 *Mean variation scores at two age ranges for subjects at lower and higher stages.*

Dominant Stage Groups	Age Ranges	
	14-18	19-26
Lower Stage	98	104
Higher Stage	113	98

[8]The Turiel middle class group showed more advanced usage of the lower stage at ages ten and thirteen than did the Kohlberg groups. Children in the Turiel population thus should advance to the higher stages a little sooner than the children in the other groups.
[9]The trends in Figure 5.4 indicate that the stabilization of the higher stages only begins in early adulthood. Stage mixture at the higher stages should be substantially less in people who are well into their adulthood. These findings indicate that the development of morality continues long past adolescence.

Rate of development and stage mixture were also examined for the three remaining groups from rural villages. Research has been done with children from rural cultures (rural USA, Turkish village, isolated Mexican village) to determine if the moral stages represent a universal sequence. The development of moral thinking is a function of an interaction between organismic factors and a general social environment: structures result from the child's attempts to order his social and moral word in accordance with particular modes. While some differences in rules and values may exist across cultures, the ways in which the growing child interprets and integrates his social environment should not differ from culture to culture.

Structural universality is also expected because the child does not attain moral stages by merely internalizing patterns in the external environment. If the successive structures were internalizations of cultural patterns, the idea of an invariant sequence would not be tenable. A fixed stage sequence implies that there are universal aspects of development that exist in all children. In contrast, the notion of stage variation from culture to culture would imply that specific environmental influences could determine the process of structural change. According to this view and insofar as children's experiences differ to some extent, different environmental pressures could result in different structural sequences even within a given culture.

Kohlberg (1966b) presented some evidence in support of the cross-cultural universality of the moral stages. Children between the ages of ten and sixteen in a Malaysian aboriginal tribal village were administered a form of the moral judgment interview. It was found that the age trends, which were similar to American children, were in concordance with the theorized sequence. However, the development of the village children differed from that of Americans in that the rate of change was slower. The village children reached stages 3 and 4 later than American children and did not show much usage of the last two stages at the age of sixteen

The results for three additional cultural groups are presented in Figure 5.5, which shows that children from Turkish, Mexican, and American villages do follow the moral stage sequence in the prescribed order. This figure also shows that children in these groups, like the Taiwanese children, progressed through the sequence more slowly and attained each stage at a later age than the American city children. An examination of the implications of these findings must await the completion of more detailed analyses of our data. [For further discussion of the cross-cultural issue, see Owen (1968).] For our purposes, we present the cross-cultural findings to further support and clarify the stage mixture hypotheses.

Figure 5.5 shows the percentage of subjects at each stage for the three rural groups at ten, thirteen, and sixteen years. Comparing Figure 5.5a with Figure 5.3a, we see that, at age ten, children in the rural cultures (who mainly use the lowest stage) were much less advanced than the city children. Consequently, on the basis of hypothesis 1 we would expect all three rural groups to have substantially less mixture than the city groups. Figure 5.6a contains variation scores for the rural groups that are lower than those of the city groups (Figure 5.2a). The rural USA group should show more mixture than the other two rural groups since it was more advanced on the moral stages. As expected, the Rural USA group had a higher mean

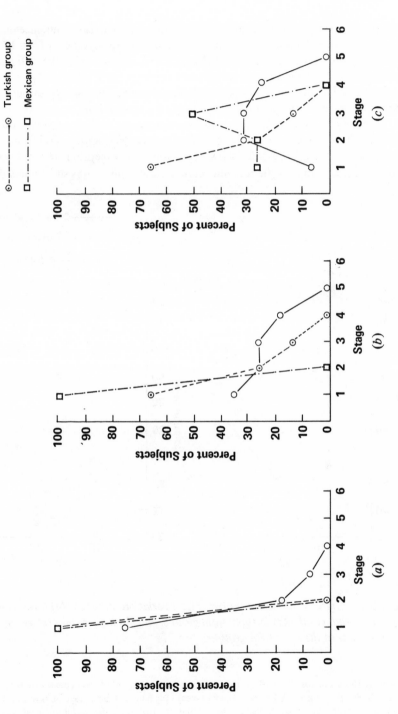

Figure 5.5 *Percent of three rural subject groups at each moral stage: (a) at age 10; (b) at age 13; (c) at age 16.*

Rural USA group
Turkish group
Mexican group

than either the Turkish or Mexican groups. The overall analysis of variance on the ten-year-old variation means of the six groups was highly significant ($F = 17\,00$; $p < .01$). A Duncan multiple range test (Kramer, 1956) showed that the differences between the rural groups and city middle class children were significant ($p < .05$).

At age thirteen, the rural groups were still advancing very slowly through the moral stages (Figure 5.5*b*) and only beginning to reach the level of the city middle class ten-year-olds. In consequence their variation scores at thirteen should still be lower than those of the ten-year-old middle class subjects. Comparisons of variation scores in Figures 5.6*a* and 5.2*a* show that, with the exception of the Turkish group,[10] stage mixture for the thirteen-year-old rural children was slightly less than

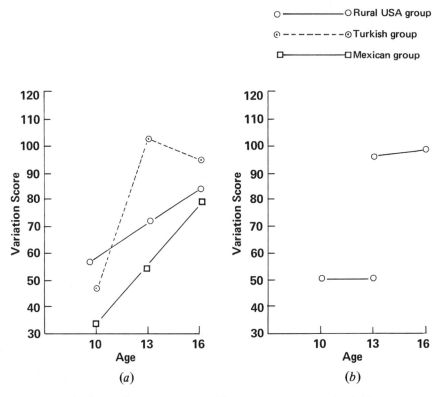

Figure 5.6   *Analysis of stage mixture: Mean variation scores for (a) lower stage (stages 1, 2, and 3) subjects in three rural groups; and (b) higher stage (stages 4, 5, and 6) subjects in the rural USA group.*

---

[10]The variation score for the Turkish thirteen-year-olds is the only serious departure from our hypotheses. We do not know why these thirteen-year-olds had such high stage mixture, as it was not expected from the stage usage of these children. However, the variation mean for the sixteen-year-old Turkish children does decrease to an expected value.

the mixture of the ten-year-old city children. It was not until the age of sixteen (Figure 5.5c) that the rural subjects reached the stages attained by the ten- and thirteen-year-old city children. The mixture of the three rural groups increases at sixteen (Figure 5.6a) and is approximately the level of ten- and thirteen-year-old lower stage city children. The combination of stages attained and degree of mixture for rural children indicates that at sixteen they are involved in an ongoing process of developmental change that is characteristic of city children between the ages of ten and thirteen. The few rural subjects who did use the higher stages have large variation scores (Figure 5.6b).

The findings thus far presented show that stage mixture within an individual is in itself an aspect of the developmental process. Furthermore, these findings have shown that degree of mixture signifies different things at different points in onto-genesis. Younger children show stage consistency at the early stages because developmental change is slow. When children are in the years of relatively rapid development through the lower stages, mixture—which is necessary for change to occur—increases substantially. Those who do not advance to higher stages begin to stabilize at the lower stages after the period of transition. While the transitional period is characterized by increasing mixture, the stabilization at lower stages results in a leveling of degree of mixture.

The earliest emergence of the higher stages brings with it the greatest amount of mixture because at that point higher stage functioning is very unstable. Subsequently there is an ongoing restructuring process with somewhat less mixture. Finally, mixture decreases substantially as the higher stages stabilize in more equilibrated functioning.

Children in more isolated rural cultures follow the same stage sequence as do children in American cities. However, moral development in the isolated societies is more gradual and progresses more slowly. This slow progression is reflected in the minimal amount of mixture displayed by the ten- and thirteen-year-olds in the rural cultures. It is not until the age of sixteen that their mixture reaches the level of ten- and thirteen-year-old city children. The ontogenetic process for the rural children is a very gradual one, taking place over many years.

These developmental hypotheses regarding stage mixture are amenable to experimental validation. Our previous experimental techniques, which involved exposing children to new modes of thought, can also be applied to this problem. Our hypotheses suggest that an age-by-stage interaction will determine partially the degree to which a child can be influenced to change. There is some evidence (Turiel, 1965) indicating that twelve-year-old children at the lower moral stages can be influenced to change to the stage above more readily than twelve-year-olds at the higher stages. Subjects in stage 2 changed more than subjects in stage 3, who in turn changed more than those in stage 4. Stage 4 functioning at the age of twelve is only in its early phases and thus rather unstable. However, we would expect opposite trends from attempts to influence older subjects. If an older child at the lower stages is fixated in his mode of thought, he could not be influenced readily. The older child at the higher stages can be influenced to change because he is in the process of development.

Some findings from the Rest, Turiel, and Kohlberg study indicate that there is an age-by-stage interaction. Fifth-grade children in stages 1 and 2 were able to more accurately recapitulate statements at stages above their own than were fifth-graders in stages 3 and 4. Conversely, eighth-graders in stages 3 and 4 showed slightly better recapitulations than eighth-graders in stages 1 and 2.

CONDITIONS OF DISEQUILIBRIUM
CAUSING DEVELOPMENTAL CHANGE

Stage mixture appears to play an essential role in the developmental process. However, mixture is functionally related to factors causing change from one structure to the next. A comprehensive understanding of moral development includes laws of transition that elucidate variables causing developmental change.

According to Piaget (1947, 1967), movement from one cognitive structure to the next occurs when the system is in a state of disequilibrium. When a child who is in a state of disequilibrium is presented with operations that are developmentally close enough for him to consider, his assimilatory and accommodatory functions may act in complementary fashion to establish greater equilibrium (Langer, 1967). The child deals with environmental events in accordance with structures available to him. Change may occur when the inability to completely assimilate events to the existing structure leads to disequilibrium that motivates attempts to achieve new equilibrium. This more highly equilibrated stage allows better assimilation of the new experience.

Some researchers have attempted to experimentally investigate developmental change. Smedslund (1961b), working with the concept of conservation, has shown that presenting contradictions in the form of "cognitive conflict" can lead to some reorganization of structure. In a study by Inhelder, Bovet, Sinclair, and Smock (1966), some children at the transitional stage between nonconservation and conservation of quantity developed the concept of conservation after being presented with a conflict situation. The most extensive discussion of structural change in terms of disequilibrium has been presented by Langer (1967), who delineated two parameters in the equilibration process: the organizational and the energetic (1967, p. 4). The energetic parameter refers to the affective experience of disequilibrium that must exist if the equilibration process is to take place. While other studies have been based on the assumption that external contradictions would lead to disequilibrium, Langer has attempted to actually measure the conflict experienced by a child presented with contradictions. The organizational aspects of equilibration include (a) the environmental conditions that facilitate mental actions necessary for the attainment of a more progressive cognitive organization, and (b) the effects of different symbolic media on cognitive reorganization.

We previously postulated that cognitive conflict may be one of the factors causing change in the development of social concepts (Turiel, 1966, p. 617) and are presently experimentally investigating conditions of disequilibrium that may cause developmental change (Turiel, 1967). In some studies dealing with concepts such as conservation or class inclusion, physical contradictions have been produced

(Inhelder, et al., 1966; Smedslund, 1961b) or subjects have been directed to per-form impossible tasks (Langer, 1967) in order to motivate children to perform the necessary mental acts. The study of change in moral thinking requires a somewhat different, though related, approach: rather than dealing with the influence of contradictions on physical and logical concepts, such study is concerned with the effects of contradictions on moral thinking.

Our analysis of disequilibrium will make use of Langer's (1967) paradigm of organizational and energetic parameters—two parameters we believe to be interre-lated. One way of inducing change in moral thinking through the equilibration process is by presenting the child with conceptual contradictions that activate disequilibrium. These contradictions must be perceived by the child in such a way that he is motivated to deal with the contradictory events. If concepts correspond-ing to the higher mode of thought are presented at the same time, the child may assimilate those concepts by performing new mental operations. In summary, change occurs when perceived conceptual contradictions energize attempts to re-structure by exploring the organizational properties of the higher mode of thought.

The experimental procedures used in our first study clarify the nature of the equilibration process. In the experimental treatment, subjects were presented with arguments supporting both sides of the moral conflict. It has been demonstrated that concepts at the stage above the subject's own stage are perceived as favorable and are somewhat understood (Rest, Turiel, and Kohlberg, in press); therefore, these arguments served to expose subjects to cogent reasons (in the exposure to the stage directly above) justifying two contradictory positions. Conceptual contradic-tions existed because two incompatible positions were being supported by the *same* moral structure. The child could have been conflicted in this experimental situation since both sets of concepts used to support incompatible positions seemed to be correct. In such a case, he could not resolve the contradictory state using the existing moral structure and may have attempted to become more competent with the concepts causing conflict. The child who resolves contradictions by becoming more competent with higher level concepts is *assimilating* those concepts by chang-ing his form of thought (*accommodation*).

Presenting external contradictions does not in itself mean the child will perceive them as contradictory. For instance, exposing subjects to concepts of the stages two above or one below did not result in significant change. A child exposed to the stage two above his own would not experience the disequilibrium experienced by a child exposed to just one stage above, because the concepts presented would not be understood. Before a child can understand the concepts of a stage two above, he must develop the thought of the stage immediately above his own. Even if the contradictions were perceived by the child, he would not be able to operate with the organizational aspects of the contradictions. The contradictions presented in exposing subjects to the stage below do not provide sufficient energizing effects for disequilibrium because those concepts, which have been rejected, are seen as incorrect.

Research on the equilibration process is presently being conducted by attempting to determine the types of situations that produce some developmental change. The general hypothesis with which we are working is that the presentation of arguments at the stage one above the child's own, supporting two incompatible positions in a moral conflict, should induce developmental change, since a two-sided argument meets the energetic and organizational criteria for equilibration. In order to experimentally explore the validity of this hypothesis, the effects of two-sided arguments are being compared with the effects of one-sided arguments. After determining the subjects' initial stages, they are exposed to moral concepts that correspond to one of the six stages. With each subject, one of the following three exposure methods is used.

1. One exposure method involves using a one-sided argument that supports the subject's choice in a moral dilemma. After the subject makes a choice in the situational dilemma, the role playing described in the first study is used to expose the subject to two sets of advice favoring the same side he has favored.

2. In the second method two sets of advice support the alternative opposite to the one the subject has chosen.

3. The third exposure method involves using a two-sided argument. In the role playing for each situation, the subject is exposed to one set of advice favoring one side of the dilemma and a second set favoring the other side.

We are interested in determining which of these experimental manipulations will cause progressive or regressive change. Such change will be ascertained through a posttest interview. Furthermore, each subject will be interviewed immediately following the treatment condition in order to assess the amount and kind of conflict experienced in the experimental session. In that way, it may be possible to relate amount of change in moral thinking to the disequilibrium felt in the experimental treatment.

It seems to us that the most effective experimental condition should be the two-sided argument.[11] Presenting a subject with one-sided arguments at the stage above his own that agree with his choices is not likely to greatly motivate him to deal with the new concepts. Rather, he is more likely to be reinforced in accepting the choice in the dilemma and he may attempt to mimic the higher level support of that choice. A subject presented with one-sided arguments that support the alternative opposite to his choice may misinterpret the concepts as a lower level or he may experience some conflict because an opposite point of view is being supported by

---

[11] In addition to exposing subjects to the stage above via the three different exposure methods, the study includes exposing subjects to the stages one below and two above their own. One purpose of these procedures is to replicate the previous experiment (Turiel, 1966). It is expected that the findings will be similar to those of the previous study, with subjects exposed to the stage one above being influenced more than the other groups, thus further substantiating that the moral stages form an invariant sequence. The present study also includes a condition exposing subjects to their dominant stage in order to determine the influence of arguments at their own level. A further interest of this study is to determine which of the stages, in relation to the subject's stage, is most effective in influencing a child to change the content of his choices in the moral conflicts.

higher level concepts. However, these subjects may not experience the kind of disequilibrium that comes from perceiving contradictions. Subjects presented with two-sided arguments can experience cognitive disequilibrium if they feel something is wrong in the situation. Perceiving the disparity in two sets of similar concepts supporting contradictory positions can lead the subject to a further aspect of the equilibration process—to mentally explore the structural properties of the conceptual contradictions in an effort to resolve them.

Any reorganization in moral thinking that is induced by the experimental treatments may occur immediately or may require time for the equilibration process to take place. The posttest is administered to some subjects immediately following the experimental exposure, while it is administered to other subjects one week later. Since disequilibrium leads to attempts at restructuring, a period of time is probably necessary for the changes to occur. Therefore, changes may not be measurable on the posttest administered immediately after the treatment; they may not be measurable until some time after the treatment. On the other hand, any real structural changes occurring immediately should endure until the delayed posttest.

Learning that represents the acquisition of verbal responses rather than restructuring could easily be retained until the immediate posttest. However, such learning might dissipate in the one-week period between the treatment and the delayed posttest. Smedslund's studies (1961b) have shown that children who acquire the concept of conservation maintain it for a period of time, while those who only learn the verbal responses do not retain them. If our one-sided conditions lead only to mimicry of verbal statements, the subjects may be able to use them immediately, but this learning should not be lasting or generalizable.[12]

It now becomes possible to elaborate on the assertion that began this discussion of transitional mechanisms—that stage mixture is functionally related to equilibration. The concept of disequilibrium refers to an internal state of apparent contradiction and cognitive disorganization, which leads to active attempts at reorganizing. Presenting external contradictions does not necessarily result in the equilibration process and it is essential to determine whether or not the child perceives the contradictions. While a child will not experience structural contradictions if they are too advanced for him, disequilibrium can be induced with structural contradictions at the stage one above. But why is the child able to perceive contradictions at a stage that is not his own? The probable reason is that he functions on more than one stage—stage mixture. A child who functioned at only one stage would experience relatively little conflict, as it would be difficult for him to perceive

---

[12]Greater effectiveness of the two-sided argument over the one-sided on the delayed posttest could be attributed to an attention factor. It is possible that a two-sided argument holds the child's attention more than a one-sided argument. A more attentive subject would, of course, be expected to change more. However, by also having an immediate posttest, it will be possible to determine to what degree one type of presentation leads to greater attentiveness. If the one-sided presentation is as effective or more effective than the two-sided presentation on the immediate posttest, it would indicate that presenting two sides does not lead to greater attentiveness.

contradictions in the external environment. The child whose functioning is mainly on one stage, but who uses other stages as well, will more readily perceive contradictions and thus experience conflict more frequently. In other words, stage mixture serves to facilitate the perception of contradictions, making the individual more susceptible to disequilibrium and consequently more likely to progress developmentally.

Experimental manipulations do provide an external impetus for disequilibrium but, in a child's natural developmental history, the perception of structural contradictions often has an internal source. Contradictions are more readily perceived by the child who uses more than one level of thought. Furthermore, equilibrium may be disrupted by the internal contradictions that result from stage inconsistency. As an example, we saw that children with very little mixture were more retarded than those with greater mixture. With low mixture there is relative developmental stagnation because a partial use of the stage above the dominant one is necessary for the perception of higher level structural contradictions. Thus children with much mixture are in an ongoing process of development that is stimulated by a constant internal source of conflict.

The amount of conflict presented by the environment is interrelated with the potentiality of an individual to experience disequilibrium. A complex heterogeneous environment that presents a variety of contradictions is more likely to facilitate the equilibration process than a more homogeneous environment. Children in the complex environment would have greater stage mixture, and children with high stage mixture are more likely to perceive higher stage structural contradictions in the environment.

IMPLICATIONS FOR SOCIAL CHANGE

Our theoretical assertions on developmental change are applicable to problems of social change. We have already noted that children in rural, isolated societies show less stage mixture and slower development through the moral stages than do children from American cities. What probably distinguishes the more advanced urban cultures from the smaller, more isolated rural societies, even though they share many institutions in common, is the degree of social complexity. A more advanced society normally affords greater opportunity for inducing cognitive conflicts. Although children in both types of societies follow the same sequence of stages, those in the more complex society—where change is more rapid—are more likely to reach a more advanced level of moral development.

There is no guarantee, however, that members of the heterogeneous society will advance to the highest moral stages. In fact, only a minority of American adults function at the more advanced stages, even though many public moral statements are at stages 5 and 6 (Kohlberg, 1968). Several factors are undoubtedly involved in explaining why people do not attain the highest moral level presented by the environment. One factor appears to be a form of assimilating higher level statements, which allows individuals to insulate themselves against disturbances to their cognitive equilibrium. This form of assimilation was observed in children who, when asked to recapitulate moral statements at levels higher than their own, misinterpreted preferred statements as their own level and misinterpreted disliked statements as the stage below their own (Rest, Turiel, and Kohlberg, in press).

These findings help explain why the majority of people in the society do not themselves attain the moral level contained in public statements, such as those expressed by social leaders and in documents such as the Constitution. Social leaders expressing moral statements at a level higher than that of their audience may elicit a positive attitude toward the content endorsed. However, the structural level of thought used by the leaders may be assimilated by the listener to his own level. Similarly, an individual having a positive attitude toward the content of an action may seek out and endorse social leaders who advocate that action. Again, the structural level of thought communicated by such leaders may be perceived by the listener at his own level. Perhaps listening to higher level statements supporting content originally approved by the listener serves to further confirm the listener's own structure when the higher level statements are interpreted by him according to his own level.

Higher stage moral statements would not be as readily misinterpreted if the statements induced disequilibrium. However, the concern of group leadership (particularly that in support of a "cause") with the content of an issue generally results in moral statements containing little structural contradiction. Therefore, such statements are more easily distortable—to one's own stage in order that one may accept the content or to a stage below to permit rejection of the content. The structural level of the audience generally does not reach that of the leaders because structural change cannot be achieved through modeling, which is the implicit mechanism of most groups and cults. Some form of structural conflict must be presented for structural change to occur. The conflict would prevent the individual from passively accepting content through distortion of structure and motivate him to actively deal with the structural elements.

REFERENCES

Bandura, A., & McDonald, F. J. Influence of social reinforcement and the behavior of models in shaping children's moral judgments. *Journal of Abnormal and Social Psychology*, 1963, **67**, 274–281.

Bandura, A., & Walters, R. *Social learning and personality development*. New York: Holt, Rinehart & Winston, 1963.

Barker, R. G., Dembo, T., & Lewin, K. Frustration and regression. In R. G. Barker, J. S. Kounin, & H. F. Wright (Eds.) *Child Behavior and Development*, New York: McGraw-Hill, 1943, 441–458.

Eysenck, H. J. The development of moral values in children: The contribution of learning theory. *British Journal of Educational Psychology*, 1960, **30**, 11–22.

Flavell, J. H. *The developmental psychology of Jean Piaget*. Princeton, N.J.: Van Nostrand, 1963.

Freud, S. (1923). *The ego and the id*. New York: W. W. Norton, 1960.

Freud, S. (1924). The dissolution of the Oedipus Complex. *Collected Papers*, Vol. 2. New York: Basic Books, 1959.

Freud, S. (1928). Dostoevski and parricide. *Collected Papers*, Vol. 5. New York: Basic Books, 1959.

Freud, S. (1930). *Civilization and its discontents.* New York: W. W. Norton, 1961.

Gesell, A. The ontogenesis of infant behavior. In L. Carmichael (Ed.) *Manual of child psychology*. New York: Wiley, 1964, 335–373.

Inhelder, B., Bovet, M., Sinclair, H., & Smock, C. D. On cognitive development. *American Psychologist*, 1966, 21, 160-164.

Kohlberg, L. The development of modes of moral thinking in the years ten to sixteen. Unpublished doctoral dissertation, University of Chicago, 1958.

Kohlberg, L. The development of children's orientation toward a moral order: I. Sequence in the development of moral thought. *Vita Humana*, 1963a, 6, 11–33.

Kohlberg, L. Moral development and identification. In H. W. Stevenson (Ed.) *Yearbook of the National Society for the Study of Education: Pt. I. Child Psychology*. Chicago: University of Chicago Press, 1963b, 277–332.

Kohlberg, L. Cognitive stages and preschool education. *Human Development*, 1966a, 9, 5–17.

Kohlberg, L. Moral education in the schools: A developmental view. *School Review*, 74, 1966b, 1–30.

Kohlberg, L. *Moral development*, 1969 (book in preparation).

Kramer, C. Y. Extension of multiple range tests to group means with unequal numbers of replications. *Biometrics*, 1956, 12, 307–310.

Kramer, R. B. Changes in moral judgment response pattern during late adolescence and young adulthood: Retrogression in a developmental sequence. Unpublished doctoral dissertation, University of Chicago, 1968.

Langer, J. Disequilibrium as a source of development. Paper read at Society for Research in Child Development, New York City, April 1967.

Langer, J. *Theories of development*. New York: Holt, Rinehart & Winston, 1969.

Owen, C. Cross-cultural studies of moral development. Unpublished doctoral dissertation, University of Chicago, 1968.

Piaget, J. *The child's conception of the world*. New York: Harcourt, Brace, 1929.

Piaget, J. (1932). *The moral judgment of the child*. Glencoe, Illinois: Free Press, 1948.

Piaget, J. (1947). *The psychology of intelligence*. New York: Harcourt, Brace, 1950.

Piaget, J. (1954). First discussion. In J. M. Tanner & B. Inhelder (Eds.) *Discussions on child development IV*. New York: Basic Books, 1958.

Piaget, J. *Six psychological studies*. New York: Random House, 1967.

Rest, J., Turiel, E., & Kohlberg, L. Level of moral development as a determinant of preference and comprehension of moral judgments made by others. *Journal of Personality* (in press).

Sears, R. R. Identification as a form of behavior development. In D. B. Harris (Ed.) *The concept of development*. Minneapolis: University of Minnesota Press, 1957, 149–161.

Smedslund, J. The acquisition of conservation of substance and weight in children: II. External reinforcement of conservation of weight and of the operations of addition and subtraction. *Scandanavian Journal of Psychology*, 1961a, 2, 71–84.

Smedslund, J. The acquisition of conservation of substance and weight in children: III. Extinction of conservation of weight acquired 'normally' and by means of empirical controls on a balance. *Scandanavian Journal of Psychology*, 1961b, 2, 85–87.

Smedslund, J. The acquisition of conservation of substance and weight in children: V. Practice in conflict situations without external reinforcement. *Scandanavian Journal of Psychology*, 1961c, 2, 156–160.

Turiel, E. An experimental test of the sequentiality of developmental stages in the child's moral judgments. Unpublished doctoral dissertation, Yale University, 1965.

Turiel, E. An experimental test of the sequentiality of developmental stages in the child's moral judgments. *Journal of Personality and Social Psychology*, 1966, 3, 611–618.

Turiel, E. Cognitive conflict in the development of the child's moral judgments. National Science Foundation, January 1967 (mimeo).

Werner, H. Process and achievement. A basic problem of education and developmental psychology. *Harvard Educational Review*, 1937, 7, 353–368.

Werner, H. *Comparative psychology of mental development*. Chicago: Follet, 1948.

Werner, H., & Kaplan, B. *Symbol formation*. New York: John Wiley, 1963.

White, R. Motivation reconsidered: the concept of competence. *Psychological Review*, 1959, 66, 297–333.

Whiting, J. W. Resource mediation and learning by identification. In I. Iscoe & H. W. Stevenson (Eds.) *Personality development in children*. Austin: University of Texas Press, 1960, 112–126.

6

SOME ORIGINS OF CONCERN
FOR OTHERS[1]

▬▬▬▬▬▬▬▬▬▬▬▬▬▬▬▬▬▬▬▬▬▬▬▬▬▬▬▬▬▬▬▬▬▬

I take it that the central message of American experimental psychology over the past fifty years has been that if man seeks anything, he seeks to avoid pain and to gain his own rewards. I take it also that a similar message seems to emerge from psychoanalytic psychology over the same period: man is a drive-reducing organism that seeks to satisfy its instinctual concerns.

Both of these psychologies have become more differentiated during these fifty years than the above statements imply. Yet this central concept has undergone little change. Man is integumented (Allport, 1960), these psychologies would hold, concerned with his own skin and little else.

There have always been phenomena that challenge this concept of man's concerns, phenomena for which there are few experimental data. An insistent one is that man sometimes seems much more concerned with the rewards and sufferings of *others*. Indeed, concern for others occurs throughout the animal

[1]It is a pleasure to acknowledge the efforts of assistants and students who have energetically facilitated the research reported here, among them Anne Burrowes Bloxom, Janet Cuca, Michael Davenport, Fred Hipp, Jr., Irene Kostin, David Mantell, Edward Nystrom, Barry Ranieri, Anita F. Thompson, and Patricia Warren. Henrietta Gallagher performed the statistical computations. Professor Glenn M. White joined me in the design and conduct of several of these studies and was a major contributor to the development of the research. A considerable debt is owed Professors James Bryan, Perry London, and Silvan S. Tomkins, all of whom contributed generously of their ideas and critique to these studies. The studies were supported in part by Grant 1 PO 1 HD 01762 from the National Institute of Child Health and Human Development to the Educational Testing Service, and by Grant MH-HD 13893 from the National Institute of Mental Health to the writer.

This paper is adapted from a colloquium given to the Department of Psychology, University of California at Berkeley, January 11, 1968.

DAVID ROSENHAN

Swarthmore College, Swarthmore, Pennsylvania

kingdom (see, for example, Hebb and Thompson, 1954; Lorenz, 1952). These theoretically troublesome phenomena include the abiding concern of parents for children; attachment to mates and lovers; courage in war and other circumstances when the actor's life is at stake; rescue behavior; devotion to altruistic causes; principled behaviors that involve enormous sacrifices; charitability; generosity to the unknown and unthanking poor. All of these phenomena are altruistic acts in the sense in which Comte intended that term: they reflect concern for others. And none of them is immediately reconcilable with current theory.

Of course, it is possible to fit altruistic behaviors into the current theoretical frameworks. Mowrer (1960, p. 435), for example, raises the possibility that what we call courage may simply be the absence of fear in situations where fear is ordinarily expected. Glover (1925), Freud (1937), and Fenichel (1945), in the psychoanalytic tradition, suggest that the dynamics of guilt and self-destruction and conflicts about masculinity may variously account for these acts. Theoretical possibility is by no means a substitute for evidence, however, and we need to begin to assemble hard data to determine whether altruistic phenomena support or injure current psychological conceptions.

This essay summarizes some of the evidence concerning the origins and dynamics of concern for others. It begins with a study of committed altruistic independence as it occurs in the everyday environment, a study that was intended to provide theoretical clues to an understanding of this phenomenon. It then examines some laboratory experiments designed to test aspects of a theory and to more clearly elucidate the phenomenon. It closes with informal observations on the psychological ingredients of concern for others.

CHILDREN OF ANAK:
THE ALTRUISM OF COMMITTED CIVIL RIGHTS WORKERS

Several years ago, as part of a project that sought to discover the relations between cognition and behavior, I and my laboratory associates assembled field data on people who were associated with, or sympathetic to, the civil rights movement. Three concerns of that study are relevant to this discussion. First, in our study we wanted to examine whether the theories of altruistic behavior were reflected in the altruism that was apparently involved in civil rights activity. Second, we hoped to compile a detailed oral history of altruistic behavior which might be valuable to scholars in many disciplines, particularly when combined with other such histories (a hope, it might be mentioned, that was not quite fulfilled). Finally, we hoped that the data emerging from this study might yield hypotheses that could be subjected to experimental scrutiny. With regard to this last intention, it is clear that field studies have the singular virtue of coming close to what is going on in the "real" world and therefore of directing one's attention to hypotheses that are maximally relevant to that world. But field studies also suffer a liability; they provide too many data whose interrelations can rarely be made clear. Nevertheless, our hope was to illuminate the matrix of variables associated with altruistic behavior and to examine, separately and together, the relative impact of these variables.

Interviewing began early in 1963 and continued through 1964. It concentrated on the events leading up to the spring and summer of 1961, when activity on behalf of civil rights appeared to reach a peak; marches and freedom rides occurred throughout the South and in Washington, D.C. With the cooperation of the Student Nonviolent Coordinating Committee and the Congress of Racial Equality we were able to obtain the names and addresses of those who had taken part in these efforts or had supported them financially. We interviewed most of the respondents in the North and also made two trips to the South. When we explained the nature of our study, nearly all who were approached consented to be interviewed. The interviewing was no small matter; sessions often lasted as long as twelve hours, in two- and three-hour periods. We are grateful for the cooperation that was given. The interview was conic in structure (it began with general questions and ended with specific ones) and concerned three areas.

Facts of involvement. Discussed were details on how the respondents became involved in the movement (precipitating circumstances), the course and nature of their involvement, dates, people worked with, perceived and actual risks (where relevant), the degree to which missions were accomplished, and the material and psychological gains and losses. We "trained" the respondents to give us as much information as possible by letting them know that everything they had to say was of interest to us.

Personal history. Information was elicited on relationships with parents, siblings, peers, teachers, authorities, vocational and educational history, family vocation and social history, estimates of perceived and actual social class, health and "cosmetic" history.

Perceptions of motivations for participating. We obtained the respondents' views of their own behaviors, of the behaviors of others who were like them or different from them, and of the opposition.

Black respondents were interviewed by a black person, and white respondents by a white. Both interviewers were well experienced. Nearly 90 people were interviewed and we obtained 68 usable interviews—36 from people who participated in civil rights work and 32 from those who sympathized with and gave financial support to it. (In the main, the other interviews were pilot studies in which we attempted to structure the interview schedule and make it fairly constant, to train the interviewers, and to begin to sense what would be the most profitable and theoretically the most interesting direction for the interview to take.)

After we examined and coded the interviews and compared the respondents who physically participated in civil rights work with those who only supported the movement—and this was to be the major comparison in the study—we did not feel much scientific compensation. There were some findings regarding the role and nature of conformity pressures that were of interest and require further examination but, on the whole, the comparisons were disappointing and I will not have much more to say about them here. Rather, I will focus on some rich and thoroughly accidental findings that emerged from the interviews of the active respondents.

On reading and rereading these interviews, we noticed that we had two subsamples among those who were committed to civil rights. The first group had been involved in civil rights only to the extent of having participated in one or two freedom rides. The second had been active for at least a year and often longer, mainly in the South, on such projects as voter registration and education of the underprivileged. The numbers of respondents in each of these subsamples is shown in Table 6.1. Because we have yet to find nonpejorative labels for these two groups, we have accepted the convenient labels of "partially committed" and "fully committed."

Table 6.1 *1961 Sample: Current (1964) activity status of civil rights workers.*

Respondent	Fully Committed	Partially Committed
Black	3	5
White	12	16

The Role and Function
of the Altruistic Socializer

It was not difficult to obtain reliable retrospective reports from the respondents regarding who they felt was the main socializing parent during their childhood. Moreover, one could confirm from the content of the interviews whether the respondent's conscious report was accurate. We found two important differences between the fully and the partially committed with regard to the function of this socializer.

Table 6.2 summarizes our judgment regarding the quality of relationship between the socializing parent and the respondent during the latter's formative years and also, as it turns out, until the time of the interview. Fully committed respondents seem to have maintained a positive, cordial, warm, and respecting relationship with their parent. True, there were disagreements, which often extended to matters of considerable substance and importance to both the respondent and his parent, including the matter of whether the respondent should be a participant in civil rights activities. Despite this, one easily sensed considerable fondness between parent and child.

Table 6.2   *1961 Sample: Affective valence toward the primary socializing parent.*

Quality of Relationship	Fully Committed	Partially Committed
Positive	12	3
Negative or distinctly ambivalent	3	18

$\chi^2 = 15.55$; $df = 1$; $p < .001$

The partially committed described the parent in negative or ambivalent terms. A substantial proportion described their relations with the socializing parent as actually hostile during their formative years and, at best, cool and avoidant at the time they were interviewed. One sensed discomfort, often anxiety and hostility, and sometimes guilt of an unspecified nature flowing from child to parent, and perhaps vice versa.

More striking than the quality of relationship, however, was the cognitive substance of the relationship. Both sets of socializers were concerned with moral issues; indeed, during the first coding when we examined "moral concerns in the socializing agent" we could locate no differences. But one or both of the parents of the fully committed were themselves fully committed to an altruistic cause during some extended period of the respondents' formative years, while the parents of the partially committed reportedly evidenced considerable ambivalence and confusion about the nature of particular moralities. At least it seemed so to the respondents— so much so that we had occasion to call their moral confrontation with their parents a "crisis of hypocrisy." Table 6.3 summarizes the coarse grain of these findings.

Some of the respondents' actual remarks may be illuminating in this regard. One of the fully committed reported that "my father carried me on his shoulders during the Sacco-Vanzetti parades"; another described how his father fought on the side of the Loyalists in the Spanish Civil War; a third told how his mother "felt close to Jesus and was warmed by His teachings. She devoted her entire life to Christian

Table 6.3 *1961 Sample: Evidence for discrepancy between teaching and practice by a socializing parent.*

Condition	Fully Committed	Partially Committed
Discrepancy present	2	13
Discrepancy absent	11	3
Evidence unclear or absent	2	5

$\chi^2 = 13.29$; $df = 2$; $p > .01$

education." Another respondent's father was outraged by the Nazi atrocities and, though over age and apparently disqualified on grounds of health, was accepted into the military during World War II. In short, we seemed to have found the presence of altruistic models in the backgrounds of the committed altruists, models whose behavior apparently influenced the course of their children's activities. The matter may not be so simple, as we shall see when we examine the laboratory studies of altruistic behavior. However, this was our working hypothesis after we analyzed the interview data.

Among parental socializers of the partially committed, there was evidence of a discrepancy between what was preached and what was practiced. A number of the respondents indicated that their parents told them one thing but practiced another. These discrepancies often reflected inconsistencies in culturally stereotyped principles of conduct but, regardless of source, it was clear that the respondents had noted discrepancies and responded angrily. One respondent literally railed against his father, who had preached a stern honesty but vigorously condoned dishonesty toward members of a cultural outgroup. The respondent was startled by the vigor of his own expressed anger, remarking that he had not even thought about these incidents in more than a decade.

Although I am not yet committed to a theoretical view of the relevance of the "crisis of hypocrisy" to partial altruistic commitment, I am tempted by the following speculation: the child who is morally polarized by his socializers and is thereby angered will be severe in his judgment of his elder if—and only if—he is able to see himself as "good" and the elder as "bad" or "hypocritical" on the moral dimension in question. Avowed sinners, as we know, are quite gentle in their judgments of others; only those who believe themselves without sin can afford to throw stones. But the child, and subsequently the adult, has little basis for internalizing or believing in his moral purity; since he has been exposed to moral models who, insofar as their deeds are concerned, are ambiguous at best and repellent at worst. In order to retain his judgment of bad others, he needs to reassure himself that he is morally good. Going on a freedom ride is sufficient to that need, and having gone on one, there is no real need to engage in another. The self, as it were, is already convinced of its worthiness.

Those who grew up in an altruistic environment, on the other hand, respond to the social need for civil rights from an entirely different matrix. They have learned, by loving precept and percept, to respond easily to the needs of others. Such a response is evoked by the structure of their perceptions of the environment. This is the meaning of identification: an intense emotional experience, rich in behavioral and cognitive contents, that imprints a relatively enduring attitudinal and behavioral matrix, a matrix that proves relatively resistant to the pressures and temptations of the immediate surroundings.

In short, these data lead us to believe that the differences between the fully and the partially committed are greater than might simply appear from the behavioral differences in involvement in civil rights activity. For the partially committed, the act of participation is concomitantly an act of personal reassurance. For the fully committed, commitment is very much a matter of concern for others. The altruist in psychoanalytic literature (Coles, 1963; Fishman and Solomon, 1964; Solomon and Fishman, 1964), who is beset by one or another conflict, is probably our partially committed. Indeed, we find support for this belief in the fact that half of our partially committed respondents had spent some time in psychotherapy, while none of the fully committed had. In short, there is more to full altruistic commitment than the reduction of tension and the dynamics of guilt.

In closing this section, I cannot resist one further observation on the difference between the partially and the fully committed, this one dealing with the length of the interviews. The average interview with the partially committed was one hour longer than that with the fully committed. This difference was totally unexpected, indeed quite surprising, since the nature of the interview gave the partially committed less to say. The first section of the interview was a detailed description of the involvement. Those who had been on one or two freedom rides surely had less to tell than those whose involvement had extended over a considerable period. And indeed, this was true. However, the partially committed more than made up for their shortcoming here in the third section of the interview, which dealt with self-perception and perception of others and which rapidly drifted into a discussion of the philosophy of civil rights. Here, the partially committed were brilliant and compelling, offering insight after insight in inexhaustible profusion. The fully committed, on the other hand, had considerably less to say. It was not that they were not as bright: on the dimensions of education and verbal intelligence (the latter assessed from the interview), there were no significant differences between the groups. Rather, the fully committed came to the point directly and simply. Perhaps they had exhausted themselves during the earlier parts of the interview. It is also possible that the relationship between cognition and behavior was affected by the length of the interview: when one of them is amplified, the other may be constricted. Amplified cognition and incisive speech may have served the partially committed as a substitute for behavioral involvement, perhaps in the manner described by sensory-tonic theory (Werner and Wapner, 1952). On the other hand, having acted, the fully committed had less need to speak at great length.

THE CONSTRUCTIVE REBEL AND THE OBEDIENT LAMB:
AN EXPERIMENT ON CONSTRUCTIVE REBELLION

The field studies were designed to provide hypotheses about the nature and development of prosocial behaviors that might be further investigated under controlled laboratory conditions. For example, one observation was that exposure to prosocial models facilitated prosocial behavior in the observer—a finding that can be subjected to experimental verification.

Our first experiment[2] was concerned, in part, with the effects of disobedient models on obedience. The experimental paradigm was similar to that used by Milgram (1963) in a series of brilliant experiments that examined the extent to which people obey a legitimate authority. Milgram's basic experimental paradigm is straightforward. Two subjects come to a psychological laboratory and are told that the scientist is investigating the effects of punishment on learning. In this experiment, the punishment—electric shocks—is administered in increasingly severe doses each time the learner makes a mistake on a paired associates test. After having been fully instructed, the subjects draw straws to determine who will be the learner and who the teacher. The teacher then straps the learner to a chair, tapes the electrodes on his hands, and returns to a large and enormously impressive instrument panel, on which are clearly marked shock dosages that range from 15 to 450 volts in steps of 15 volts. Above each dosage is a lever, and the teacher's task is to press one of these levers each time the learner makes a mistake. To convince the teacher that the shock levers actually give shocks, the experimenter gives him a sample shock of 45 volts. The "learner," however, is a stooge: he only pretends to receive the shock and to feel pain.

The experiment then begins. The teacher reads a long list of paired associates to the learner. He then reads a second list in which the second element of each pair is embedded in four alternatives and requires the learner to produce the correct alternative to the first member of the pair. Each time the learner fails to answer correctly he is given a shock: first 15 volts, then 30 volts, then 45, and so on. The learner protests, at first weakly then more vigorously as the shock increases. The teacher turns to the experimenter to ask advice. The experimenter responds, "Please continue the experiment." And the experiment continues. The critical question is: At what point will the teacher refuse to continue to administer shock?

Milgram's findings were as distressing as they were unexpected: nearly 70 percent of his subjects continued to shock the learner through the entire shock series. The teachers protested vigorously to the experimenter and some of them were emotionally upset, but they nevertheless continued to participate in the experiment simply because the experimenter told them to continue.

In our experiment, four conditions were used. The first was quite similar to that used by Milgram, as described above. For the remaining three, the subject who was

[2]A more elaborate description of this study, including its rationale, method, precautions taken to ensure the welfare of the subjects, and the methods used to determine the degree of insight the subjects had into the experimental procedures, will be found in D. Rosenhan, "Obedience and rebellion: Observations on the Milgram three-party paradigm," in preparation.

subsequently to be the teacher arrived in the experimental room and was asked to wait until another subject finished "teaching." He thus could watch another subject—a model—perform in one of three ways.

The humane model. In this condition, the model teacher continued to protest but nevertheless to obey the experimenter until he had passed 210 volts and the learner's protests seemed unbearable. He then turned to the experimenter and courteously informed him that he simply could not continue the experiment because the learner was in great pain. The interchange between model and experimenter stressed the plight of the learner and resulted in the teacher's refusal to continue and his leaving the room.

The delegitimizing model. The model continued to protest but to deliver shock, as in the first condition. When he passed 210 volts, he turned to the experimenter and asked if the experimenter was a member of the faculty. The experimenter shook his head. The model then asked with some surprise if he was a graduate student. The experimenter looked away in some embarrassment. Model then asked with indignation whether the experimenter was an undergraduate. Again, no answer. Model: "Is your professor in town?" Again, no answer. "You mean you're just a college freshman and you're conducting an experiment like this? Asking me to fry someone? . . ." In evident outrage, the model refused to continue and stomped out of the room.

The obedient model. In this condition, the model protested as had the others, but unlike them, continued to administer the full 450 volts.

The results of this experiment are shown in Table 6.4. Of the subjects (as teachers) in the no-model condition, 85 percent obeyed the experimenter and administered the full complement of voltage. A similar proportion of the subjects who had observed an obedient model obeyed the experimenter. There was no significant difference between subjects who had observed either of the two disobedient models: more than 50 percent of these subjects obeyed the experimenter.

Even after observing a disobedient model, a majority of the subjects continued to obey the experimenter, despite the fact that nearly all subjects protested in the course of their effort that the shock was terribly painful, if not downright dangerous, to the learner. On a subsequent interview, the "teachers" showed that they were aware of the averseness of the procedure; almost all of them refused to participate in the experiment again, this time as learners.

While we had verified our hypothesis that observation of a prosocial model, whether humane or delegitimizing, facilitates prosocial disobedience in the observer, when one considers the painfulness of the procedure and the elaborateness of our disobedient model conditions, the effects obtained were weak indeed. Such weak effects will be found throughout the series of experiments described here, and also are found in other studies relevant to these issues (Bryan and Test, 1967; Darley and Latané, 1968). Noting that similar weak effects are found in the natural environment, the reader may want to speculate on this matter.

We tested two areas of hypotheses from the civil rights study on children. First, we examined the hypotheses about hypocrisy in a series of experiments (see Rosenhan, Frederick and Burrowes, 1968; Rosenhan and Hilmo, in preparation[3]) that I shall not discuss here. Second, we began a series of studies designed to assess what impact prior social relationships and observation of altruistic models had on the acquisition and elicitation of charitable behavior.

Table 6.4 *Obedience and disobedience according to experimental condition among subjects who believed the experiment was "real."*

Experimental Condition	Obedient	Disobedient	Total
Base rate	17 (85%)	3	20
Obedient model	15 (88%)	2	17
Prohumane model	11 (58%)	8	19
Delegitimizing model	10 (53%)	9	19
Total	53	22	75

$\chi^2 = 8.99$; $df = 3$; $.05 > p > .025$

EXPERIMENTS ON CHILDREN'S CHARITABILITY

In an early study (Rosenhan and White, 1967), we attempted to simulate positive and negative relationships with children during brief interaction periods. Establishing a positive relationship was, for that experiment, a matter of positively reinforcing a variety of the child's behaviors, while the negative relationship was established by negatively reinforcing his behaviors. The child and the adult then took turns playing with an attractive miniature bowling game. Each time the adult won, he took two gift certificates and ceremoniously reached past the child in order to contribute one of his gift certificates to the Trenton Orphans' Fund, a fund we had established for our own experimental purposes. The gift certificates were, in fact, money surrogates, redeemable at a well-known neighborhood toy and candy store (with parental signature), and used in these experiments because we wanted to be certain that the children were really giving up something prized if they decided to contribute anything to the orphans' fund. While the child played, the experimenter looked the other way, jumping up and down and pounding his hands as if waiting impatiently for his turn. This was an attempt to minimize the degree of tacit approval or disapproval that the child might feel was warranted by his donation behavior.

---

[3]D. Rosenhan and J. Hilmo, "Maintenance of an imposed behavior standard as a function of method of socialization " (in preparation).

When this game was completed, the experimenter pretended he had to leave and asked the child if he would like to play the game by himself. Each child agreed, and the experimenter told him to "lock the door so that no one bothers you" and to return to class when he had finished. It was made clear that he would not see the experimenter again. He was left alone with several hundred dollars' worth of gift certificates and allowed to play until the game's buzzer went off.

In this experiment, some of our hypotheses were put to a difficult test. Note that there was a minimal prior relationship with the experimenter. Note also that the child's donation behavior was not reinforced. And note finally that we encouraged the child to believe that he was alone when the experimenter left. The concern was with the child's internalized behavior, not with his ability to conform or comply. We were successful in the formal aspects of the experiment. Each child was interviewed after the game-playing by an experimenter (not the one with whom he had played) who was ostensibly signing up volunteers for extracurricular activities. Since one of these activities was bowling, she was able to indicate that she had heard that there had been a bowling game in the school, and to ask the children what their perceptions of it had been. Even when the interviewer encouraged the child to give expression to his experimental insights ("You mean you were left there alone with all that money and no one was watching you?"), no child realized that he had been observed, though several said that there might have been "some trick."

Our first concern was whether the observation of a charitable model elicited internalized charitability in the children. As Table 6.5 shows, this was true. None of the control children who had not observed a model contributed to the charity, while nearly half of the experimental children did. Altruistic models, even in a narrow laboratory situation, serve to facilitate altruism in children.

Our second concern turned on the question of the relationship between conformity in the model's presence and internalization in his absence. As Table 6.6 indicates, 51 of the 57 children who internalized the charitable behavior—nearly 90 percent—had conformed in the presence of the model. (This is to be considered a state phenomenon, not a trait; by statistical test, these 51 children differed also from the 10 controls.) Thus, it was both observing an altruistic model and the opportunity to corehearse with that model that elicited altruistic behavior in the child.

We felt that this finding added a new dimension and meaning to our interviews with the civil rights workers. When a respondent says, "My father carried me on his shoulders during the Sacco-Vanzetti parades," he may be describing not only an observational phenomenon but also one of rehearsal—that is, "I was with him during those parades." Similarly, respondents whose parents sought military duty in World War II may very well have vicariously experienced something of that war with the parent. Although we did not think to obtain this material explicitly during these interviews, it is just possible that on some level they corehearsed the altruistic behavior with the parent.

Table 6.5 *Altruistic responses of subjects who were or were not exposed to models.*

Response		Exposed to Model		
		Yes	No	Total
Gave in model's absence	Yes	57	0	57
	No	63	10	73
Total		120	10	130

Fisher Exact Probability = .0046

In the matter of demonstrating the effects of prior relationship with the model on altruistic behavior we were not at all successful, as Figure 6.1 indicates. No real differences were obtained between the positive and negative relationships. Some interesting sex differences in conformity and internalization seemed to emerge as a function of prior contact with the model, but in the matter that was of central concern to us—the effects of prior positive and negative relationships—there were no significant findings. Of course, this may be due to the briefness of the period of prior relationship to which the children were exposed, and we intend to examine this matter in greater detail in subsequent experiments.

Table 6.6 *Relationship between giving in the presence and in the absence of a model.*

Response		Gave in Model's Presence (conformity)						
		Yes			No			All Ss
		Boys	Girls	Total	Boys	Girls	Total	
Gave in model's absence (internalization	Yes	28	23	51	3	3	6	57
	No	9	16	25	20	18	38	63
Total		37	39	76	23	21	44	120

χ^2 (corrected for continuity) = 29.84; df = 1; $p < .001$

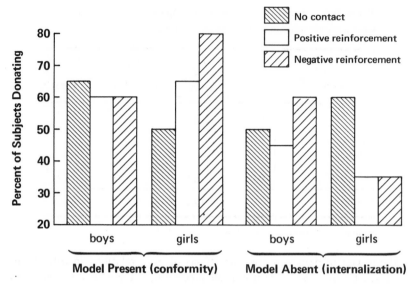

Figure 6.1   *Conformity and internalization as a function of prior relationship with the model (from Rosenhan and White, 1967).*

OBSERVATION, REHEARSAL, OR BOTH?

As a result of this experiment, we became interested in understanding more about the nature of the observation-rehearsal sequence and its effect on internalization. If you look carefully again at Table 6.5, you will notice that nearly 90 percent of the children who donated in the absence of the model, donated also in his presence. This finding raises an interesting question: Was it the observation of the model that was most influential for the subsequent internalization, or was it the rehearsal? Or was it the combination? This experiment could not possibly answer these questions, since observation and rehearsal were purposely confounded. The next experiment, however, performed by Glenn White (1967), seemed a first step towards understanding this matter.

Three experimental treatments were employed. In the first, called *enforced rehearsal*, the child was required to contribute to the charity in the presence of the experimenter without, however, having observed a model do so. This situation was designed to assess the impact of giving in the presence of an adult (rehearsal) on subsequent internalization. The second condition was identical to the one we examined earlier in the section, *observation and voluntary rehearsal*. The third condition examined the effects of observation alone. In it, the child observed a model play the game and donate to the charity, but did not play or rehearse in the presence of the model. In a third situation, a control condition was imposed. The child was simply asked to play the game, and, if he wanted to, to contribute to the orphans. As in the earlier experiment, the experimenter or model departed after describing the treatment and the children played the game again while alone.

We had no doubt that the enforced rehearsal condition would have the greatest immediate impact on the child's private behavior because any instructional condition gives a child a fixed structure within which to play the game. But we expected that a second exposure to the game would loosen the structure considerably and that children in this condition would be more variable after a few days had elapsed than they had been immediately after training. The experiment therefore was designed in such a way that children in all of the experimental conditions could play twice: once immediately after they had been trained, and again several days later.

As Figure 6.2 indicates, we were not disappointed. When children in the enforced rehearsal condition were tested immediately after training (Session 1), they contributed an enormous amount to the Trenton Orphans' Fund, much more than did children in the other conditions. However, when tested again several days later, their performance fell considerably: to or below the level of performance provided by children in the observation and voluntary rehearsal condition. Similar findings resulted when we examined the *number* of children who internalized (as opposed to the average amount they gave) in the first and second sessions (Figure 6.3). While most of the enforced rehearsal children gave in the first session, slightly more than half gave during the second session. Their performance was clearly less stable than those in the observation and voluntary rehearsal condition.

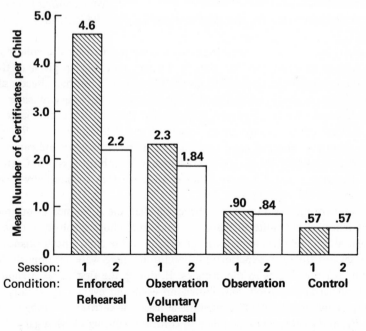

Figure 6.2 *Mean number of certificates contributed according to experimental treatment and session (modified from White, 1967).*

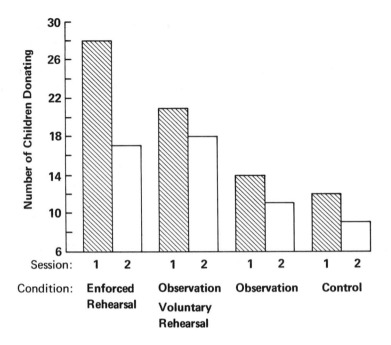

Figure 6.3   *Number of children who contributed according to experimental treatment and session (modified from White, 1967).*

One might argue that the variable behavior demonstrated by the children in the enforced rehearsal condition was due to the fact that, having given in the first session, they experienced no need to give in the second. They had already satisfied their obligation, whereas children in the observation and voluntary rehearsal simply had not. Internal analyses, however, indicate that this position is untenable. Correlations between contributions during Sessions 1 and 2 for subjects in the observation and voluntary rehearsal condition was .67. Further analyses indicate that this figure was not inflated by the number of nongivers in both sessions. Correlations between Sessions 1 and 2 for the other conditions were substantially lower (enforced rehearsal, .38; observation, .40).

We have two further reasons for believing that the dynamics associated with enforced rehearsal are quite different in kind from those involved in observation and rehearsal. The first has to do with the rigidity of the child's performance during the first session. In each experimental condition, there were six opportunities to contribute gift certificates to the orphans. If, during the first game, a child in the enforced rehearsal condition contributed on each and every opportunity, it was extremely likely that he would contribute at least one certificate during the second session. If, on the other hand, he failed to contribute during the first game on *every* trial, it was extremely *unlikely* that he would contribute at all during the second session. In short, if the child had broken the rule at all during the first game, he broke it with impunity during the second. Such rigidity did not mark children in the observation and voluntary rehearsal conditions. Although they observed a model donate on every trial, they commonly did not give on every trial during the first game. However, such rule flexibility did not eliminate giving during the second game.

The second reason is related to stealing behavior during the experiment. You will recall that, during the internalization trials, the children were left alone with several hundred dollars' worth of gift certificates, strewn about the table in such a way that it was clear no one would miss a few if they were taken. Stealing was, thus, a salient alternative to giving. As might be expected from the rigidity argument, children in the enforced rehearsal condition did not steal at all—during the first session. During the second session, however, 25 percent of them stole. Compare this to stealing among the children exposed to observation and voluntary rehearsal, where less than 5 percent stole in either session. We hold, therefore, that effects of enforced rehearsal on charitability during the first session were marked because the instructions established rigid rules for the task. But they are not enduring because, as subjects begin to test the rules and fail to suffer consequences, they make up more convenient rules. For children in the observation and voluntary contribution conditions the central focus is on the orphans' fund and on their freedom to give or not to give to the orphans. For these children the structure is considerably less rigid: such rules as exist are voluntary and reasonable, and attention is more easily centered on the plight of the orphans. Consequently, greater consistency and less cheating is found. Similar findings in the context of adult helpfulness have been reported by Horowitz (1968).

All of this, of course, is speculative, but the reader may be interested in one further bit of evidence that is consistent with this formulation. Three weeks after a subsequent experiment that involved some of these conditions and several new ones, a new experimenter presented herself to the children in each class and thanked them for their help in testing the bowling game. It so happened, she said, that there were still quite a few gift certificates left, and she wanted to give each of the children some additional gift certificates in appreciation of their assistance. She did this, and then mentioned that there was another envelope in the envelope that contained the gift certificates. This envelope contained empty contribution envelopes. If any child so desired, he could put some of his gift certificates in this unmarked envelope and contribute them to charity. For approximately half of the children, the charity was the Trenton Orphans' Fund, while the remaining children were permitted to contribute to UNICEF. Contributions were relatively anonymous, since the contribution envelopes were unmarked and the children left their donations in a basket as they were leaving class.

We had, of course, recorded the gift certificate numbers and could trace the contributions to the donors. It soon became clear that children in the enforced rehearsal condition gave less, and generalized in voluntary giving to UNICEF less than did children in the observation and voluntary rehearsal conditions. This is precisely what we expected. For children in the enforced rehearsal conditions, donating was rigidly associated with the game context, so they gave considerably less outside of that context.

COGNITIVE DEVELOPMENT AND
CONCERN FOR OTHERS

Observation of an altruistic model the child liked and voluntary corehearsal with this model may be necessary to the promotion of altruism in the observer (the child in these experiments) but, according to our current thinking, they are by no means sufficient. Also necessary is a well-prepared *cognitive-affective* matrix in the observer.

There is abundant evidence that norms of social responsibility (Berkowitz, 1968; Berkowitz and Connor, 1966; Berkowitz and Daniels, 1963, 1964; Daniels and Berkowitz, 1963; Goranson and Berkowitz, 1966) and reciprocity (Gouldner, 1960) are necessary in the performance of altruistic acts. The bases for these norms presumably lie in the altruist's capacity to relinquish his personal perspectives and to perceive and experience the universe from the perspective of another—in this instance, a person in need. To the extent that this capacity is developed, we hold, is the observation of an altruistic model meaningfully internalized.

The results of experiments with children appear to be consistent with this view. Six-year-old children are still relatively egocentric, unable to take easily the role of another (Piaget, 1926; Flavell, 1966). Also, as Figure 6.4 indicates, fewer six-year-olds than older children (who have observed a model contribute to charity and have had the opportunity to corehearse with him) contribute to the Trenton Orphans' Fund when alone. The lower incidence of contributions among six-year-olds is clearly *not* a matter of their failure to *acquire* the necessary behaviors from the model, since the behaviors involved are neither mentally nor physically complex. Rather we would urge that young children's feelings for others and their capacity to understand the needs of others are relatively muted compared to their capacity to experience their own desires for as many rewards as they can earn. Because the

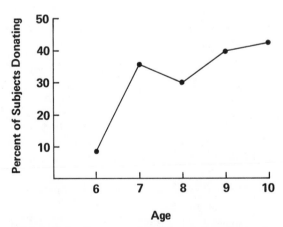

Figure 6.4 *Percent of children who observed a model contribute and who subsequently internalized, by age.*

behavior of the model is only vaguely relevant to their own understandings, they do not implement it when alone.

If this is the case, then an experimental treatment that heightens momentarily the neediness of others should also increase the incidence of donors among young children. That this is true is seen in Figure 6.5. The model elaborates on the needs of orphans ("They don't have parents . . . no one to buy them toys or candy or even shoes or clothing . . . And when you and I have Christmas they just won't have any because there's no one to care for them . . . If you want to give some of your pennies to the orphans you can, but you don't have to."). Because the model then makes a donation, many six-year-old children internalize his behaviors and contribute in his absence. Their number remains far below the number of contributing eleven-year-olds, since for the latter the model's elaboration mobilizes elements of a cognitive-affective structure that is already well-formed and quite salient.

SUMMARY

We have made some headway in dealing with the problem posed in the first pages of this paper. Some forms of altruism, particularly that of the partially committed, seem clearly compatible with the descriptions emerging from psychoanalytic literature. Others do not. Nor do these others fit the reward-seeking, punishment-avoiding conceptions of man that arise from experimental psychology. As further evidence is accumulated, the match and fit between these theories and particular kinds of altruistic behavior should become clearer.

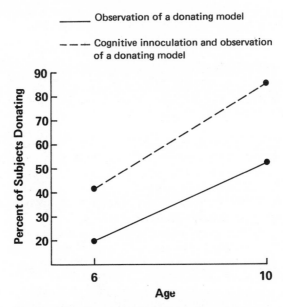

Figure 6.5 *Percent of children who observed a model contribute and who subsequently internalized, by age and experimental treatment.*

We know from these studies that observation of a positively regarded altruistic model facilitates altruism in some observers. Moreover, voluntary rehearsal of altruistic behavior with the model greatly increases the likelihood that altruism will be internalized in the observer. Finally, we speculate that certain cognitive and affective structures must be relatively well-formed if the model's altruistic behavior is to result in altruism on the part of the observer.

When a child observes a model's performance, it is by no means automatic that he will imitate the performance. Even experimenters who utilize "salient" models [models who engage in a variety of "outlandish" tactics designed to capture the observer's attention (Bandura and Walters, 1963)] find that some children do not imitate the demonstrated behavior. One can imagine some children saying "That looks like fun, I think I'll try it," and others saying "What a silly thing to do. Not me!" The model's behavior is cognitively processed, and whether or not the child imitates it depends on the linkages that exist between the observed behavior and other structures in the knowledge assembly—the cognitive and affective components that are organized around a particular dimension. With regard to the altruism dimension, we speculate that among the elements in such an assembly are abilities: to experience the role of a needy other; to share a social responsibility norm; and to experience joy because the receiver will be happy (Aronfreed and Paskal, 1965; Midlarsky and Bryan, 1967). When these elements are present, an altruistic model's behavior is easily incorporated and integrated. Conversely, when they are either absent or muted, or when a nonaltruistic knowledge assembly is salient ("Why should I help orphans. I want all I can get."), observation of an altruistic model is not likely to give rise to internalized altruism.

REFERENCES

Allport, G. W. The open system in personality theory. *Journal of Abnormal and Social Psychology,* 1960, **61**, 301–310.

Aronfreed, J., & Paskal, V. Altruism, empathy, and the conditioning of positive affect. Unpublished manuscript, University of Pennsylvania, 1965.

Bandura, A., & Walters, R. H. *Social learning and personality development.* New York: Holt, Rinehart & Winston, 1963.

Berkowitz, L. Responsibility, reciprocity, and social distance in help-giving: An experimental investigation of English social class differences. *Journal of Experimental Social Psychology,* 1968, **4**, 46–63.

Berkowitz, L., & Connor, W. H. Success, failure and social responsibility. *Journal of Personality and Social Psychology,* 1966. **4**, 664–669.

Berkowitz, L., & Daniels, L. R. Responsibility and dependency. *Journal of Abnormal and Social Psychology,* 1963, **66**, 427–436.

Berkowitz, L., & Daniels, L. R. Affecting the salience of the social responsibility norm. *Journal of Abnormal and Social Psychology,* 1964, **68**, 302–306.

Bryan, J. H., & Test, M. A. Models and helping: Naturalistic studies in aiding behavior. *Journal of Personality and Social Psychology,* 1967, **6**, 400–407.

Coles, R. Serpents and doves: Non-violent youth in the South. E. Erikson (Ed.), *The challenge of youth.* New York: Basic Books, 1967.

Daniels, L. R., & Berkowitz, L. Liking and response to dependency relations. *Human Relations,* 1963, **16**, 141–148.

Darley, J. M., & Latané, B. Bystander intervention in emergencies: Diffusion of responsibility. *Journal of Personality and Social Psychology*, 1968, 8, 377–383.

Fenichel, O. *The psychoanalytic theory of neurosis.* New York: Norton, 1945.

Fishman, J. R., & Solomon, F. Youth and social action. *The Journal of Social Issues*, 1964, 20, 1–28.

Flavell, J. H. Role-taking and communication skills in children. *Young Children*, 1966, 21, 164–177.

Freud, A. *The ego and the mechanisms of defense.* London: Hogarth, 1937.

Glover, E. Notes on oral character formation. *International Journal of Psychoanalysis*, 1925, 6, 131–154.

Goranson, R. E., & Berkowitz, L. Reciprocity and responsibility reactions to prior help. *Journal of Personality and Social Psychology*, 1966, 3, 227–332.

Gouldner, A. W. The norm of reciprocity: A preliminary statement. *American Sociological Review*, 1960, 25, 161–178.

Hebb, D. O., & Thompson, W. R. The social significance of animal studies. G. Lindzey (Ed.), *Handbook of social psychology, Vol. I.* Cambridge, Mass.: Addison-Wesley, 1954, 532–561.

Horowitz, I. A. Effect of choice and locus of dependence on helping behavior. *Journal of Personality and Social Psychology*, 1968, 8, 373–376.

Lorenz, K. *King Solomon's ring.* London: Methuen, 1952.

Midlarsky, E., & Bryan, J. H. Training charity in children. *Journal of Personality and Social Psychology*, 1967, 5, 408–415.

Milgram, S. Behavioral study of obedience. *Journal of Abnormal and Social Psychology*, 1963, 67, 371–378.

Mowrer, O. H. *Learning theory and behavior.* New York: John Wiley, 1960.

Piaget, J. *The language and thought of the child.* New York: Harcourt, Brace, 1926.

Rosenhan, D., Frederick, F., & Burrowes, A. Preaching and practicing: Effects of channel discrepancy on norm internalization. *Child Development*, 1968, **39**, 291–302.

Rosenhan, D., & White, G. M. Observation and rehearsal as determinants of prosocial behavior. *Journal of Personality and Social Psychology*, 1967, 5, 424–431.

Rosenhan, D., & Hilmo, J. Maintenance of an imposed behavior standard as a function of method of socialization. In preparation.

Solomon, F., & Fishman, J. R. Youth and peace: A psycho-social study of student peace demonstrators in Washington, D.C. *The Journal of Social Issues*, 1964, 20, 54–73.

Werner, H., & Wapner, S. Toward a general theory of perception. *Psychological Review*, 1952, 59, 324–338.

White, G. M. The elicitation and durability of altruistic behavior in children. Unpublished doctoral dissertation, Princeton University, 1967.

7

A MODEL FOR THE UNDERSTANDING OF
SCHOOL AS A SOCIALIZING AGENT

No one would deny—from personal experience or from observation of children growing up—that both home and school have a profound influence on the development of children: on their adjustment to others, their attitudes, values, and aspirations, their self-images, their problem-solving abilities, skills, and knowledge, their success at school and later as adults. However, no one looking at the socialization literature by psychologists, particularly that published in America,[2] would realize that this is the case; only one member of this partnership—the home—is studied in depth and, consequently, given overriding importance.

Two main groups have been responsible for this trend: Freud and Piaget with their emphasis on undeniably important early learning experiences, and the sociologists who have focused attention on the different value systems held and child-rearing techniques practiced by families differentially located in the social hierarchy. Studies of the authoritarian family, of delinquency, neuroticism, and schizophrenia, and the work of Symonds (1946), Sears (1957), Maccoby (1960), Bronfenbrenner (1965), Mussen (1963), and others, have all shown that we appreciate the parents in their setting and view them historically as the results of their own upbringing and of the lives they lead, if we are to understand the values, attitudes, aspirations, and behavior they encourage in their children and the processes by which they do this.

Kohn's work (1959) provides an excellent example in point. He showed that the working classes' emphasis on respect, order, and obedience, and the middle classes'

[1] The longitudinal study was financed by the Science Research Council and the development of the model of the school by a grant from the Department of Education and Science. The authors would like to express their gratitude for the help received.
[2] Outstanding exceptions are the writings of Erikson (1952) and Friedenberg (1956).

154

HILDE T. HIMMELWEIT AND BETTY SWIFT

London School of Economics and Political Science, London, England

emphasis on understanding, ability to empathize, decision-making, and long-term planning ability, make sense if we recognize that families in both classes seek to develop in their children those skills that they see as necessary for effective adjustment to adult life as they know it.

In all these studies, and perhaps best illustrated by looking at the type of data collected by two major American longitudinal studies [those of the Fels Research Institute (Kagan and Moss, 1962) and the Institute of Human Development, Berkeley (Macfarlane, 1938)], the family—particularly as represented by the parents—is studied as the major socializing agent. Because the parents do indeed affect outlook and behavior, interest is focused on the how and why.

Taking the same longitudinal studies, let us now consider how the other partner in the task of educating and socializing is treated. Few measures have been developed for understanding how, why, and with what effect the school seeks to influence behavior and outlook. The tendency appears to be toward collection of measures of the child's liking for and adjustment to school, his examination records, leaving age, and ratings of his behavior by peers and teachers. Moreover, these measures are used essentially as dependent measures to be related to the child's emotional, social, or intellectual ability. Where performance deviates from that expected, explanation is often sought in terms of deficits in parent-child interaction or learning opportunities, or of misfit between values taught at home and at school. Little consideration is given to the contribution that the school makes by *its* values, *its* learning opportunities, and teacher-child relationship—school is not seen as an *active* socializing agent exerting an effect independent of that of the home. To our knowledge, there are no studies of teacher-child teaching comparable to the laboratory studies that Hess and Shipman (1967) carried out on the way mothers teach their children, or those of Bernstein and Henderson (1969) on teaching different language communication patterns. The fact that the schools often do not succeed in what Hess calls "resocialization" simply means that the school, by virtue of its history and outlook, has failed to adjust to the diversity of needs of its pupils in much the same way as an authoritarian parent fails because he does not adjust his mode of upbringing to the needs of his children. The importance of the school as a socializing agent, and similarly that of the home, cannot be denied by the citing of particularistic examples of failure to achieve a desired effect.

It is worth emphasizing that the school's explicit function—a function assigned to it by society and underwritten by parents—is to socialize the child, that is, to affect his behavior and outlook, and that for this task the school has as much contact, if not more, with the child during ten crucial years as do the parents.

This makes it all the more surprising that psychologists neglect to consider seriously school as an active socializing agent. One of the reasons for neglect in the United States may lie in the fact that the American education system is comprehensive and unified: the children all proceed from primary to secondary schools where any separation of children into different grades or preparatory courses is a minor division within a unified whole. Therefore, when attempts are made to account for differences in pupil performance, attention is focused on factors outside the apparently shared school environment. Outstanding exceptions to this approach are the studies by Coleman (1966), Yates (1966), Turner (1961), and Pace (1963), which draw attention to relevant features in the school itself.

In England and on the Continent it is more difficult to ignore the school as an independent socializing force. This part of the world has divided secondary school systems in which, at the age of eleven in England and at ages ten, eleven, and twelve in other countries, children are separated into different types of secondary schools. In England, 90 percent of children attend state schools. Of these, approximately the top 20 percent are *selected* on the basis of intelligence and performance tests and teacher reports, to fill available grammar school places. With minor exceptions (those who go to technical schools or to the more recently instituted comprehensive schools), the remainder are *placed* into secondary modern schools. Input policy, teacher and pupil composition of the schools, curricula, and objectives of these two principal types of secondary state school differ considerably. Indeed, it is no exaggeration to say that the school to which a child is allocated influences far more his life chances than do his ability, social background, motivational states, or personality predispositions.

Because the English educational system forces recognition of the fact that school is an active socializing agent, two longitudinal studies carried out in this country have been concerned with both school and home. One of these, carried out by Douglas (1964, 1968), was based on a large, representative sample of children studied from birth to age twenty-one and showed that very good schools may offset the deficits derived from home, provided these are not extreme, and that very bad schools produce negative effects of varying severity. (The most negative effects were noted for children of moderate ability from lower working class backgrounds).

DESCRIPTION OF THE LONGITUDINAL STUDY

The second longitudinal study is the one to be discussed in this article. In 1952, we studied 600 thirteen- to fourteen-year-old middle and working class adolescent boys who were then reinterviewed 11 years later at age twenty-five, when they had completed their education and settled into a job (Himmelweit, 1964, 1966).

Our study was designed explicitly to examine the interplay of home and school, to determine how applicable to England were American theories of social class differences in upbringing, such as that of Davis and Havighurst (1946), and to what extent such differences would be modified or transformed by our divided secondary school system with its inbuilt, sponsored mobility.[3]

To explore this interaction, we needed a population that would permit us to study the effect of *different schools* on children from comparable social backgrounds and the effect of the *same school* on children of different backgrounds and/or ability levels. We therefore tested the entire intake of the third forms of four grammar and five secondary modern schools in the Greater London area. A secondary modern and a grammar school were selected from each of three types of neighborhoods: a primarily working class, a mixed, and a primarily middle class neighborhood. For each child we obtained measures of his anxieties, self-image, involvement in school, relation to peers and teachers, school performance, educational and job aspirations, attitude to his family and perception of their attitude to him, and his attitude toward a range of social issues. In addition we obtained personality measures (including a measure of authoritarianism), sociometric ratings, details of social background, intelligence tests results at age eleven and, from the teachers, ratings of each child's performance and behavior in class.

The results of the study were clear and pointed to the dominant influence of the school. Information about the type of school a child attends enables better prediction of his behavior, outlook, values and attainments than does information about his I.Q. or his family's social background.

We were able to assess the long-term effects of school when we reinterviewed 75% (463) of the boys eleven years later. We traced with them their educational and occupational histories and asked them about their adjustment to work, their aspirations, goals, and values, and their attitudes toward a variety of social issues (including some inquired about at the adolescent stage). In addition, we obtained measures of neuroticism and of the individual's self-image, together with an account of his relations with his parents as an adult and his recollections about his adolescent attitudes toward them.

Analysis of the adult data confirmed the findings obtained in adolescence— namely that school rather than home affected the individual's subsequent occupational history, job level, and aspirations. Moreover, his evaluation of his own career

---

[3]The term "inbuilt, sponsored mobility," coined by Turner (1961), denotes that a working class boy becomes potentially upwardly mobile as the result of a grammar school education, as this opens the way for middle class occupation and for entry into higher education, while a secondary modern school pupil from a middle class background becomes potentially downwardly mobile since the majority of secondary modern school pupils go into manual work.

achievements was determined far more by reference to the achievements of his classmates than to those of his family. Thus, a grammar school boy saw being a clerk as a failure or nonsuccess while a secondary school boy in such a position felt that he had done well; these judgments were made with almost total disregard for whether, in terms of his own family, being a clerk would constitute upward or downward social mobility (Heckhausen, 1967).

THE SCHOOL AS A SOCIALIZING AGENT

To provide a context for assessment of the relative strengths of influences from home and school, we developed a general model of socialization in which we made school the central feature: we made school the independent variable and treated the other socializing forces as mediating forces. In a study that emphasized *different* outcomes of the socializing process, the family could be made the focus of attention and school regarded as one of the mediating variables. Such an approach might well provide an understanding of the types of changes over time in child-rearing practices, such as those reported by Bronfenbrenner (1958).

Our model was designed to chart and order relevant variables and to set up hypotheses concerning the focus of their influence and the links between them. Demonstration of the full usefulness of the model would require another study in which the sampling of environments and children and the collection of data were specifically geared to the purpose. Although the model was developed with reference to the English educational system, it has general applicability and could be particularly useful for cross-cultural comparisons, such as those carried out by the International Project for the Evaluation of Educational Achievements (Husan, 1967). In the IPEEA project, variations in educational attainment were explained in terms of the differences in the social and family structures and the school systems of the countries concerned.

The model, as presented in Figure 7.1, shows the child progressing through the school system. It lists two types of agents: those that affect the pupil directly—his parents, the school he attends—and those that affect him indirectly by influencing the objectives and resources of the direct agents. The major indirect agent is society itself, which affects the goals of the parents, defines the objectives of the school, and often sets down the methods the school may employ and the conditions under which it may operate. Arrows have been used to indicate the direction of the influence. In some cases there is a two-way effect. This effect is indicated in the figure by arrows that point in both directions; the darker arrows represent the direction of major influence, and the broken arrows indicate a relatively weak influence.

Interaction Effects

The child at any one time is subject to varied pressures, conflicting or reinforcing, from peer groups, family and school. The extent to which he is influenced by school depends on:

1. The extent to which the school's values are consistent, coherent and inclusive.

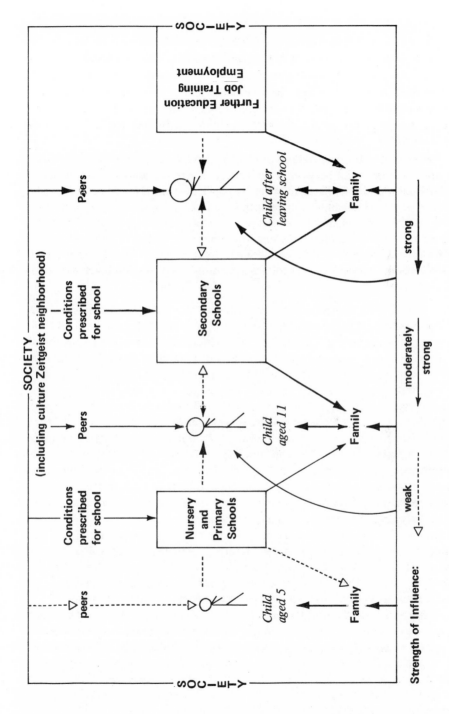

Figure 7.1 *A model for the socialization process, with special reference to the secondary school.*

2. The extent to which the school's values and ideology conflict with or are reinforced by other values to which he is, or has been, exposed.

3. The kind of rewards, both long-term and short-term, that the school can offer the pupil in return for his acceptance of its values and norms.

4. The kind of sanctions that the school can use, or threaten to use, for noncompliance with its rules and for non-acceptance of its objectives. For example, can it expel a child, or withhold a good school report when a pupil applies for a job or for university admission?

5. The kind of status (well defined or ill-defined, relevant to the school's objectives or irrelevant) the child has within the school. Where the school structure makes available clearly differentiated roles for its pupils they are involved *actively* in the working of the school and are more open to the values it wishes to inculcate. Thus, both the child who achieves or is assigned a "success" status (for example, membership of an "elite" stream) and the one who occupies a "failure" status are likely to be strongly influenced, so that they accept or react against its values. Where a pupil is less actively engaged by the roles he plays at school, its influence on him is relatively weak.

Each of the features listed above characterizes the competing socializing agents of family and peer group, as well as school. Thus, the family can be assessed in terms of the coherence of its ideology, the extent to which its values are supported by those of other socializing agents, the kinds of rewards it offers, the sanctions it can use, and the extent to which the roles it offers engage the child.

Socialization outcomes for the child depend on the relative strength of the "competing" agents and on complex interaction between the forces they bring to bear. Thus, parental encouragement may help a child to overcome the effects of early failure so that he persists at school and does well. Nursery school may provide for a child from a deprived home an enriching experience and affect his later school performance, yet not significantly aid a child from a "good" home. Peer group norms may negate pressures to stay on at school from both home and school. Later in the paper, we give examples from our study of more complex patterns of interaction between influences from parents, peers, and school.

The model is an oversimplification. School is not a separate entity, or one that influences only the children who pass through it. Parents can affect its goals, and can be affected by school through their children. Further, the goals defined for the school by society are interpreted by individuals, by teachers and pupils, so that each school has a unique style of functioning and thus of affecting its pupils.

Finally, it is quite clear that no one part of the educational system can be studied in isolation. Changes in any institution have profound effects on those that precede it and on those that follow. The primary school, for instance, in its policy, curriculum, and structure, is affected by the form and content of the eleven plus examination which is used for allocating pupils to different types of secondary school. Similarly, the secondary school is affected by the requirements and demands of universities and other institutions of further education.

Inputs and Outcomes

The term "input" refers to those characteristics that the pupil brings to the school, including age, sex, knowledge, and skills, as well as cognitive style, curiosity, interpersonal skills, personality predispositions, motivations, attitudes, and values. The child's intellectual potentiality, emotionality, and reactivity are highly relevant input variables since they set limits for the achievement of given objectives.

"Outcomes," as referred to in this article, apply only to the individual, and do not include outcomes for the social system (Bowman, 1967), or for the economy (such as those resulting from failing to provide an adequate number of adults with requisite mathematical skills), or for the university which must accommodate to the way the schools have prepared entrants.

Outcomes must be clearly distinguished from objectives; the latter can be ascertained either by asking those who operate the system what their objectives are or by inferring the objectives from a study of the manner in which the system allocates its resources and the types of behavior that it rewards or punishes. These objectives—precise or vague, salient or nonsalient, direct or indirect—should be related to a measurable outcome characteristic. For example, if one of the objectives of a grammar school is retention of a large number of pupils to do A-level work, the extent to which the objective has been realized should be ascertained by determining the proportion of pupils who stay. Once this is known, further questions must be asked: To what extent can this particular objective be regarded as having a successful outcome? What has been its cost to the system and its members (the ones who stayed or left and their teachers)? Did its achievement justify the cost?

Some of the outcomes will be intended and will have been made explicit—as in the case of examinations; others will be more nebulous—such as learning to behave like a good citizen—and may have been conveyed either directly ("one does not behave this way") or indirectly through the role models provided in the school.

Some outcomes are desirable, others undesirable. Some of the latter may be a by-product of a strategy aimed at an explicit, apparently desirable objective. As we shall see later, the division of an age group into hierarchically ordered classes (streams) usually results in higher motivation and better performance on the part of those students selected for the top stream. However, this benefit is achieved at the cost of conveying (perhaps unwittingly) to students not selected the information that they are failures or at least not successes. This, we find, leads to a lowering of morale and performance.

Outcomes relate to all levels of the individual's functioning. Some of these are obvious and easily measured. Others, though less tangible, are no less important and need to be considered as an investigator orients himself to the problem. Further, outcomes are often interrelated. For example, the successful attainment of one objective, such as the passing of an examination, is likely to have consequences for self-image and attitudes and so bring other outcomes in its train.

Outcomes include acquisition of knowledge and skills, and the development of a cognitive style—ability to absorb, store, and organize new information, to form abstract concepts, to use language effectively as a tool for thought and communication. Outcomes also may be measured in terms of aspirations, attitudes, values, norms, self-image, and skill in interpersonal relationships. They may be attainment qualifications giving access to new experiences, for example, to those experiences available at university. It should be stressed here that, since a different type of experience results from failure to qualify, such experience of failure should also be seen as an important outcome.

Socializing Agents Outside the School System

Family, peers, and his home neighborhood are all socializing agents that affect the individual's outlook and behavior and interpret for him many of the school's attempts to socialize. In fact, these agents play a triple role because they are themselves influenced by what happens to the child and may attempt to influence the school system. For example, when parents find that their children are disturbed by certain school selection procedures, they may seek to influence the school to adopt different approaches. In addition, if many parents experience the same reactions, they may (with or without the help of teachers) enlist the assistance of influential individuals or institutions (political leaders, the medical profession, mass media) to change or at least alleviate the requirements that society makes on the school.

In Figure 7.1 the culture of "Zeitgeist" has been assigned a somewhat elevated position, with arrows leading from it to all directions. It represents the values, norms, fashions, roles, conduct, and communication patterns current in that society. Culture might be subdivided into generation cultures, the culture of the country, and world culture. Individuals, in their turn, affect the culture but with an impact far weaker than culture's impact on the individual. Culture can exert a dominant impact, particularly at times such as adolescence when the individual seeks for identity through models away from home and school (Erikson, 1952).

Because of the very important ways in which society, the economy, the government, and other agents set limiting conditions for the school and help to define its objectives, a separate description of these will be given.

The Educational System

Children's reactions to school are influenced not only by the learning modes and general motivation that they bring to school (for which the primary influence will have been the family) but also by the different ideas they have developed about school. What parents and perhaps siblings have told them about the purpose of school and what the teachers expect of them defines school for the child, creating a mental set that influences initial behavior and serves as a filter for experiences. Hess showed, for instance, that middle and working class mothers define school and its role in relation to the child quite differently for their respective children.

This influence of parental interest, assistance, and interpretation persists throughout the child's school career. The influence the parents continue to exert is by instruction, example, cognitive style, values, and interpersonal skills already taught, and also by the provision of further socializing experiences that may help or hinder the child's response to school. Douglas showed the strength of such impact as partially dependent on the quality of the school.

In our model, we treated the educational system in three phases: (a) education received prior to entry into secondary school—nursery and primary schools; (b) secondary school; and (c) further education, industrial training, or employment obtained after leaving secondary school.

Each of these institutions operates as a socializing agent in its own right. Each has demands put on it by society. Each school defines its objectives within the limits set by society. The types of methods it adopts depend on the teaching staff's outlook, their belief regarding the fit between given teaching methods and phases of child development, their perception (which is more important than the facts) of the values and potential the child brings to the school, and on the support the parents will give the school. The school's strategies are determined by its resources (intake characteristics, number and quality of teachers, degree of support for its objectives from the neighborhood) and are evidenced by organizational features—whether all subjects are taught by the same teacher, whether the teachers stream their students, impose homework, concern themselves with extracurricular activities, the curriculum priorities they select, and the methods of discipline they adopt.

Nursery and primary schools. The role of nursery school is to accustom the child to being away from home and to help him develop behavior and motivation appropriate for the tasks demanded of the pupils in primary school; the primary school's task consists of teaching basic skills and in preparing pupils for the critical examination that decides their secondary school assignments.

Outcomes of the primary school are often measured in terms of the number of pupils who gain entrance to grammar school. However, the success of these schools should be assessed in much broader terms, in particular, by how far they have helped to develop the potentialities the child brought to the school.

The secondary school. The organizational features, strategies, and methods of the secondary school system reflect considerations similar to those of the early education institutions as it seeks to meet the objectives—as it interprets them—set by society.

One major difference must be emphasized: pupils in primary schools comprise the entire intake from one neighborhood, but pupils enter their assigned secondary schools bearing badges of success or failure. They have passed through a critical selection point, having been *selected* for a grammar school or *placed* in a secondary modern school.

Further education, industrial training, or employment. The final phase in our model relates to transition either to further education, to industrial training, or to employment.

We cannot fully understand the role of the secondary school as a socializing agent without relating it to the other parts of the educational system in which it functions in an interesting mid-position: it is affected by the way schools for the younger age groups socialize and also by the demands made on the school's output by subsequent educational and industrial institutions.

Our data show clearly that, to understand the impact of the school on the individual, we need to consider the school systems in juxtaposition to one another and also in terms of the conditions and demands that society imposes on them (Himmelweit and Wright, 1969).

Conditions Set by Society that Affect the School

Factors outside the school—historical, ideological, and economic—help to shape the school's structure, objectives, and techniques, and affect its maneuverability[4] and the probability of effective outcome. These factors are set out below under four broad headings.

The Basic Educational System

1. The importance attached to educational qualifications as a prerequisite for entry into particular occupations or educational institutions.
2. The extent to which the educational institutions are linked—primary school as a preparation for secondary school, secondary school as a preparation for further education.
3. The degree of insistence on comparative, external standards of selection procedures for (a) admission to secondary school and (b) admission to further education.
4. The use of school examination results as the sole criterion for judging suitability for further education; if other attainments are taken into account, the importance of school examinations is reduced; and if other institutions prepare pupils for equivalent examinations, the importance of particular school attendance is reduced.
5. Adequacy of provision of schools of different types designed to deal with the diverse needs of pupils, and the status assigned to these different types of schools.
6. Adequacy of provision of places in schools to meet the demand at various stages on the educational ladder. Entry can be *candidate-* or *institution-centered*. Where candidate-centered, all those suitable can go on; when institution-centered, assessment is competitive, aimed at selecting the best because there are not enough places for all.

Resources

1. Supply of teachers, which depends on the status and conditions offered.
2. Caliber of teachers, which is related to the nature and availability of training.
3. Building and equipment resources.
4. Access to technical advances in teaching methods (computer-based teaching, programmed learning).

Ideology and Tradition

Ideology and tradition have significance for educational priorities because they help define the permissible, the desirable, and the feasible.

---

[4]By "maneuverability" we mean the school's capacity to change in response to input and other pressures, and its freedom to adopt strategies appropriate for desired outcomes.

1. Traditional view of requirements of different educational institutions in terms of the ability levels of their members.

2. Concept of child care: the school's demands must not be damaging to the child's mental and physical health.

3. Strength of demand for equal opportunity for all.

4. Acceptance of responsibility for education of the underprivileged.

5. Acceptance of research that shifts emphasis from the view of given intellectual potential to one emphasizing the importance of environmental influences as releasers or inhibitors.

6. Inertia regarding change (a general predisposition toward the status quo).

7. Parent's comprehension and support of school's aims. Constraints are imposed where these apply to one social group only (Parsons and Bales, 1955).

8. Philosophy of education: emphasis on self-discovery versus directed methods of teaching; restrictions of the child's work to the school premises versus extending it outside (homework, museum visits); views on the educational potential of given types of pupils (Sealy and Himmelweit, 1966).

Legal and Other Institutional Factors

1. Legal minimum school-leaving age in relation to the age at which important examinations are given. (The grammar school has a problem of retention because pupils must stay beyond the legal minimum age in order to take A-level examinations: its population changes from a captive to a voluntary one.)

2. Sphere of influence of school relative to that of other social institutions, such as juvenile courts and child guidance services.

3. Variety of types of school provided by the state.

Influence of Other Educational Institutions

1. Influences of the range of methods adopted by other schools of the same type, their objectives, and success rates.

2. Reappraisals necessary after introduction of a new type of school, such as comprehensive schools.

3. Methods of teaching in primary schools on which the secondary schools draw.

4. Provision for further education in the local area and in the country.

5. Channels of communication (formal versus informal) with other educational institutions (readiness to transfer students from one type of secondary school to another often depends on this).

Application to English State Secondary School System

The above listed factors have implications for the objectives, organization, and impact of the two major types of secondary schools in England—the grammar school and the secondary modern school.

The grammar school has a clear input policy: it selects the best pupils available. Its output policy is equally clear since it acts as the filter for access to further education: successful completion of A-level examinations is the necessary entry qualification for university and other further education, as well as for given forms of professional training; passing of O-level examinations facilitates entry into other jobs. The significance of this is enhanced by two factors: (a) although preparation for these examinations can take place outside school, very few early leavers make use of these facilities, and (b) educational attainment is highly related to occupational success. (We obtained a correlation of .662 between educational attainment and occupational level at age twenty-five.)

The grammar school has become important because of its selective input and its clear objectives; due to society's understanding and support of its system, the school is able to make demands of both pupils and parents. However, one problem exists—the school must woo its pupils to stay on after they are legally free to leave. Thus a preponderance of working class boys in a school creates a problem of motivation—how to retain a sufficient number; and a high proportion of pupils of relatively low ability creates a problem of a different and equally relevant kind— how to maximize on the ability of its pupils.

By contrast, the secondary modern school has no input policy—it accepts those not selected for grammar school—and its pupils may easily see themselves as rejects. Since it has no external examinations and since there is no link between school performance and subsequent occupational success, also it lacks a clear output policy. There is nothing tangible to indicate to parents and pupils (and perhaps to some teachers) what constitutes success and what constitutes failure. Definitions affecting the minority do exist, of course: at the failure end, there are the persistent truants and delinquents; at the success end, those students who are prepared to attempt O- or even A-level examinations. These characterizations of success and failure, however, do not touch the majority of parents and pupils.

Both types of schools aim to develop appropriate cognitions, attitudes, motivation, and behavior on the part of their pupils. However, beyond generally doing "good," no special role is assigned to the secondary modern school. As in the case of its entry policy, its objectives are more easily specified in negative terms. It would seem that the main role assigned by society to the secondary modern school is that of retention or custodial care of an educational kind (at least this was the case in the 1950s, when the first part of this study was carried out).

SURVEY APPLICATION OF THE MODEL

The general model was conceptualized after initial inspection of the data, then it was developed specifically and in greater detail to guide subsequent analysis of the data. Because of the close link between the model and our data, the findings presented here should be regarded as an example of the usefulness of this type of approach and not as a full exploration of the potentialities it offers.

A school's impact can be assessed by what happens to the individual while at school and also by how long-lasting and decisive the impact is after the individual leaves school. In our survey, the latter was assessed by comparing the occupational attainments at age twenty-five of the secondary modern and grammar school pupils in our sample. To test the proposition that the impact of the school is strong, we needed some way of evaluating that strength. We argued that if attendance at a given type of school made such a lasting impact, it should prove more important than other characteristics (family background, intelligence) relevant to occupational attainment. Table 7.1 indicates that this was so with regard to social background: *school had in fact taken over.* In both schools, boys of middle class background did better than those of working class background but such differences were small compared with the enormous differences that existed between the overall occupational attainments of the two school populations.

Table 7.1 *Percentage distribution of occupational level of subject at age 25 by social class of father within type of school.*

Social Class of Father Within Type of School	N	Occupational Level of Subject at Age 25					
		Upper Middle	Lower Middle	**All Middle**	Upper Working	Lower Working	**All Working**
Grammar							
Middle Class	(125)	70	19	89	11	0 (1)	11
Working Class	(138)	62	22	84	12	4	16
Total	(263)	66	21	87	11	2	14
Secondary Modern							
Middle Class	(31)	29	22	51	39	10	49
Working Class	(156)	14	16	30	46	24	70
Total	(187)	16	17	33	45	22	6.7

Further examination provided us with grounds to refute the possible contention that grammar school pupils possibly do better later in life because they are more intelligent: despite the high correlation between IQ results and school assignment, we found 63 pupils who were "wrongly" assigned—that is, they possessed ability more appropriate for attendance at the other type of school. It must be remembered that the ability level of the grammar school intake depends on the supply of grammar schools in a particular neighborhood. Wiseman (1964), in his survey of a large number of grammar and secondary modern schools, showed that within each type of school there are wide variations in average ability level and range and that, consequently, there is a significant overlap between the least intelligent of the grammar school pupils and the most intelligent of the secondary modern schools.

In our sample, we compared the "11+ overassigned"—those whose ability level was more in line with that of the secondary modern pupils—with the "11+ underassigned"—those of grammar school calibre who had been assigned to the secondary modern school. If occupational attainment was a matter of ability alone, then these two groups with similar ability levels should have performed almost equally well and should have been sharply differentiated from the remainder of the school population to which they had been assigned. On the other hand, if our proposition holds (namely, that the school influence is the most important influence on occupational attainment), it should follow that wrongly assigned pupils would differ less from the remainder of the school population to which they had been assigned than from one another. Our results, as presented in Table 7.2, support this proposition.

Table 7.2 *Occupational attainment of "11+ overassigned" and "11+ underassigned" pupils relative to the rest of the school populations to which they had been assigned.*

| Type of School Attended | N | Occupational Level at Age 25 | | | |
		Percent Upper Middle	Percent Lower Middle	Percent Upper Working	Percent Lower Working
Grammar					
11+ overassigned	(17)	59	35	6	0
Remainder	(177)	66	20	10	4
Secondary Modern					
11+ underassigned	(46)	26	18	44	13
Remainder	(142)	13	18	45	24

We suggested earlier that the two types of schools comprise different systems. We now submit that the grammar school is a relatively strong system and the secondary modern a relatively weak one. By "strong," we mean that a school has coercive power over its pupils, deriving from the nature of the objectives assigned to the school and their salience for the individuals within the system. To prove this we would have to establish that the strong system is more effective than the weak in reducing the significance of those characteristics that pupils bring with them that are seen as potentially harmful to its objectives. For example, the grammar school should be more capable than the secondary modern school in offsetting the potentially low achievement motivation of working class pupils (Swift, 1968).

The grammar school system is stronger in this regard, as demonstrated by the *within school* comparison of attainments of middle class and working class boys (Table 7.1). Although in both types of schools a higher proportion of middle class boys went into middle class occupations than did working class boys, the difference was insignificant in the grammar school but highly significant in the secondary modern school where 51 percent of the boys from middle class homes entered middle class jobs, as compared with 30 percent of those from working class homes. This difference was even sharper for the higher level occupations which required training or were achieved as a result of rapid advancement (29 percent:14 percent).

In the secondary modern school, correlation between occupational levels of father and son was .31 [it remained unchanged (.30) when IQ was partialled out], while in the grammar school, correlation was insignificant (.09). This difference is understandable because, at the time of the initial survey, secondary modern school pupils did not take the public final school examinations that would have provided a yardstick of their capabilities. Consequently, the forces of home and neighborhood continued to play an important part. Since middle class parents place greater emphasis on occupational achievement and have more knowledge of available opportunities outside school than do working class parents, they are better able to direct their children into suitable occupations. "For the middle class parent, having a boy at a secondary modern school constitutes a threat to the boy's future; not so for the working class parent who expects his boy to go to a secondary modern school" (Himmelweit and Wright, 1969).

Grammar and secondary modern schools constitute separate systems: different things are expected of each school system and the pupils of each can expect a very different future. Therefore, in all subsequent analyses we treat the two populations separately. For the purpose of illustrating the usefulness of our model, we will concentrate on the grammar school system which has a clear objective—to prepare its able pupils for the A-level examination at age eighteen. To meet this objective, the school must persuade pupils to stay at school voluntarily after age fifteen, as they cannot be forced to do so.

We sought factors inside and outside the grammar school system that might account for differences in student performance. As the Ministry of Education's *Early Leaving Report* (1954) and its more recent *Statistics of Education* (1966) show, more pupils from middle than working class homes stay at school, a difference that held in our sample. We directed our attention, however, to the crucial stage of sixth-form entry—the important step for those who want to prepare for A-level examinations. There was a strong relationship between entry and social class: 52 percent of boys from middle class backgrounds entered as compared with only 28 percent of those from lower working class homes. Yet when we looked at the proportion of pupils who entered the sixth form in each of four grammar schools, we found no relation between the proportion of boys entering the sixth form and the proportion of middle

Table 7.3 *Percent proportion of sample of four grammar schools by social class of father and by entry into sixth form.*

Social Class of Father				Entry into Sixth Form	
Middle	Working	*N*	School	Entered	Left Before Entering
30	70	(86)	*A*	48	52
51	49	(70)	*B*	32	68
58	42	(66)	*C*	29	71
59	41	(41)	*D*	39	61

class boys in the school. Indeed the school with the highest percentage of working class pupils also had the highest percentage of entry into the sixth form (Table 7.3).

It was clear that the usual approach of regarding the school environment as equivalent for all pupils was unsatisfactory and that we needed to look *within each school* for strategies that served to offset the general trend of differential leaving rates among pupils from different backgrounds. D. Young (1964) and W. Brandis, who carried out this part of the analysis, thoroughly examined the organizational structure of each of the four grammar schools in relation to its intake and the boys' final school performance. It turned out that all of the schools used the streaming device, but that schools *A* and *D* made a special feature of this device. Brandis found that the latter schools had particular intake problems: school *A* had a retention problem because 70 percent of its pupils came from working class homes and school *D* had an ability problem in that the average ability level of its pupils was low for a grammar school. He suggested that schools should attempt a rescue operation by emphasizing those good characteristics of its intake that are in ample supply and deemphasizing good characteristics that are in short supply. Thus, school *A* developed an "express" stream with a demanding curriculum, designed to make it possible for its able pupils to take the A-level examination in the minimum length of time; school *D* created an "elite" stream, with students selected on the basis of their readiness to work in order to compensate for low ability.

Once analysis was carried out within streams (designated "1," "2," or "3"; Table 7.4), a clear picture emerged: more students in stream 1 stayed and entered sixth form than did students in stream 2, and almost everyone in stream 3 left school before entering sixth form.

In relating these findings to our model, it was obvious that we again were dealing with differences in clarity of objectives and in input and output policies. Boys in the top stream (stream 1) know they are expected to continue—they are the chosen. The position of the stream 2 boys is more ambiguous but that of boys in stream 3 is clear—it is expected that few of them will stay beyond the sixth form.

Table 7.4 *Percentage of pupils in streams 1, 2, and 3 who entered the sixth form in each of the four grammar schools.*

School	N	Percent Entering Sixth Form in		
		Stream 1	Stream 2	Stream 3
A	(86)	84	43	15
B	(70)	56	27	10
C	(66)	39	36	6
D^1	(41)	86	–	14

Pupils in stream 3 are placed, not selected; they constitute all those who did not make the grade because the teachers thought them less able or less compliant. Before looking at the implications of the proposition that when a boy is assigned to a stream, stream takes over and sets a level for attainment, we first must demonstrate that stream assignment is not always based on characteristics usually associated with high attainment. Here the most salient characteristic is ability. Our evidence is based on our finding that the two schools that placed great emphasis on streaming used quite different selection criteria. School A streamed by ability [correlation of .40 ($p < .001$) between IQ and stream]. School D looked for the students' capacity to work hard because the level of ability was low: the correlation of ability with stream was insignificant (Himmelweit and Wright, 1969).

The effect of stream can also be examined by its correlation with IQ and with educational attainment. In our survey, these were .30 and .51, respectively. Partialling out IQ did not reduce the correlation with educational attainment (.48), but partialling out stream reduced to zero the initial (already weak) correlation between educational attainment and IQ of .13 ($p < .05$).

Just as the type of school attended is a better predictor of future attainment, outlook, and aspirations than is ability, so *within* the grammar school, the stream to which the pupil has been assigned has more predictive power than has the level of his ability. *Allocation to stream, for whatever reason, affects the boy's ultimate performance far more than does his ability or motivation.*

The role of the school and its structure has been discussed as a determinant of school leaving and attainment and its importance ascertained relative to that of the boy's social background and his ability.

Further analyses aimed at studying the *processes* involved were based on other factors suggested in the model for which data was obtained from our longitudinal study, including the following:

Other relevant data about the boy's background (the size of his family; his ordinal position; the secondary school experience of his parents and siblings).

The quality of his relations with his family as he perceived it (ease of communication; degree of mutual trust; strictness of parental discipline; warmth of mutual relations).

His orientation to school (identification with school values; own assessment of performance; age at which he would like to leave; desire to attend university).

His teachers' and peers' ratings of him (sociometrics; teachers' evaluations of his performance and behavior).

Orientation toward society (preference for peer or adult values; preference for fighting, adventure, and risk; measures of authoritarianism; appreciation of "status quo"—that is not wanting to stand out from the crowd; desire for an undemanding job). From our range of social attitudes we selected those that previously distinguished between grammar and secondary modern pupils.

To understand the relative contribution of these factors in accounting for the age at which the boys actually left grammar school, we used a two-stage stepwise regression analysis developed by M. Garside. This type of analysis allows an initial specified set of variables to make its maximum contribution, after which the other variables enter in order of their contribution to the variance. For the specified set of variables we selected those that could be described as "structural": they are given in the school situation (assignment to stream), in the home situation (parents' social background and education, the grammar school experience of siblings, size of family, and ordinal position), and the boy's IQ. The percentage variance accounted for by these structural factors was 20.2. Of these factors, stream was by far the most important, with family background variables and ability contributing only marginally. When social-psychological data were added, the percentage variance substantially increased, from 20 to 37 percent (yielding $R^2 = .61$). Table 7.5 sets out those variables that significantly contributed to the overall variance.

The most powerful contributing variable was the age at which the boy said he would want to leave school if he was free to choose (this correlated .44 with his actual leaving age).[5] Other contributing variables were: (a) how well he did in class, (b) to what extent he accepted peer values regarding adventure and risk (qualities not particularly valued by school authorities), and (c) whether he wished to go on to university. The last contributed only marginally.

How valid was our forecast? Compared with the results obtained by sociologists using the variables of social class and ability, our prediction was excellent, particularly in view of the fact that we chose to restrict our analysis to data collected when the subjects were age thirteen and excluded their performance at O-level. The latter is a powerful factor in determining entry into the sixth form. However, while the prediction generally was good, it was not spectacular in view of the wealth of data we had about each boy. We tried to improve it by transforming some variables—making them operate at an apparently critical level—but this made no difference.

[5]Fishbein (1968) has always maintained that the best way to find out how a person will behave is to ask him what he intends to do. The age variable is an apt illustration of this principle, despite the fact that the behavior in question could not occur for at least two years and that the boy was not a free agent as teachers and parents also had a say in the final decision.

Table 7.5 *Contribution of variables to the prediction of the actual leaving age of grammar school pupils, using a two-stage stepwise linear regression model.*
(*N*: 263; Number of Variables: 40)

Variable	Correlation with Leaving Age	Direction for Late Leavers	Stage of Entry	Overall % of Explained Variance'
Specified set of structural variables: background			1 (specified)	20.2
Age at which boy said he wanted to leave school	.442	late	2	31.9
Teacher's rating of class position	.169	high	3	34.1
Enjoyment of adventure and risk	.258	low	4	35.9
Wanted to attend university	.282	yes	5	37.3
Multiple R = 61				

Non-metric multiple regression analysis (AID program: Morgan and Songuist, 1963) was utilized to explore further our theories about the manner in which a boy's behavior is shaped and for identification of complex processes and interactions. This method successively dichotomizes variables or sets of categories at an optimum "split" to produce increasingly "purer" groups in terms of the criterion variable. As we were not interested in maximal prediction but rather in using the technique to learn as much as possible about the checks and balances that determine a child's behavior, we decided to exclude our measure of the age the boy wanted to leave school since it had the highest correlation of all of the variables employed. The non-metric characteristic of the technique enabled us to add one important variable—the four individual grammar schools—making it possible to determine whether the process whereby a boy leaves school early or late was different for individual schools and, if so, in what way.

Figure 7.2 shows the manner in which the groups separated and illustrates well the operation of our model. It shows that very favorable or very unfavorable events (such as assignment to a particular stream) can be offset only by very strong favorable or unfavorable counterbalancing factors provided by peer group or home influences. Thus, group I had everything in its favor: it was assigned to the right stream and had the right attitude—nearly everyone stayed until age eighteen.

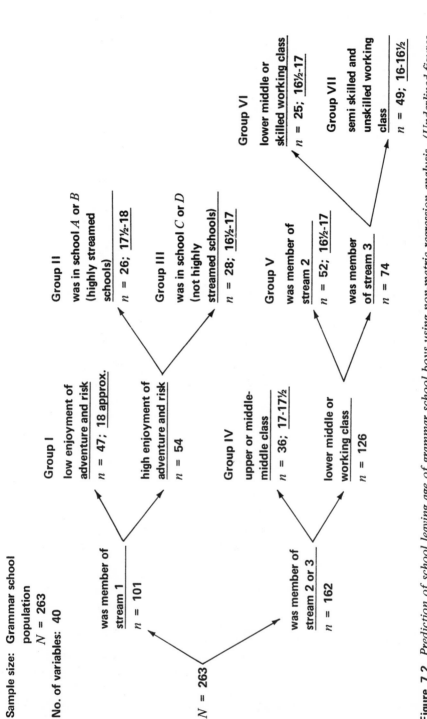

Figure 7.2 *Prediction of school leaving age of grammar school boys using non-metric regression analysis. (Underlined figures denote the approximate leaving age of each of the seven final groups; size and defining characteristic is given for each group.)*

However, those stream 1 subjects who held peer group (antischool) values and were in a school where stream was not given as much importance tended to leave fairly early—an unfavorable attitude offset the favorable assignment. The opposite was true for group IV, for which unfavorable assignment to stream 2 or 3 was offset by the group's positive attitude to continuing in school—an attitude stimulated by parents of middle class backgrounds who were well aware of the importance of A-level examinations. These boys left relatively late, but not quite as late as the group II boys who, although they had the "wrong" attitudes, had been assigned to stream 1 in a school that stressed stream and thus were members of an élite.

The lower part of Figure 7.2 shows the result of an accumulation of adverse factors: the group that left earliest (group VII) had the disadvantage of being assigned to stream 3 and of coming from families with little awareness of the importance of acquiring grammar school education (the fathers were semi- and unskilled workers).

We feel that Figure 7.2 illustrates well our contention that background factors are significant where school structure is weak (schools *C* and *D*) and less so where it is relatively strong (*A* and *B*). Our further suggestion that stream 1 constitutes the stronger structure as opposed to streams 2 and 3 is confirmed by the fact that the social background of our subjects did affect reactions to assignment to streams 2 or 3 and, for stream 1 boys, leaving school depended not on the home outlook but rather on their adherence to peer values.

As this type of analysis seemed promising, we carried out a second analysis of the same type, this time using entry into the sixth form as our criterion variable—a more critical variable than leaving age because it indicates the boy's readiness to prepare for the A-level examination and excludes those boys who stayed on in the fifth form to complete their O-levels. We also included another crucial determining variable—results of the fifth-form O-level examination, because these results provide the first external assessment of a boy's achievement level for the boy himself, his teachers, and his parents. Otherwise, the variables were the same as in the first nonlinear analysis.

One further analysis alteration was made: the first analysis was stopped at the point at which a further split would produce a group with no less than 25 cases, as this time we felt that smaller and more homogeneous groups would produce more significant results. The statisticians we consulted agreed this was permissible as long as the splits added significantly to the variance explained.

As expected (Figure 7.3), the population first divided on a high O-level performance versus a lower one—the variable that indicated whether the pupil was capable of advanced work.[6] Within these two major groups, features of school structure and factors associated with the individual boy (his attitudes, his home life) were important. It would take too long to discuss every feature of this complex figure, so only a few of the groups will be discussed. First, it is significant that almost as many students from school *A* with fewer than five O-level credits stayed on as did those

[6] As stream and O-level performance were so highly correlated, stream was the next best single predictor of entry into sixth form.

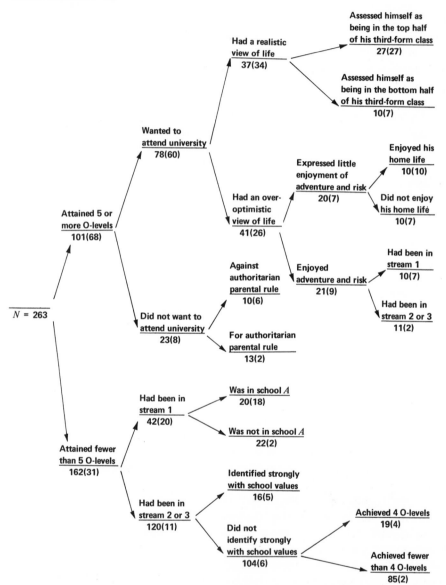

Sample size: **Grammar school population** $N = 263$

No. of variables: **40**

Had a realistic view of life
37(34)

Assessed himself as being in the top half of his third-form class
27(27)

Assessed himself as being in the bottom half of his third-form class
10(7)

Wanted to attend university
78(60)

Expressed little enjoyment of adventure and risk
20(7)

Enjoyed his home life
10(10)

Did not enjoy his home life
10(7)

Had an over-optimistic view of life
41(26)

Attained 5 or more O-levels
101(68)

Against authoritarian parental rule
10(6)

Enjoyed adventure and risk
21(9)

Had been in stream 1
10(7)

Had been in stream 2 or 3
11(2)

$N = 263$

Did not want to attend university
23(8)

For authoritarian parental rule
13(2)

Had been in stream 1
42(20)

Was in school A
20(18)

Was not in school A
22(2)

Attained fewer than 5 O-levels
162(31)

Identified strongly with school values
16(5)

Had been in stream 2 or 3
120(11)

Did not identify strongly with school values
104(6)

Achieved 4 O-levels
19(4)

Achieved fewer than 4 O-levels
85(2)

Figure 7.3 *Prediction of entry into sixth form using non-metric stepwise regression analysis. (Numbers in parentheses denote the number of students who entered sixth form; size and defining variable given for each group.)*

from all the schools who had five O-level credits and also wanted to go to university. This can be attributed to the fact that school A, in its endeavor to induce its best pupils to do A-level work as early as possible, required its stream 1 pupils to obtain only a minimum number of O-level credits (those required for university entrance in addition to the necessary A-level performance). The same policy clearly did not hold for boys in streams 2 or 3 in school A—these boys tended to leave school if they had fewer than five O-level credits. The policy therefore was specific to stream 1.

Another interesting group comprised 11 boys, only two of whom entered the sixth form even though they had five O-level credits. These boys had the double handicap of possessing inappropriate attitudes (they lacked a realistic outlook, and had peer rather than adult values) and of having been allocated to stream 2 or 3. In contrast, of the 10 boys who possessed the same attitudes but who were in stream 1, 7 entered the sixth form.

The rock-bottom group, of which only 2 of the total of 85 boys entered the sixth form, showed nothing but deficits. The boys in that group did poorly on the examination, had been in stream 2 or 3, and had little interest in school.

To generalize from this analysis, it seems feasible that within a given situation many variables have equivalence: "good" (functional) features are associated with staying on at school, and "bad" (dysfunctional) ones with leaving school. Furthermore, the greater the predominance of functional attitudes, the greater the likelihood that those who have done well at O-level will stay—several functional attitudes or attributes may cancel out one or more dysfunctional ones. Strong identification with school values, for instance, prompted almost one-third of the boys from streams 2 and 3 to stay on, even though they had done poorly in the examination; of those lacking this strong identification, only 6 of 104 boys did so.

It is interesting to note that those attitudes that offset initial disadvantages and those that led boys to leave school despite good examination results were the same attitudes that differentiated between secondary modern and grammar school pupils. It would appear that there are attitudes and aspirations—some related to school and work and others reflecting the boy's view of society and of his place in it—that are characteristic of good school performers and also, even among these, indicate further ability to make full use of any opportunities afforded by school.

CONCLUSIONS

This article has presented a model of the socializing process, featuring the school as a powerful socializing agent. Particular attention has been paid to the way in which society determines the school's objectives and often defines its input and output policy.

Using a longitudinal study in which middle and working class boys who attended two different types of secondary schools were studied at age thirteen and again at age twenty-five, we were able to illustrate the conditions under which school is likely to make maximal impact. We showed that a strong system is one that *selects* its pupils—as opposed to a system that simply *accepts* pupils not selected by others—and one that has explicit goals tailored to significantly shape its pupils' futures. Under these circumstances and by specific strategies such as streaming, school can offset the poor motivation generated by a family that is little interested in education.

Linear and non-metric stepwise regression analyses were carried out on the longitudinal study to demonstrate the workings of the model. The results showed that a boy's performance is influenced by a combination of checks and balances and a combination of the functional and dysfunctional attitudes and attributes of the boy, his family, and his school. The non-metric technique of analysis, which enables one to identify factors that operate in one setting without necessarily operating in another, proved more useful in highlighting the socializing process than did the linear one.

As we have shown, the model provided a means for setting a longitudinal study in a theoretical context. The results of our experiment suggest the validity of using this approach for other such studies—of asking different questions of the data than are commonly asked. Instead of trying to determine to what extent early childhood characteristics persist into adult life (an exercise doomed to failure except in rare, extreme cases), researchers should be concerned with examining the attitudinal and behavioral patterns that the young person brings to *each* important new socializing experience—patterns that are modified, expanded, or transformed by that experience. This process would have to repeated as many times as the character of the socializing agents or institutions changed. The input to experience A changes, as a result of that experience, into output A which, in turn, becomes the input for experience B and so on.

Further, the results of our longitudinal study have shown that there are critical incidents in children's lives. These effects are immensely powerful and often persist into adulthood, determining access to subsequent experiences and defining the individual's position in society. Some of the critical incidents are imposed on him (allocation to secondary school); others are determined, in part at least, by the individual himself (decision to stay on at school). Whether imposed or selected, these are critical events. As a consequence of one such event, a grammar and a secondary modern school child live in different worlds as distinct from one another as the world of the manual worker from that of the professional man. There is a need for further studies which identify critical events, examine the effects of differential access to experiences, and analyze searchingly the relevance for its members of the goals and methods of each institution.

From our analysis, it follows that if England changed from a divided secondary school system to a comprehensive one (but retained the current objectives of the grammar school, such as acquisition of A-levels), the comprehensive school might well turn to streaming as a means of attaining these objectives. If this were done, we would in fact continue to have a divided secondary system, but under one roof. Our model demonstrates that, if there is to be genuine innovation, it cannot be achieved without redefinition of the objectives not only of the school, but also those of all institutions that relate to it.

It is hoped that the model will serve to draw attention to the many factors that must be considered in studying the effect of school. We need such documentation—sometimes in order to understand why the school did not make more of an impact or, as in the present study, why it had such a powerful effect. A useful concept to introduce into such consideration is that of the strength of a system. We have shown in our study that the grammar school represents a strong system, the secondary modern school a weak system, and have indicated that strong systems prevail while weak ones influence a child less strongly than do outside factors.

Finally, the model has implications for cross-cultural research concerned with the socialization process. It points to factors that should be studied at a comparative level when the impact and influences of home or school are to be assessed. Above all, it directs attention to the necessity of considering critical incidents, conditional processes, and the strength of the systems of which a child is a captive member.

While the authors are responsible for the formal presentation of the model and its elaboration, it is the result of the work and discussion of several research workers who have been connected with the longitudinal study: D. Young, W. Brandis, Judy Wright, and A. P. Sealy. The authors owe a special debt of gratitude to Dr. Sealy for his essays on model building and for his helpful comments at all stages.

REFERENCES

Bernstein, B., and Henderson, D. Social class differences in the relevance of language to socialisation. *Sociology*, **III**, No. 1, 1969.

Bowman, M. J. The "fit" between education and work. Cross National Conference, Mohonk, 1967.

Brandis, W. Functional requisites and the grammar school structure (to be published).

Bronfenbrenner, U. Socialization and social class through time and space. In E. E. Maccoby et al. (Eds.) *Readings in social psychology*. New York: Henry Holt, 1958.

Bronfenbrenner, U. Toward a theoretical model for the analysis of parent-child relationships in a social context. In J. Glidewell (Ed.), *Parent attitudes and child behaviors*. Springfield, Ill: C. C. Thomas, 1965.

Coleman, J. S. *Equality of educational opportunities*. Washington: U.S. Department of Health, Education and Welfare, 1966.

Davis, A., & Havighurst, R. J. Social class and color differences in child-rearing. *American Sociological Review*, 1946, **II**, 698–710.

Douglas, J. W. B. *The home and the school*. London: MacGibbon and Kee, 1964.

Douglas, J. W. B., Ross, J. M., Simpson, H. R. All our future. London; Peter Davies, 1968.

Erikson, E. H. *Childhood and society*. New York: W. W. Norton & Co., 1950.

Fishbein, M. *Readings in attitude theory and measurement*. New York: J. Wiley & Sons, 1968.

Friedenberg, E. Z. *The vanishing adolescent*. New York: Dell Publishing Co. Inc., 1959.

Heckhausen, H. *The anatomy of achievement motivation.* New York: Academic Press, 1967. (Also to be published in *Sociology*, 1968.)

Hess, R. D., and Shipman, V. C. Cognitive elements in maternal behavior. *First Minnesota Symposium on Child Psychology,* Minneapolis: University of Minnesota Press, 1967.

Himmelweit, Hilde T. A ten-year follow-up study, its objectives and methods. Paper read at the annual conference of the British Psychological Society, Leicester, England, 1964.

Himmelweit, Hilde T. Social background, intelligence and school structure—and interaction analysis. In J. D. Meade, & A. S. Parkes (Eds.) *Genetic and environmental factors in human ability.* Edinburgh: Olver and Boyde, 1966.

Himmelweit, H. T., and Wright, J. C. The school system, social class and attainment after school. Paper read at the annual conference of the British Psychological Society, Swansea; 1967 (to be published in *Sociology*, 1969).

Husen, T. *International study of achievement in mathematics.* Stockholm: Almquist and Wiksell, 1967.

Kagan J., & Moss, H. A. *Birth of maturity: A study in psychological development.* New York: J. Wiley & Sons, 1962.

Kohn, M. L. Social class and the exercise of parental authority. *American Sociological Review,* 1959, 23, 352.

Maccoby, E. Choice of socializing variables. *Sociometry*, 1960, 23, 357.

Macfarlane, J. W. Studies in child guidance. I-Methodology of data collection and organization. *Monographs of the Society for Research in Child Development,* 1938, 3, No. 6, 1–254.

Ministry of Education. *Early leaving report*, 1954.

Ministry of Education. *Statistics of education*, 1966.

Morgan, J. N., & Songuist, J. A. Problems in the analysis of survey data, and a proposal. *Journal of the American Statistics Association*, 1963, 58, No. 302.

Mussen, P. H., Conger, J. J., Kagan, J. *Child development and personality.* (2nd ed.) New York: Harper & Row, 1963.

Pace, C. R. Differences in campus atmosphere. In W. Charters, Jr., & W. W. Gage (Eds.) *Readings in the social psychology of education.* New York: Allyn & Bacon, 1963.

Parsons, T., & Bales, R. F. *Family socialisation and interaction process.* Glencoe: Free Press, 1955.

Sealy, A. P., & Himmelweit, H. T. The school as a socializing agent. Review of British studies carried out for the U.S. Social Science Research Council's Committee on Socialization, 1966.

Sears, R. R., Maccoby, E., & Levin, H. *Patterns of child rearing.* Evanston: Row Peterson & Co., 1957.

Swift, B. Job orientations and transition from school to work of 450 adolescent school boys. Paper read at a working conference "Into work" organized by the National Foundation for Educational Research, Wolverhampton; 1968. (To be published by the N.F.E.R., 1969.)

Symonds, P. M. *The dynamics of human adjustment.* New York: Appleton Century, 1946.

Turner, R. H. Modes of social ascent through education: Sponsored and contest mobility. In A. Z. Halsey, J. Floud (Eds.) *Education and society.* Glencoe: Free Press, 1961.

Wiseman, S. *Education and environment*. Manchester: University Press, 1964.
Yates, A. *Grouping in education*. New York: J. Wiley & Sons, Unesco Institute of Education, 1966.
Young, D. Early leaving of grammar school boys. Paper given at the annual conference of the British Psychological Society, Leicester, 1964.

8

RELATION OF BODY SIZE,
INTELLIGENCE TEST SCORES,
AND SOCIAL CIRCUMSTANCES[1]

This paper describes and attempts to analyze (rather warily) the relationship that exists among mental ability, physical size, and social circumstances in the cases of both children and adults.

THE RELATION OF BODY SIZE
AND MENTAL ABILITY IN CHILDREN

In 1892, William Townsend Porter[2] (then professor of physiology at St. Louis Medical College) organized a survey of the heights, weights, and various other measurements of some 33,500 boys and girls in the public schools of St. Louis. The school classes were organized in grades and a pupil moved up a grade when he had successfully completed the work of the previous grade, irrespective of his age. On compilation of the survey results in 1893, Porter found that the pupils in the higher grades were taller and heavier than pupils of the same age in lower grades. Not only was this true of the average figures: Porter, a close follower of Galton, who

---

[1] Parts of this paper are based on the Galton lecture delivered to the Eugenics Society in London on June 1, 1966. I am indebted to the Society and the Eugenics Review for permission to quote some passages. I am also most grateful to Dr. Cedric Carter and Mr. Harvey Goldstein, who read the manuscript, made valuable suggestions, and drew my attention to several points and papers with which I was unfamiliar.

[2] Porter (1862–1949), at this time aged thirty, later became a famous figure in American physiology. His pioneer work in the field of analyzing children's growth in relation to mental ability prompted Henry Bowditch, the first professor of physiology at Harvard and the first serious student of children's growth in America, to call him to Harvard the following year as assistant professor of physiology. Porter later became professor of comparative physiology at Harvard (1903–1928); founder, first editor (1898–1914), and financial sponsor of the American Journal of Physiology; and founder of the Harvard Apparatus Company.

J. M. TANNER

Department of Growth and Development
Institute of Child Health
University of London, London, England

invented percentiles, calculated the 20th and 80th percentiles in higher and lower grades and showed that the whole distribution of weight of pupils of the higher grade was shifted upward.

Figure 8.1, redrawn from one of Porter's papers, shows the weight at each year of age of children who were above average in grade and children who were below average. Although the difference shown in the figure does not look very impressive, it corresponds to the amount an average child grows in about six months. The data, of course, are cross-sectional. The figures for height are similar: for example, twelve-year-old girls in Grade 2 were 5 cm shorter than girls of the same age in Grade 5. The same difference existed between ten-year-old boys in Grades 1 and 4. Size in children, then, appeared to be linked in some way with ability.

Porters' findings aroused incredulous but ill-documented opposition then as, sometimes, now. Porter (1893) thought that physical strength—which he equated with size and weight—conditioned the amount of mental effort that a child could make and wrote "Precocious children are heavier and dull children lighter than the mean[3] child of the same age. This establishes a basis of precocity and dullness." By "precocious," however, he did not mean "temporarily advanced," but rather the opposite of dull—what we might term "bright." He pointed out that the growth curves of precocious and dull children followed a parallel course and that the adolescent increase in weight occurred at about the same age in the two groups. He thus indirectly implied (though he did not directly commit himself) that he believed these differences of size and mental ability would persist into adult life.

[3] By "mean" Porter meant "median." In this he followed Galton's terminology (*Natural Inheritance*), which is somewhat confusing to us nowadays. Our modern mean, $\Sigma X/N$, was referred to as the "average."

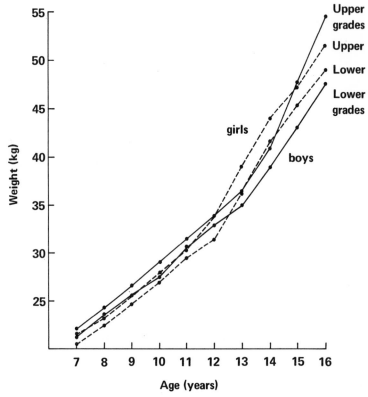

Figure 8.1 *Weight of boys and girls of above-average grade and below-average grade in schools of St. Louis in 1892. Cross-sectional data (Porter, 1893).*

To this conclusion Franz Boas, the greatest American anthropologist of his generation and the foremost pioneer of studies of human growth, objected strongly (Tanner, 1959, p. 82):

> I should prefer to call the less favorably developed grade of children retarded, not dull, and these terms are by no means equivalent, as a retarded child may develop and become quite bright . . . . Furthermore I do not believe that the facts found by Dr. Porter establish a basis of precocity and dullness, but only that precocious children are at the same time better developed physically. Dr. Porter has shown that mental and physical growth are correlated, or depend upon common causes; not that mental development depends on physical growth. (Boas, 1895)

Boas was the first man to realize fully that children developed at different rates; it was he who invented the phrases "tempo of growth" and "developmental age." Thus he naturally saw the relation between ability and size as probably being caused by differences in rate of development—some children being advanced both physically and mentally and others retarded in both aspects. If so, then by adulthood the retarded child would have caught up to the advanced one and there would no longer be any difference between them in either physique or ability.

Seventy years later the controversy still rages. Only very recently have we made any substantial progress toward clarifying an issue that is, after all, an important and practical one to both educationists and human biologists. The writings of Porter and Boas predated Binet's publication by more than a decade, yet even today intelligence tests are constructed and usually interpreted entirely on the basis of the terms "bright" and "dull." They do not distinguish between the advanced child who will end up, early, with average ability and the bright child who is not advanced and who will end up, at the average age, with high ability. Worse, they fail to identify the slowly developing child of potentially high ability. Modern longitudinal studies of intelligence test scores indicate clearly that differences in rates of maturing occur in mental ability just as they do in height and weight (Bayley, 1956; Tanner, 1961, p. 92).

Porter's factual observations on the relation of body size to school grades have been repeatedly confirmed over the years. Boas himself found that children in Worcester, Massachusetts, who were one grade ahead were on the average bigger by about six months' height growth than their coevals a grade below. When psychological testing was introduced and the school system reorganized so that promotion was less dependent on passing graded examinations, the relevant statistic became the correlation between height[4] and test score, or IQ, at a given age.

In 1947, a sample of 6,490 pupils drawn at random from all eleven-year-old Scottish school children, gave a correlation of 0.25 ± 0.01 between height and score in a Moray House group test of attainment, the effect of age differences from 11.0 to 11.9 having been allowed for (Scottish Council, 1953). An approximate conversion of the test scores to Terman-Merrill IQs leads to an average increase of about 0.67 IQ points for each centimeter of height, or roughly 1.5 points of IQ for each inch.

In 1959 and 1960, a survey of approximately 4,000 ten- and eleven-year-old pupils in London showed a correlation of 0.23 between height and verbal reasoning test scores (Moray House Test 61 or NFER Test 9B). The correlation does not look high but the effects can be very significant for individual children. Among the ten-year-old girls there was a 9-point difference in IQ between those whose height was below the 15th percentile and those whose height was above the 75th percentile—two-thirds of the standard deviation of the test score.

The children included in the National Survey of Health and Development provided measurements at ages eight, eleven, and fifteen. This survey consisted of a stratified sample of all boys and girls born in the first week of March, 1946; the sample considered comprised 2,864 children. To children of each age, four pencil-and-paper tests were given; the heights were taken by school doctors. The correlations between height and the results of these tests were 0.14 at eight years,

[4]It is likely that the true relationship is with body size rather than height, both in children and in adults. Weight, however, is a poor measure of size since it is so affected by fat.

0.14 at eleven years, and 0.12 at fifteen years (Douglas, Ross, and Simpson, 1965). Actually, height was taken at age seven and the first test at age eight, but the results were adjusted for this.

None of these data tell us, however, whether the correlation represents simply coadvancement in height and in ability and hence will disappear in adult life (Boas' view), or whether it represents something more persistent (Porter's view).

Longitudinal studies have shown that early maturing children—that is, children with an early puberty—do score higher in tests, from at least age six, than do late maturing children (Tanner, 1962, p. 211; Nisbet and Illsley, 1963). The early maturing children are also taller, of course, because children with an early puberty generally are advanced throughout their growing period, from early infancy on. However, for a number of reasons this does not settle the matter. First, the longitudinal data, as so often, become very poor after about age fifteen and, for this reason, we cannot really be sure what happens at full maturity. Shuttleworth's (1939) data (Tanner, 1962, p. 212) suffered a sharp reduction in numbers at the older ages, due to causes that probably introduced bias; the same is true of Abernethy's (1936) and Freeman and Florey's (1937) data. The National Survey of Child Health and Development data showed the usual higher scores in early maturers and also demonstrated that this held good even for children matched for occupational category and number of siblings: at age fifteen the difference not only did not diminish, it was actually slightly greater for both boys and girls than it was in the same children at ages seven and eleven (Douglas, Ross, and Simpson, 1965). Thus it is dubious whether the difference between early and late maturers disappears in adulthood.

Most writers on the subject, however, (including myself at one time) have adopted Boas' view that the correlation probably represented only coadvancement and would disappear at maturity. This view has important implications for education. According to it, early developers are at an advantage in tests for admission to selective education, gaining an increasing educational advantage simply as a result of passing these tests. Hence they would remain always ahead, an example of the classical self-fulfilling prophesy or positive feedback. This effect would also bias the results of a longitudinal study to maturity, unless allowances could be made for differences in educational opportunity.

However, adoption of Boas' view should be preceded by some very serious thought—even though Boas seldom lost an argument. In 1956, Dr. Nancy Bayley published correlations between height and intelligence test scores at each year of age from eleven to sixteen in a group of some 40 Berkeley children who were followed longitudinally until the age of twenty-one. The correlations were high, mostly between 0.30 and 0.50, and showed no tendency in either sex to drop between seven and sixteen. Furthermore, Dr. Bayley developed an absolute score for the intelligence test, so that it was possible to compute for each individual the percentage of his final twenty-one-year-old score attained at each age. Similarly the percentage of mature height attained at each age was calculated. The correlation between these two measures—mental and physical advancement—proved, in these admittedly limited data, to be slightly negative. There was no evidence that an early maturing boy or girl in the height-growth sense was early maturing in the mental attainment sense. Indeed, there was some suggestion that children who were slower in physical maturing reached their twenty-one-year-old level of intelligence sooner. In other words, the less able, though slow in maturing physically, nevertheless reached their twenty-one-year-old intelligence level relatively early, slowing down in mental attainment as they approached adulthood. (This could be wholly or partly a result of poor teaching associated with poor social circumstances; the latter could also contribute to slow physical growth.) Dr. Bayley's study, therefore, provided some evidence against the coadvancement hypothesis.

Perhaps a model will help clarify the foregoing pro and con arguments on coadvancement.

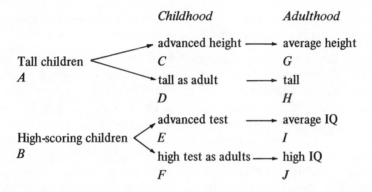

Tall children may be divided into those who are advanced in height but will end up average as adults, and those who are tall and will be tall adults. We can classify the high-scoring children similarly. (In practice, no such crude dichotomies can be made, of course; the true situation is a continuum.) Our information is that there is a connection (on the average) between A and B. This must come about either by connection between C and E, D and F, C and F, or D and E. C–E represents the coadvancement or Boas' hypothesis, D–F the adult-persistent or Porter hypothesis. We must assume that C and D, and E and F are independent. We know that this is almost true of C and D: advanced children end up very slightly shorter than others so there is small negative interaction, larger in girls than boys. About E and F we know nothing, except possibly from Dr. Bayley's study as outlined above, which might lead us to think that E and F could be negatively interacting also.

In relation to these connections, we must remember ruefully that, though we can distinguish C and D in childhood (by bone age and pubertal age), we cannot as a rule distinguish E and F. We therefore cannot say anything about the connections except by reference to the situation at adulthood, shown in the right-hand column. The adult correlations indicate that, on the average, tall adults have high test scores: H is connected with J. This then is evidence that D, the generator of H, is connected with F, the generator of J, since we know that C and H are practically independent and we suppose that the same is true of E and J. This, then, leads us to the connection $D\text{-}B$.

The evidence for the $C\text{-}E$ or coadvancement connection is, on the whole, not as good. In most data the connection $C\text{-}B$ exists, though whether it is more or less important than $D\text{-}B$ is not clear. In the National Child Health Survey data, $D\text{-}B$ was probably more important since the height-ability correlation was lowered very slightly by allowing for different stages of puberty—that is, eliminating the effect of C (Douglas, Ross, and Simpson, 1965). However, assuming $C\text{-}B$ exists, our problem is whether this is via $C\text{-}E$, $C\text{-}F$, or both. The evidence on $C\text{-}F$ is conflicting. Early maturers may perhaps have persistent high test scores when they are adult, which means that the connection $C\text{-}E$ need not necessarily exist. Dr. Bayley's data suggest directly that C and E are independent or slightly negatively related and carry the consequence that, in her small series, the connection $C\text{-}F$ does exist.

THE RELATION OF BODY SIZE
AND MENTAL ABILITY IN ADULTS

The main argument against coadvancement as the sole cause of the height-ability correlation in children rests on recent data about the same relationship in adults. The older literature, summarized in Patterson (1930), primarily concerned students. The restricted nature of their intellectual range (in the statistical sampling sense, that is) makes them a poor guide to analyzing the population as a whole. However, because there is a difference in height among individuals belonging to different socio-economic groups and a similar difference in intelligence test scores, one might expect to find a positive correlation between height and test scores in the population at large. This does appear to be the case, based on the findings of several researchers: Husen (1951) reported a correlation coefficient of 0.22 for 2,250 Swedish conscripts; Schreider (1956), 0.29 for 566 French conscripts and a similar figure for industrial workers; Scott, Illsley, and Thomson (1956), 0.24 for a random sample of Aberdeen women pregnant for the first time (Wechsler test); Udjus (1964), 0.16 for twenty-year-old Norwegian conscripts.

These figures undoubtedly reflect to a large extent the association between occupation, or socio-economic class, and height and intelligence (Udjus, 1964; Schreider, 1964). But even within certain admittedly crude occupational or educational groups, the relation persists to a significant degree. In Udjus' data, high school graduates averaged 179.7 cm in height, compared with a general mean of 177.5 cm. Nearly all were in the top three of the nine ranks given by the intelligence tests, but those in the top two ranks of the test were taller—by about 2 cm—than those in the third and lower divisions. (Indeed the regression within this educational group was no different than the general regression, though its members contributed only about 50 percent of the top two divisions and 17 percent of the third one). However, when the Aberdeen women were classified by husband's occupation, the height-ability correlation disappeared in the Registrar-General's Groups I and II but persisted significantly in the less prosperous occupational groups: 0.16 in Group III and 0.25 in Groups IV and V.

With some confidence we can therefore assert that there is currently a small but significant tendency for taller adults to score higher in some intelligence tests than short adults of the same sex, even within certain (if not all) crude occupational categories such as "unskilled" and "semiskilled" workers.

At this point it is necessary to dispose of an objection sometimes raised by tall men on behalf of their shorter and brighter friends. Hard cases make bad law and soft friends make worse statistics. Just because on average large boys do well in school, it does not follow that every large boy is a paragon of educational virtue. On the contrary, school teachers frequently query the statistical relationship because they have had the experience of a large, unintellectual, uninhibited boy who remains obstinately in their memory when the visions of more tractable pupils have long faded. Similarly with adults: the correlation is far too low, of course, for it to indicate anything as applied to individuals. Perhaps the best analogy is with accident statistics. No one can tell if he will be killed in a motor accident next week, yet the total number of people who will be killed in this period can be predicted rather accurately. Equally the correlation we are discussing, like road deaths, tells us something of sociological but nothing of individual importance. It is a sociological symptom calling for diagnosis and perhaps treatment.

We may sum up the situation to date by saying there is evidence in most data that both the Boas and Porter links—the coadvancement and the adult-persistent—between height and ability exist. Their relative importance probably varies according to circumstances. We must now clarify these circumstances and at the same time consider how each of the links is brought about.

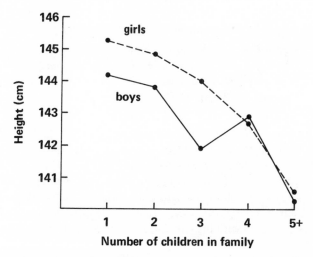

Figure 8.2 *The relation of height and number of children in the family in boys and girls aged 10¾ to 11¾ [London County Council, 1959 (from Scott, 1962, Table 1)].*

VARIABLE I:
NUMBER OF CHILDREN IN THE FAMILY

One factor that is clearly associated with the height-ability relationship in childhood is the number of children in the family. In all surveys reported, children are taller if they have few sibs[5] and shorter if they have many. This is illustrated in Figure 8.2 with data obtained from the London County Council (Scott, 1962, Table 1). The data on intelligence test results are also quite consistent: here again children with fewer sibs scored higher, as shown in Figure 8.3 (LCC data, Scott, 1962, Table 1: the test was Moray House Test 61, standardized to a mean of 100 and S.D. 15; see also Nisbet, 1958).

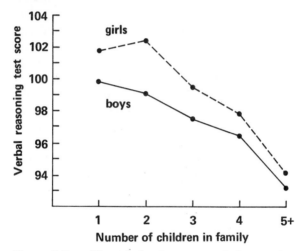

Figure 8.3   *The relation between verbal reasoning test scores and number of children in the family in boys and girls aged 10¾ to 11¾ [London County Council, 1959 (Scott, 1962, Table 1)].*

Hence all or part of the childhood correlation between height and ability might be associated with differences in number of sibs. In fact, approximately half of the correlation in the LCC data is so associated and half is not. Figure 8.4 shows the regression for girls in families with one, two, three, four and more children (Scott, 1962, Table 4). Figure 8.5 shows the regression of height on test score in families of one or two children only (Scott, 1962, Table 3). The average correlation in these data is 0.17, as compared with the correlation of 0.23 for all children irrespective of sib number.

The association with number of sibs certainly seems unlikely to spring from factors present in the zygote. Probably it reflects differences in nutrition affecting

[5]By "sibs" most surveys mean children living in the same household, whether or not they are natural brothers and sisters.

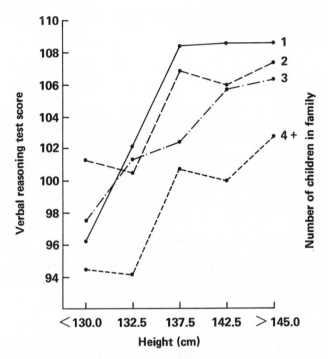

Figure 8.4 *Regression of verbal reasoning test scores on height for girls aged 10¼ in families of various sizes [London County Council, 1959 (Scott, 1962, Table 4)].*

height and differences either in nutrition or, more likely, in parental attention affecting attainment. The height relationship probably is established by the age of 4½ (Douglas and Blomfield, 1958), and certainly by age six (Grant, 1964). The National Survey of Child Health and Development data showed a difference of height between girls with no sibs and girls with three or more sibs amounting to 3.6 cm at age seven, 3.2 cm at age eleven, and 1.3 cm at age fifteen, suggesting that by full maturity the association might have disappeared. For boys, however, the figures were 1.6, 2.5, and 2.3 cm, respectively (Douglas and Simpson, 1964).

Udjus' Norwegian data show that at age nineteen men with no sibs or only one sib averaged 178.0 cm tall; those with two or three sibs, 177.7 cm; and those with four or five sibs, 176.9 cm. The regression is therefore small. Further, a follow-up study showed that, on the average, the conscripts grew an approximate 0.8 cm to maturity; hence it could well be that the conscripts with many sibs were a little delayed and made up the 1.1 cm deficit in the ensuing years. In twenty-year-old French army recruits in the period 1946–1948, there was still a difference of 2 cm in height between those from families of one or two children and those from families of five or more (Trémolières and Boulanger, 1960). However, full adult

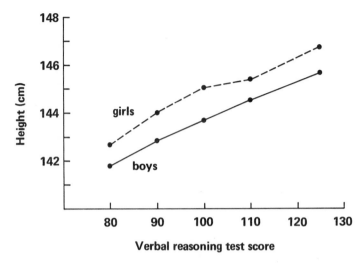

Figure 8.5 *Regression of height on verbal reasoning test score in boys and girls aged 11¼ of one-child or two-child families only [London County Council, 1959 (Scott, 1962, Table 3)].*

height probably was not reached by age twenty, due to the effects of war. The relationship of intelligence test scores to number of sibs is established by age eight (Douglas and Simpson, 1964; Douglas, 1964) and probably persists into adult life (Vernon, 1951).

All in all, it seems likely that the sib-number effect is concerned chiefly or entirely with the coadvancement link of height and ability and not with the adult-persistent link. If the effect is purely environmental in origin, as we suppose, then it should be less noticeable in the prosperous home than in the poor. This appears to be the case. Results of tests on children of the upper middle class families in the National Survey of Child Health and Development showed no relation at all between height and number of sibs, at ages seven, eleven, or fifteen. In girls the regression was present to much the same degree in lower middle, upper manual, and lower manual groups, but in boys it became progressively greater as the parents' social class declined. In the same data, at ages eight and eleven, the regression of intelligence test scores on sib number in the upper middle classes is about half the amount that it is in the other three groups, among which there is again little difference (Douglas, 1964). In the Scottish eleven-year-olds it is striking that the only occupational group (other than the professional-managerial) not to show a decline of height and weight with increasing numbers of sibs was that which comprised farmers and agricultural laborers (Scottish Research Council, 1953, Tables 32 and 33).

Ministry of Food statistics show that families in the UK spend less per capita on food as the number of children in the families increases. Recently Abel-Smith and Townsend (1965) produced data that challenged the widely held notion that, in the

UK, poverty (particularly poverty in the case of children) is a thing of the past. Defining "poverty" as the level of living of National Assistance Board applicants, they showed that one-third of all the poor were children. As many as 25 percent of households with four children or more were poor, but only 10 percent of households with three children and only 6 or 7 percent of households with one or two children fell into this category. Thus there is ample reason to suppose that a substantial number of children in large families in the poorer classes are not adequately fed. Children in these circumstances also have a higher incidence of childhood diseases such as bronchitis, though whether this causes retardation of growth is in dispute (for discussion, see Tanner, 1962, p. 130). Undernutrition and possibly disease may well account for retardation of growth in height, and even, perhaps, for smallness at maturity. However, it is not known whether suboptimal feeding has any effect on either the rate of development of mental ability or on the level of mature ability. For many years, opinion has been against any such notion, except perhaps in cases of extreme starvation in early infancy. However, opinion is a poor guide and controlled observations are lacking.

In summary, according to present data, children with many sibs in the family are retarded in their height growth from an early age, compared with children of the same social class with few sibs. This is particularly true of children in poor families, who also score lower in tests of intelligence or attainment. By the time adulthood is reached they have completely or nearly caught up in height but not in intelligence test scores (Vernon, 1951). However, this may be the result only of the vicious circle of educational opportunity. The sib-number effect on height would appear to be due to suboptimal nutrition. The effect on intelligence in childhood may be a direct consequence of the retardation of physical growth rate—factors underlying mental development being perhaps to a small extent linked with rate of development of body size—or it may simply be due to the influence of parental contact, this being less in families with many children. The sib-number effect explains to some extent that part of the height-ability relationship present in childhood and due to coadvancement, but it does not explain the part that persists into adulthood.

VARIABLE II:
OCCUPATIONAL OR SOCIO-ECONOMIC CLASS

To explain the adult-persistent link, we must examine the association of height and intelligence test scores with occupational or socio-economic class. (Bear in mind that occupational groups are enormously heterogeneous in terms of income and of social behavior. Occupational classifications should be supplemented with assessments of maternal efficiency, child-centeredness, and sociological affiliations, but these are not available for large-scale data.) Here we have a different type of variable than sib number because occupational class differences, which begin in early childhood, obviously persist into adult life. In the five West European longitudinal studies coordinated by the International Children's Centre (at London, Paris, Brussels, Zurich, and Stockholm), children in the prosperous classes were already a little taller at age one (though not at one month) than poorer children of the same age, and by age five the difference in height between those in the top two and those in the bottom two of five classes amounted to an average of 3 cm in boys and 1½ cm in girls (Graffar and Corbier, 1966; Graffar, Asiel, and Emery-Hauzeur, 1961).[6] In the 1947 survey, this difference rose to about 6 cm for Scottish eleven-year-old boys, in large part independent of the number of sibs. Not all of this difference persists into maturity (some is due to advancement in height growth in the more prosperous classes), but some part does persist (Tanner, 1962, pp. 139, 140). Udjus' nineteen-year-old conscripts, for example, showed a difference of about 3 cm between sons of fishermen, farmworkers, and unskilled laborers and sons of white-collar executives, with the latter being the taller. This difference is clearly too great to be eliminated by growth after age nineteen.

The same difference arises and persists in intelligence test scores. In the International Children's Centre studies, Terman-Merrill IQs at ages three and five already showed a marked differential (Graffar and Corbier, 1966). At age seven, clear differences in reading and arithmetic attainment tests were present in children of the National Child Development Study 1958 Cohort (Kellmer Pringle, Butler, and Davie, 1967). They were also present at this age in the Aberdeen children (Illsley, 1966).

SOCIAL STRATIFICATION AND THE STEADY STATE

Much of the adult-persistent correlation between height and ability is associated, then, with differences in social class. We now must consider two further curious facts: (a) people who migrate from one part of the country to another as children or as young adults are taller and score higher in tests of mental ability than the stay-at-homes; (b) women who migrate upward in social class on marriage are taller and brighter (perhaps prettier too?) than those who do not.

Concerning the first of these facts, the major reports are those of Martin (1949), Vernon (1951), Lee (1957), Scottish Council (1953). Martin showed an average height difference of 0.8 cm between soldiers who, on call-up in 1939, resided outside their county of birth and those who still resided in it. Vernon showed a corresponding difference of some three points in intelligence test scores. Both facts appear to indicate that people who move away from their place of birth are taller and more intelligent, on the average.

Concerning the second fact, the classic demonstration is that of Baird and his associates in Aberdeen (Scott, Illsley, and Thomson, 1956; Thomson, 1959). From 1950 to 1957 they measured the height of some 7,500 women pregnant for the first time and showed that, whatever the occupation of the father, the taller women took a more skilled job before marriage and the shorter a less skilled job. Their survey also showed that, whatever type of work they did before marriage, the taller women married husbands with more skilled jobs and the shorter women took

[6]Numerous studies, including the Perinatal Mortality Survey, have shown that small differences do exist in birth weights of the different classes, but in the International Children's Centre studies the weight differential at one month of age was insignificantly small. In most data there is a significant correlation between birth weight and later (e.g., age seven) IQ (Illsley, 1966).

husbands with less skilled jobs. At each choice-point, so to speak, the tall rose in the social scale and the short sank. This effect is best shown in the record of daughters of skilled manual workers (Figure 8.6). Of these, 23 percent were less than 5′ 1″ in height; of those who took unskilled manual jobs before marriage, 28 percent were less than 5′ 1″ tall, as compared to only 17 percent of those who took nonmanual jobs. Some of the girls in nonmanual jobs married men in similar jobs; others married skilled manual workers. Of the former, only 10 percent were under 5′ 1″ in height; of the latter, 19 percent.

It is a pity that it was not possible to measure and test the sisters of these women to see what happened to taller or shorter women brought up in the same family surroundings. Naturally, a greater proportion of the height differences between sisters is genetically controlled than that of height differences between women from different families. Thus if the taller sib rose socially more than the shorter one, we could more clearly infer, at least in the absence of prenatal differences, that this was due to something associated with the inherited element in height, if not due simply to height itself.[7]

Recently, Schreider (1964), in an excellent discussion of the whole problem, tabulated the results of the British perinatal mortality survey (Butler and Bonham, 1963) and found support for the Aberdeen results. Figure 8.7 shows the percentage of women 5′ 5″ and taller according to the occupations of both father and husband. Height increases as the husband's occupation is more skilled. Furthermore, this occurs for women of all social origins, as judged by father's occupation. Thirty-one percent of the daughters of unskilled British laborers who married professional husbands were 5′ 5″ or taller. Only 24 percent of the women who married men of their own class of origin were this height. On the other hand, of the women born into professional homes who married semiskilled or unskilled laborers, only 32 percent were 5′ 5″ or taller as compared with 46 percent of those who married men of their own class of origin.

The same process is reflected in data on the weights of fourteen-year-old school boys, as reported by Berry and Cowin (1954). Among boys in grammar schools and secondary modern schools in the same town, consistent weight differences existed that could be related to parents' social classes. But still larger differences existed between the boys in the grammar schools, which offered a more academic program, and those in the secondary modern schools, offering a less academic program, whose fathers shared the same type of occupation. The process of social selection had apparently begun.

In a similar vein, Parnell (1954) showed that Oxford University students from

[7]Recently this approach was used by Laycock and Caylor (1964) in studies on the height-ability relation in children. They surveyed children with IQs of 120 or greater who had an older or younger sib with an IQ of at least 20 points less. The gifted sibs were bigger in all five body measurements taken, but the differences were insignificantly different when measured from zero. For instance, the average height difference was the equivalent of 0.5 cm. Some objections to the details of this study can be raised—for example, the sibs should each ideally be measured at the same age—but the results do support the notion that much of the height-ability correlation is due to factors operating between, rather than within, families.

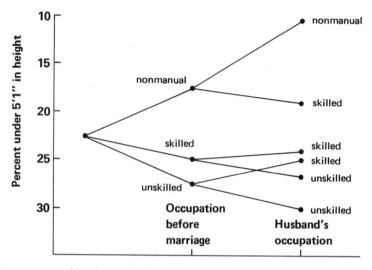

Aberdeen primiparae born to skillled manual workers

Figure 8.6 *Percentage of daughters of skilled manual workers under 5' 1" tall taking nonmanual, skilled, and unskilled manual jobs and marrying men in nonmanual, skilled-manual, and unskilled-manual occupations (redrawn from Thomson, 1959).*

state schools were not only considerably taller than the average of young men from such schools, but also a little taller than private school graduates who failed to attain university entrance requirements.

One must evidently think of social migration or selection acting for body size as it does for intelligence. Gibson and Young (1965) quote data showing that some 30 percent of English persons per generation now move from one broad class division into another and that it is the less intelligent who move down and the more intelligent who move up. Evidently the same is true of height. We have a steady state in the population in that the mean height presently rises very slightly from one generation to another, while the persons contributing to that mean reassort themselves so that a social class gradient is always maintained.

In an extensive study of a nationally representative sample in Belgium, Cliquet (1968) showed that young men whose occupations or occupational aspirations were socially higher than the occupations of their fathers, were significantly taller and heavier and had larger head circumferences than men whose occupations were in the same category as those of their fathers. Downwardly mobile men, on the other hand, were smaller in size than socially static ones. The upwardly mobile also were somewhat larger in body size and had more subcutaneous fat than the static or downwardly mobile. In contrast, there were only slight differences in size and in subcutaneous fat between young men of different social origins. Evidently the link with large size is not social origin itself, but whether the individual is moving

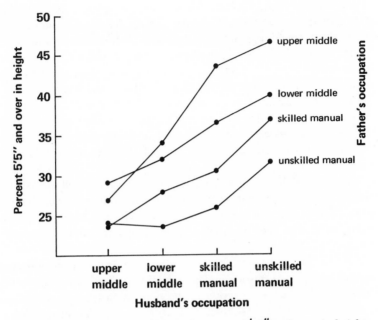

Figure 8.7 *Percentage of British women 5' 5" and over in height according to occupations of father and husband [data of perinatal mortality survey (Butler and Bonham, 1963) tabulated by Schreider (1964)].*

upward or downward. Thus a slight social gradient in body size in a population is maintained by a considerably greater gradient existing between persons moving upward or downward. Cliquet found the same relationships in measures of intellectual ability, with naturally more pronounced gradients. Burt (1961) has described this with characteristic clarity in relation to intelligence.

There are probably other examples of such a steady-state process in social selection. Some years ago, Morris (1959) and Heady (1955) pointed out that, although infant mortality had greatly decreased in all social classes since 1911, the gap between the classes surprisingly had not narrowed. At the same time, while the over-all incidence of various adult diseases had risen or fallen, their social class affinities had not changed at all.

It is easy to understand why people who are clever tend to rise in the social scale, but much harder to comprehend why the same is true of tall people. Surely tallness itself carries no social cachet. It is true that the perinatal mortality in tall mothers is less than that in short ones, even if both are in the same social class (Illsley, 1966), so there is selection at birth acting in favor of the tall. The effect may well be balanced by an excess of tall women who do not produce children, but this would only influence the general level of height in the next generation and not the ability of a given tall child to rise in the social scale.

It appears likely that, in fact, tall people rise because they are marginally better at certain mental tasks. Schreider (1964) puts this accurately when he stresses that the height correlation is probably with certain aptitudes only, not with some measure of global intelligence. The Aberdeen women showed a higher correlation between height and Wechsler score than between height and the score on the progressive matrices (Scott, Illsley, and Thomson, 1956), perhaps because the Wechsler is more verbal. The National Child Development Survey 1958 Cohort preliminary results suggest that there is a significant relation at age seven between height and reading ability—independent of sex, sib number, and social class—but none at all between height and skill at arithmetic.

This collection of hypotheses is interesting, but we are still in the dark about whether the tall, bright, upward-moving children are this way primarily because of excellence of antenatal and postnatal care and intelligent, responsible feeding and upbringing, or because they inherited a gene complex that was predisposed toward developing in this direction.

We have no formal estimate of the proportions in which hereditary and environmental factors are involved. There is the curious fact that, in all countries, students are the tallest group in the population (Parnell, 1954) and mental defectives are the shortest (Mosier, Grossman, and Dingman, 1965). Among the latter, the degree of shortness and the degree of mental defect are correlated, which does seem to argue that, on the average, lack of complexity of brain is linked with lack of skeletal growth.[8] We are totally unable to say whether such a link reflects genetic factors or minimal brain damage during intrauterine development. In principle, intrauterine damage could provide a phenocopy of any genetic predisposition. However, we cannot yet tell to what extent the small, not very bright, socially-sinking persons in the community represent phenocopies and to what extent they represent the results of gene complexes. We are also unaware of the extent to which bad maternal care in the early years can irrevocably fix the constitution of the infant.

It is safe to say that some of the effect must be genetic. Consider those small, unintelligent women who fall from grace to marry two social classes below—they cannot all be daughters of drunken, eccentric academics whose homes are in squalor and whose wives are incompetent. Many must have received excellent childhood care but were unable to benefit fully from it. Conversely, there are many persons—academics particularly—who, born into squalor and penury, emerged not only with outstanding minds but with outstanding physiques as well. Obviously, investigation of the multiple interactions between gene complex and successive environments, though difficult and exacting, is of paramount importance in unraveling causes in this small area of social biology or biological sociology.

[8]Perhaps it is significant that Figure 8.4 contains possible indications of a threshold for test scores of children taller than 137.5 cm who come from families with few children. The chief relationship may be that a significant number of small children are low in ability.

SUMMARY

● Among school-aged children, a significant though low correlation exists between body size and scores in various tests of ability and attainment, such that larger children score higher than smaller children of the same age. Though the correlation between height and test score is only 0.15 to 0.25, the possibility of a large child passing an age-linked examination is substantially greater than that of a small child.

● This correlation diminishes when maturity is reached, but does not disappear entirely. In samples of young adults representing the whole population, correlations of up to 0.2 remain. Thus the height-ability relation in children is partly due to coadvancement in both physical and mental growth, but it is also partly adult-persistent.

● The greater the number of children in the family, the lower their height and the less their scores in mental tests. This effect probably is due entirely to coadvancement, and disappears when maturity is reached. The effect is more pronounced in poor families than in prosperous ones.

● There are also differences in height and mental ability between children in different socio-economic groups and these persist to a large degree into adulthood.

● On the average, taller men and women tend to rise in the social scale, both occupationally and in marriage; shorter men and women tend to sink. This probably is due to height being related to ability. The social structure represents a steady state in which socio-economic group differences remain, while individuals change from one group to another.

● We do not know in what proportions heredity and environment contribute to these effects. Minimal intrauterine damage may well be an important factor.

REFERENCES

Abel-Smith, B., & Townsend, P. *The poor and the poorest.* London: Bell, 1965.

Abernethy, E. M. Relationships between mental and physical growth. *Monographs of the Society for Research in Child Development,* 1936, **1**, No. 7.

Bayley, N. Individual patterns of development. *Child Development,* 1956, **27**, 45–74.

Berry, W.T.C., & Cowin, P. J. Conditions associated with the growth of boys, 1950–51. *British Medical Journal,* 1954, **1**, 847–851.

Boas, F. On Dr. William Townsend Porter's investigation of the growth of the school children of St. Louis. *Science, New Series,* 1895, 1, 225–230.

Burt, C. Intelligence and social mobility. *British Journal of Statistical Psychology,* 1961, 14, 3–24.

Butler, N. R., & Bonham, D. G. *Perinatal mortality.* Edinburgh: Livingstone, 1963.

Cliquet, R. L. Social mobility and the anthropological structure of a population. *Human Biology,* 1968. In press.

Douglas, J.W.B. *The home and the school.* London: MacGibbon and Kee, 1964.

Douglas, J.W.B., & Blomfield, J. M. *Children under five.* London: Allen and Unwin, 1958.

Douglas, J.W.B., Ross, J. M., & Simpson, H. R. The relation between height and measured educational ability in school children of the same social class, family size and stage of sexual development. *Human Biology*, 1965, 37, 178–186.

Douglas, J.W.B., & Simpson, H. R. Height in relation to puberty, family size and social class. *Millbank Memorial Fund Quarterly*, 1964, 42, 20–35.

Gibson, J., & Young, M. Social mobility and fertility. *Biological Aspects of Social Problems* (Eds. J. E. Meade & A. S. Parkes). Edinburgh: Oliver and Boyd, 1965.

Graffar, M., & Corbier, J. Contribution à l'étude de l'influence socio-économique sur la croissance et le dévelopment de l'enfant. *Courrier*, 1966, 16, 1–25.

Graffar, M., Asiel, M., & Emery-Hauzeur, J. La taille et le périmètre cephalique pendant la première année de la vie. *Acta paediatrice belgica*, 1961, 15, 61–74.

Grant, M. W. Rate of growth in relation to birth rank and family size. *British Journal of Preventive and Social Medicine*, 1964, 18, 35–42.

Husen, T. Undersokninger rorande sambanden mellan somatiske for hallanden och intellektuell prestations formaga. *Militar. Halsovand*, 1951, 76, 41–74.

Illsley, R. Early prediction of perinatal risk. *Proceedings Royal Society of Medicine*, 1966, 59, 181–184.

Kellmer Pringle, M., Butler, N., & Davie, R. *Eleven thousand seven-year-olds*. Bristol: Longmans, 1967.

Laycock, F., & Caylor, J. S. Physiques of gifted children and their less gifted siblings. *Child Development*, 1964, 35, 63–74.

Lee, J.A.H. Regional variations in intellectual ability in Britain; a discussion of their importance and of the possible effects of selective migration. *Eugenics Review*, 1957, 49, 19–24.

Martin, W. J. The physique of young adult males. *Medical Research Council Memo*, 1949, No. 20. London, HMSO.

Morris, J. Health and social class. *Lancet*, 1959, 1, 303–305.

Morris, J., & Heady, J. A. Social and biological factors in infant mortality. V. Mortality in relation to father's occupation. *Lancet*, 1955, 554–560.

Mosier, H. D., Grossman, H. J., & Dingman, H. F. Physical growth in mental defectives. A study in an institutionalized population. *Paediatrics*, 1965, 36, 465–579.

Nisbet, J. D. Intelligence and family size. 1949–56. *Eugenics Review*, 1958, 49, 4–5.

Nisbet, J. D., & Illsley, R. I. The influence of early puberty on test performance at age eleven. *British Journal of Educational Psychology*, 1963, 33, 169–176.

Parnell, R. W. The physique of Oxford undergraduates. *Journal of Hygiene*, 1954, 52, 369–378.

Patterson, D. G. *Physique and intellect*. New York: Century, 1930.

Porter, W. T. The physical basis of precocity and dullness. *Transactions Academy Science St. Louis*, 1893, 6, 161–181.

Schreider, E. Taille et capacités mentales. *Biotypologie*, 1956, 17, 21–37.

Schreider, E. Récherches sur la stratification sociale des caractères biologiques. *Biotypologie*, 1964, 26, 105–135.

Scott, E. M., Illsley, I. P., & Thomson, A. M. A psychological investigation of primigravidae. II. Maternal social class, age, physique and intelligence. *Journal of Obstetrics and Gynaecology of the British Empire*, 1956, 63, 338–343.

Scott, J. A. *Report on the heights and weights of school pupils in the County of London in 1959.* London County Council, 1961.

Scott, J. A. Intelligence, physique and family size. *British Journal of Preventive and Social Medicine,* 1962, **16**, 165–173.

Scottish Council for Research in Education. *Social implications of the 1947 Scottish mental survey.* London: University Press, 1953.

Shuttleworth, F. K. The physical and mental growth of girls and boys age six to nineteen. *Monographs of the Society for Research in Child Development* 1939, **4**, No. 3.

Tanner, J. M. Boas' contributions to knowledge of human growth and form. *The Anthropology of Franz Boas: Essays on the centennial of his birth.* (Ed. W. Goldschmidt). *Memoir of American Anthropological Association* 1959, No. 89. (American Anthropologist, **61**).

Tanner, J. M. *Education and physical growth. Implications of the study of children's growth for educational theory and practice.* London: University Press, 1961.

Tanner, J. M. *Growth at adolescence* (2nd ed.). Oxford: Blackwell Science Publications, 1962.

Trémolierès, J., & Boulanger, J. J. Contribution a l'étude du phénomène de croissance et de stature en France de 1940 à 1948. *Recueil des travaux de l' institut nationel d'hygiène,* Paris: 1950, **4**, 117–212.

Udjus, L. G. *Anthropometrical changes in Norwegian men in the twentieth century.* Oslo: Universitatsforlaget, 1964.

Vernon, P. E. Recent investigations of intelligence and its measurements. *Eugenics Review,* 1951, **43**, 125–137.

INDEX

Relationship (*Continued*)
 of height and number of children in
  family, 189–191, 199
 of intelligence test scores to sib
  number, 192
 of size and ability in different
  socio-economic groups, 188, 196–197
 of schoolboys with family, 172
 rate of eye-gaze, 55
Response
 as function of reinforcement, 113
 conditioning of anxiety, 92
 reflective of thought structure, 115
 resulting from altruistic modeling, 145
 self-imposition of, 111
 to reflect attainment, 112
Responsibility, 150, 152
Rest, J., 103, 110
Reversibility, 44
Rewards, 134
Role-Playing, 101, 111

St. Louis Medical College, 182
Schizophrenics, 65
School
 admission standards, 164–165
 as predictor of future attainment, 171
 comprehensive, 165, 178
 conditions set by society, 164–166
 divided secondary system, 156, 178
 effects of, 157, 166
 effect of same school on different
  children, 157
 function of, 156
 identification with values of, 177
 influence of, 154–178
 measures of adjustment to, 155
 nursery, primary, secondary, 160,
  163–165
 rewards and sanctions, 160
 state, 156
 strong:weak systems, 168, 179
 structure and role of, 171
Schreider, E.
 height:aptitude correlation, 198
 tabulation of mortality survey, 195
Score
 dominant stage of profile, 114
 "variation," 117, 120
Sears, R. R.
 internalization of social rules, 93
 parents' effect on children, 154

Selection
 as factor in size and intelligence, 196
 by strong system, 177
 for placement in English schools, 156
Self, 95
Self-Image, 161
Self:World
 attitudes, 38
 polarity, 39
Self-Worth, 139
Sensory-Tonic Theory, 24
Sequence Tasks, 43
Serial Learning Apparatus, 43, 45
Seriation, 17
Shaftel, F R., 70
Siblings
 gifted, 195
 intelligence and number of, 190–191, 199
 variations in IQ, 195
Simulation, 143
Sinclair, H., 3, 17
Size, 183, 198–199
Skills
 associated with attitude, 84
 development with training, 69
 improvement in thinking, 71, 84
 and programmed material, 73
Smedslund, J., 7, 31
Social Complexity, 130
Socialization, 158, 159, 161
Solution, 43
Speech
 as a form of action, 18
 as substitute for action, 140
Stages
 of intermediary development, 4
 analysis of mixture of, 118
 in developmental process, 116–126
 influenced by interview, 117
Status
 assigned to different schools, 164
 of child in school, 160
Stimulus
 and physical arrangement variations, 58,
  63
 asymmetrical auditory, 59–60
 with instructions, 59
Stream
 elite stream in English schools, 160, 175
 express and elite, 170–171, 175
 1, 2, and 3, 175
Stress, 106